W9-ANA-587

American Drama, 1940–1960:
A Critical History

TWAYNE'S CRITICAL HISTORY OF AMERICAN DRAMA

Jordan Y. Miller
GENERAL EDITOR
University of Rhode Island

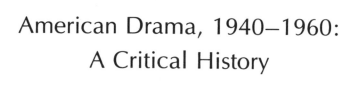

American Drama, 1940–1960:
A Critical History

Thomas P. Adler
Purdue University

Twayne Publishers ◊ New York
Maxwell Macmillan Canada ◊ Toronto
Maxwell Macmillan International ◊ New York Oxford Singapore Sydney

American Drama, 1940–1960: A Critical History
Thomas P. Adler

Twayne's Critical History of American Drama Series

Copyright © 1994 by Twayne Publishers

Twayne Publishers   Maxwell Macmillan Canada, Inc.
Macmillan Publishing Company   1200 Eglinton Avenue East
866 Third Avenue   Suite 200
New York, New York 10022   Don Mills, Ontario M3C 3N1

Library of Congress Cataloging-in-Publication Data

Adler, Thomas P.
    American drama, 1940–1960 / Thomas P. Adler
      p.   cm. — (Twayne's critical history of American
    drama series)
    Includes bibliographical references and index.
    ISBN 0-8057-8957-X
    1. American drama—20th century—History and
    criticism.   I. Title.   II. Series.
    PS351A35   1994
    812'.5409—dc20   93-33791
                                                          CIP

The paper used in this publication meets the minimum requirements of American National Standard for Information Sciences—Permanence of Paper for Printed Library Materials. ANSI Z39 48-1984. ⊚™

10 9 8 7 6 5 4 3 2 1

Printed in the United States of America.

For Winnie
and 25 years of love

contents

preface

Any discussion of a nation's literature that separates out a 10 or 20-year period will be artificial in some ways, since decades are not hermetically sealed off one from another. And yet the period between 1940 and 1960 is contained within itself better than most, since historically these are the decades of war and its aftermath, of conflagration and victory and seeming confidence—though revealing to those who look closely enough fissures of inner unrest. And from the point of view of American drama and theater, the decades of the 1940s and 1950s indisputably comprise the classic period, for they are the years of the later Eugene O'Neill and the early Arthur Miller and the nascent Edward Albee, as well as of virtually every major work by Tennessee Williams, perhaps the period's pivotal figure. As such, these years witnessed the first productions of *The Iceman Cometh* and *Long Day's Journey into Night*, of *Death of a Salesman* and *The Crucible*, of *The Glass Menagerie*, *A Streetcar Named Desire*, and *Cat on a Hot Tin Roof.*

The history of this period of theatrical activity in America, the story of its richness and lasting contribution to world drama and literature, can best be recaptured and written not in a season-by-season rundown of hits and misses, or even a discussion of types of plays and a variety of movements (modern tragedies, psychological melodramas, family problem plays, expressionism, absurdism), although these necessarily figure into the discussion at certain points. Instead, it is best told by a comprehensive overview of each of the dominant voices in American drama in the post–World War II years. So, except for an opening chapter that sets the scene by surveying a large number of plays about war and politics, and a middle chapter that examines a half-dozen popular but admittedly lesser playwrights, this book devotes a chapter (or in one case—Williams—two) to each of the central figures: O'Neill, Hellman, Miller, Inge, Williams, Hansberry, and Albee. Each of these chapters is, in a sense, deliberately self-contained in that it, first, offers a careful analysis and interpretation of the author's major plays—that is, of those works from the period 1940–60 that will probably be the most lasting in all of American drama; second, attempts to provide a coherent reading of his or her characteristic style and motifs; and, finally, offers an assessment of his or her achievement and position vis à vis other dramatists. What emerges from such an approach is an awareness of the consistency with which certain themes and attitudes recur.

With a minimum of reference back to the works discussed in Twayne's *American Drama Between the Wars*, chapters 2 and 3 focus on the continuation and completion of the playwriting careers of O'Neill and Hellman. An examination of O'Neill's dramas from the years after he won the Nobel Prize through those of the posthumous productions— plays that were, in fact, written in the late 1930s and early 1940s—reveals an absorbing concern with humankind's need to belong, to discover a sense of at oneness with something outside of the self, yet simultaneously retain a space for the self; with the need for developing a love unafraid to criticize the loved one in order to be creative; and with the need for commitment, seen particularly in a mutuality of concern for the other that can help counter a dawning awareness of meaninglessness, exacerbated by a society that is increasingly materialistic. Hellman's cultural critique zeroes in more pointedly on the ways in which the valorization of power and money, the ends of commerce, reduces people to commodities, increases the economic dependency of certain groups, particularly women, and generally threatens the continuance of civilization and the ascendancy of historical progress.

Miller shares with Hellman an overarching fear that authority, in whatever form, threatens the freedom and autonomy of human conscience, particularly of the individual in the minority. Miller's playwriting career falls neatly into two chronologically uneven parts, with a hiatus of several years between the first half and his re-emergence on the New York stage in the mid-1960s and continuing on into the 1990s. Here only the first flowering will be discussed, with consideration of the later works left for the next volume in this series. Even more emphatically than Hellman or O'Neill, Miller dissects the debasement of the American dream of material success, exposing the mismeasuring of love in terms of competition and winning. His characters, in trying to secure their dignity and integrity, image themselves wrongly, so that the dream and the actuality never coalesce. By valorizing a win-at-any-cost ethic, society and fathers fail to be moral authorities for citizens and sons.

The marginalization of women in O'Neill and Miller becomes more generalized in Inge, as he explores not only women as victims, sometimes willingly, of a domestic servitude that thwarts youthful dreams, but the more general stigma that attaches to sexual difference. Many of his characters, in fact, in plays that have much to do with issues of gender politics and the negotiation of power, find themselves attempting to escape imprisoning stereotypes, especially those that, in an attempt to define societally acceptable notions of manliness, actually end by restricting and diminishing the individual.

Virtually all of these themes find further articulation in the dramas of Williams. Although what have come to be regarded as his major works were all written by the time of *The Night of the Iguana* in the early 1960s, the later plays warrant a chapter of their own and are most appropriately considered here in relation to the earlier ones, rather than in the next volume about post-1960s drama. Williams's outsiders, whether separated by sexuality or ethnicity or race, tend to be artists/illusionists who insist on and who practice the little acts of grace—of magnanimous, nonjudgmental acceptance of those whose moral codes differ—that are all contemporary humankind has in place of God. In Williams's near-apocalyptic world, culture and beauty are threatened at the hands of materialism and violence; an open heart and an imagination that can intuit moral truth are at war with a facticity that denies the existence of any ethical value, and so reduces potentially sacramental sexuality to merely a using and abusing, increasing loneliness and isolation. In such a world, art in all its manifestations, including the theater, becomes a civilizing agent, a salvific, grace-filled moment in the face of time's inexorable movement toward oblivion.

As the 1960s approach, the dramatists tend to replace cautionary tales with more openly revolutionary and subversive texts. Hansberry, in writing the womanist text, examines oppression and subservience in class and gender as well as racial terms, proposing a resurgence of an engaged activism. Albee, countering a widespread complacency that sees everything as "peachy keen," pens the text of the archetypal outsider, resorting to violence if necessary to break through shells of indifference and incommunication. Although the audience for avant-garde drama such as Albee's early one-act plays might be similar to the elitist one attracted to modernist fiction and poetry, modernist issues and concerns arise in virtually all of these dramatists writing in the post–World War II years. They are recurrently concerned with role playing, with masking, with the fragmentation of self and even loss of self in a succession of poses. They explore issues of moral relativism and cultural pluralism. And they write works about the creating of texts and the staging of narratives. Yet in their repeated emphasis on the power of language as an attribute and evidence of a reasoning mind and the potential of art as a civilizing force, finally they remain firmly in the liberal humanistic tradition.

No one can complete a project of this scope without considerable help along the way. I will always be deeply appreciative of Jordan Miller, the general editor, for asking me to contribute this volume in the series; the kindness, common sense, and astute criticism of this too rare blend of "gentleman scholar" and the virtually complete latitude he allowed me has indeed helped make my work a pleasure. Thanks also to the editors at Twayne, John Fitzpatrick and, more recently, Anne Kiefer, and most especially to my copy editor, India Koopman, for her extraordinary care and attention to detail. For help in securing appropriate illustrations, my gratitude goes to Kenneth Holditch and Don Lee Keith; to the curatorial staffs at the Billy Rose Theatre Collection of the New York Public Library for the Performing Arts and of the Beinecke Rare Book and Manuscript Library at Yale University; to Janice Weir, director of the Independence (Kansas) Community College Library; and, most particularly, to Melissa Miller, assistant curator of the Theatre Arts Collection of the Harry Ransom Humanities Research Center at the University of Texas at Austin, who cut through red tape when no one else seemed able to. I will always be seriously indebted to my dear friend and department head, Margaret Moan Rowe, and to my dean, David A. Caputo, for their unfailing understanding and support over many years. And, finally, to my sons, Jeremy and Chris, and to my wife, Winnie, who give it all meaning and make it all worthwhile.

1

Setting the Stage:
America at War and at Peace

I n the narrative passages interspersed throughout *The Glass Menagerie,*
produced near the end of World War II but set in St. Louis just before
the conflict, Tennessee Williams's authorial character, Tom Wingfield,
reflects on the sociopolitical background of the late 1930s: "In Spain there
was revolution. . . . Here there were disturbances of labor, sometimes
pretty violent, in otherwise peaceful cities. . . . In Spain there was Guer-
nica! But here there was only hot swing music and liquor, dance halls,
bars, and movies, and sex. . . . All the world was waiting for bombard-
ments!" Were the play set 20 years later, with Tom called upon to provide
a capsule overview of the 1940s and 1950s, he might have commented:
"Abroad there was Pearl Harbor, the Holocaust, the Bomb, the Iron
Curtain, Korea, Hungary and Suez, the Cold War, and Sputnik. At home
there was internment of Japanese-Americans, investigations of suspected
Communists, suburban sprawl, rock'n'roll, the ascendency of TV, and
racial unrest. America was poised and waiting for upheaval." Although
cataclysmic events seldom find their way directly onto the stage, they
supply the undercurrents rippling through works for the theater between

1940 and 1960 that, as a part of the nation's literature, provide in the words of Frederick Hoffman "a genuine means of realizing the major issues of the time."

The Sociocultural Milieu

In his introduction to *The 1940s: Profile of a Nation in Crisis*, Chester Eisinger delineates "the prevailing mood" of that decade as "one of fear, terror, uncertainty, and violence, mingled with sad satisfactions and a sense of relief at victory" quickly giving way to an "abject fear of the bomb and of government." In his analysis, the depersonalization and regimentation of the war years are succeeded by the conformity and organization-man mentality of the 1950s, both of these contributing to an assault on individualism. Paralleling this shift, the literature of the period demonstrates a decided move "away from the social consciousness" of the 1930s to focus instead on "the quest for identity" and "the alienation of man from the self and from society." Indeed, many of the forces that Tom Wingfield would have needed to acknowledge about the 1940s and 1950s worked to exclude and marginalize, even to exterminate, the "other" on the basis of race or color or ideology. In short, according to Eisinger it was a period witnessing the culmination of an entire nation's "loss of innocence," signalled by a retreat from a secure isolationism and a new recognition of the potentially destructive power, and thus moral responsibility and culpability, of science left to its own devices. [1]

    This tension between a nostalgia for a supposedly innocent past and an awareness of an increasingly dangerous present plays itself out in a major icon that the American stage of the time contributed to popular culture. Many attribute the enormous success (over 2200 performances after it opened in 1943) of Richard Rodgers and Oscar Hammerstein's now classic musical *Oklahoma!*, with Agnes de Mille's innovative ballet sequence, to audiences' desire for escape from the realities of war into a simpler time of seemingly infinite progress around the turn of the century. Yet the nuptials of Curly and Laurie are nearly interrupted by the dark presence of Judd, who in his malignity seems almost a representation of the barbaric forces of evil threatening the continuance of civilization during World War II. After Curly kills Judd in self-defense, the commu-nity demands its right to exonerate their protector. If the men are justified in fighting to secure the society, the women are reminded of their complementary role in supporting the effort by waiting and working and nurturing on the homefront.

The widespread certainty about the moral rightness of the war's stand against nazism and fascism created a unifying effect among the people. As John Updike, who in the 1950s would inaugurate a long career as an astute novelist of contemporary mores, has remarked: "at least for Europeans and North Americans, [World War II] has become the century's central myth, a vast imaging of a primal time when good and evil contended for the planet."[2] Existing alongside this commitment to sacrifice in fighting a visible enemy and a consequent glorification of those who died was, however, a more gritty subtext. As Paul Fussell demonstrates in *Wartime: Understanding and Behavior in the Second World War*, the savagery experienced by the participants who fought in a kind of "ideological vacuum" was "systematically sanitized and Norman Rockwellized, not to mention Disneyfied" in representations to the uninitiated "laity" back home.[3]

Economically, the Truman era immediately after the war witnessed enormous expansion and prosperity at home and reconstruction abroad through the Marshall Plan. In America, the growth of the automobile industry and the development of a network of interstate and other highways led to greater mobility. At the same time, these advances contributed to spatial dislocation: the middle and upper classes moving from city to suburb, people leaving the countryside for urban areas, African-Americans migrating from the South to the North—the last two of these movements fostering ghettoized living in what sociologist Lewis Mumford would term "urban crematoriums." The country, never as unlimitedly open and egalitarian as the myth of the melting pot had fantasized it to be, was sowing seeds for increasing divisions along class and ethnic and racial lines. Yet America's booming economy at home gave it a renewed conviction of Manifest Destiny, of intervening as the world's police force to ensure the security and spread of democracy that was an offshoot of what D. W. Brogan has called "the illusion of American omnipotence." In one of the last speeches of his presidency, former General Dwight Eisenhower would in fact find it necessary to caution against unfettered growth of the "military-industrial complex" in carrying out America's mission.

Politically, the late 1940s and early 1950s in America ushered in a mood of increasing conservatism and even paranoia over perceived threats to unanimity of viewpoint, while abroad a policy of containment of communism prevailed, particularly after the Korean War fueled the

Red Scare and exacerbated the arms race. What began with loyalty oaths for federal employees, suspicion of scientists like J. Robert Oppenheimer who expressed skepticism over continued development of thermonuclear weaponry, and blacklisting of Hollywood screenwriters thought to have past ties, however tenuous, to communist cells, accelerated into a full-scale witch-hunt by the House Un-American Activities Committee. During the McCarthy era, this atmosphere made possible the imprisonment and even execution of suspected traitors such as Julius and Ethel Rosenberg and fostered a virulent homophobia and widespread anti-Semitism. With Senator Joseph R. McCarthy as their standard bearer, the most reactionary anti-Communists—seeing the spread of socialist communism not primarily as a military threat but rather as a political movement that must be stopped no matter where it sprang up—regarded all liberals as suspect. In such a chilly atmosphere, suspicion of guilt by association with "fellow travelers" meant that many leftist intellectuals, several of whom admittedly held uncritical pro-Stalinist leanings back in the 1930s, found themselves called to testify and "name names" to avoid contempt charges.

Socially, the Eisenhower years have ordinarily been seen, rightly or wrongly, as a time of homogeneous belief in traditional values of family, religion, and work and of conformity to a commodity mass culture in which what one acquired and consumed defined who and what one was. Many regard the 1950s as a regressive time for women, a period of retrenchment from the work world and anything hinting at feminist notions, accompanied by a glorification of the white, upper-middle-class nuclear family, which found its apotheosis on television in *Father Knows Best*. Popular writers, in short, would characterize it as the time of the lonely-crowd-organization-man-in-the-grey-flannel-suit. Sociologists David Riesman, in *The Lonely Crowd* (1950), and William H. Whyte, in *The Organization Man* (1956), respectively, describe and to some extent decry the "other-directed" and anonymous company worker who retreated from healthy self-determination and entrepreneurship into a corporate world in which adaptability to commonly shared business and community values and approval by one's peer group were the measuring sticks.

Beneath the apparent conformity and unquestioning acceptance that, in some cases, bred apathy to personal and social problems, seeds of change could, nevertheless, be detected. Alfred Kinsey's research and reports on sexuality in the late 1940s helped to generate discussion and demystify the physiology and psychology of sex; the restlessness of the young found expression in the adulation accorded an actor like James Dean in films such as *Rebel without a Cause*; the writers of the Beat Generation, such as poet Allen Ginsberg in "Howl" and novelist Jack Kerouac in *On the Road*, subverted long-standing cultural values and community mores. And, perhaps most important, the movement for racial equality, which would culminate in the Civil Rights and Voting Rights Acts of the mid-1960s, began in the late 1940s with President Truman's desegregation of the military and the integration of professional athletics, together with the court-ordered outlawing of restrictive housing covenants. It reached its watershed in the 1955 Montgomery, Alabama, bus boycott begun by Rosa Parks and supported by Martin Luther King, Jr., and in the 1954 Supreme Court decision in *Brown v. Topeka Board of Education*, which ordered the end of segregated "separate but equal" schools with "all deliberate speed."

Popular cultural historians surveying the events between the end of World War II and the beginning of the 1960s have given the period quite different interpretations. Marty Jezer, for example, titles his history *The Dark Ages: Life in the United States, 1945–1960*, to emphasize the way in which certain elements of the time, especially inequalities and discrimination on the basis of gender, race, class, or sexual preference, were consciously hidden and repressed and would be unleashed only by the rebellious movements of the tumultuous 1960s. Whereas Jezer foresees a tearing down before a rebuilding can begin, William O'Neill, on the other hand, calls his study *American High: The Years of Confidence, 1945–1960* to denote a "confident, expansive mood" and an "anything could be accomplished" mentality that promised easy amelioration of society's vague ills through positive corrective programs.

Two groups of plays, one focusing on the war and its aftermath and the other on politics—several of which either themselves won the Pulitzer Prize for drama or were stage adaptations of novels that had received the Pulitzer for fiction—will illustrate many of the sociopolitical currents mentioned thus far. Furthermore, these plays demonstrate that America's dramatists of the 1940s and 1950s are much more likely to support Jezer's reading of the times by pointing to the darker underside of the American experience in the decade and a half following World War II. These plays set the stage for the discussion that follows in later chapters in the sense that they form the background against which the major figures—O'Neill, Miller, Williams—will be highlighted. They help reveal the sociocultural milieu in which dramatists with sometimes more substantive and oftentimes more sustained output were writing; they also establish certain central motifs that American playwrights of the period 1940–60 persistently explore: the tension between the individual and the community; the abuse of power, both political and personal; gender stereotypes that limit self-fulfillment; and racial and ethnic difference.

Staging the War

Three plays by dramatists who actually came to prominence in the 1930s, Lillian Hellman and Robert E. Sherwood, explore what happens when the powers of reasoning have been exhausted, when diplomacy has proven ineffectual, when the time for temporizing is over, and so only the avenue of physical force in the defense of freedom is left. By the time Sherwood, who served Franklin Roosevelt as speech writer and adviser, completed *There Shall Be No Night* (1941), his own isolationism (earlier still he had been a pacifist) had given way to interventionism in response to the Fascists and Nazis as America's mood itself soon would; in fact, *Night* stands as unique in the annals of the stage for the way it helped shape public opinion about entry into World War II. During the playwright's personal odyssey what had, paradoxically, deepened rather than diminished was Sherwood's humanistic faith in humankind when all experiential evidence seemed to point to the contrary.

Decorating the Finnish home in *Night* of Dr. Kaarlo Valkonen and his American-born wife, Miranda, are portraits of her family in which southern sensitivity meets dour New England Puritanism; the ancestors furnish a capsule history of America's decline, "rugged heroism . . . developing into ruthless materialism . . . and then degenerating into [the] intellectual impotence and decay that eventuates in anarchy," a progress (or regression) not unlike that which denotes the successive generations in O'Neill's projected cycle, "A Tale of the Possessors Self-Dispossessed." In Sherwood's view, America can redeem itself from its downward spiral only through discovering a new energy and commitment against the threat posed by the German megalomaniac who "seeks to create a race of moral cretins whom science has rendered strong and germless in their bodies, but feeble and servile in their minds," precisely what George in Edward Albee's *Who's Afraid of Virginia Woolf?* (1962) will claim is the agenda of Nick, the purveyor of "biological inevitability."

In *There Shall Be No Night*, two men of science demonstrate the antithesis between the proper and improper use of human reason. The

German Dr. Ziemssen argues for "admit[ting] the necessity" for the Nazis to assert their power by reducing "inferior races" to "animals"; while the new Nobel laureate Valkonen speaks with conviction of man's coming to "consciousness" about the ethical dimensions of his actions and the presence of God through "the mysteries of his own mind." Humankind, however, has temporarily bypassed words and language, the outward sign of its inner reasoning faculty, as an antidote for brutality, and so people and nations must respond by taking up arms; though antithetical to the law of Christian love, this may under certain conditions, Sherwood insists, be not merely justified but required. Remaining behind with Miranda, who stays to protect the sanctity of her home rather than retreat to the safety of America, is Valkonen's Uncle Waldeman. Throughout the play, he has been a prophet of despair, of the apocalypse and the reign of the Antichrist, yet as the curtain falls, he calls upon his Finnish heritage through a folksong that brings "a kind of peace" to the house. At this juncture in history, any chance for permanent peace can be arrived at only through the sword.

Although geographically America never became a theater for battle as Finland did, World War II still manages to invade the Washington drawing rooms in Lillian Hellman's two plays about the conflict, one portraying the movement from isolation to involvement, the second providing a backward look at events that set the stage for the conflagration. In *Watch on the Rhine* (1941), Fanny Farrelly has insulated herself from the outside world in the closed space of her country drawing room outside the nation's capital, where she naively plays hostess to aristocratic German Nazi supporter Teck de Brancovis and his wife, Maria, who is involved in an affair with Fanny's son, David. The return of her daughter, Sara, with her children and German husband, Kurt Muller, a freedom fighter in the anti-Nazi underground movement, makes Fanny realize this "is not the world they once knew." Kurt hates all violence as a moral sickness, yet finds it necessary to kill Teck in his mother-in-law's drawing room so that he can maintain the best possible chance of saving his compatriots. Fanny, newly "shaken out of the magnolias," shows her mettle by giving money to the cause despite knowing this will "mean trouble." Her late husband's convictions that "For every man who lives without freedom, the rest of us must face the guilt," as well as his perception that all acts of oppression are linked, that "We are liable in the conscience-balance for the tailor in Lodz, the black man in our South, the peasant in—" have worn off on her and guide her response.

Hellman's structurally most complex play, *The Searching Wind* (1944), with its time shifts between the present and Italy in 1922, Berlin in 1923, and Paris in 1938, becomes a meditation on—perhaps even an admission of and act of reparation for—the moral failure of left-leaning intellectuals who fooled themselves about historical events that it was easier to countenance and condone than to challenge. The sexual dalliance that has been continuing for almost 20 years between former ambassador to France Alex Hazen and his wife Emily's closest friend, Cassie, becomes symbolic of how governments supposedly committed to democracy have closed their eyes in disbelief over villainy, have "just [sat] back and watch[ed]" tyranny unfold: Victor Emmanuel's welcome of Mussolini into Rome, the early anti-Jewish pograms, and the Munich Pact. Hazen excuses his myopia by rationalizing that it "is rare to be able to see our own time as clearly as if it were history"; Cassie, meanwhile, makes no excuse for their irresponsibility as "frivolous people" who failed to analyze what they were doing or why. Hellman assails the excuse of helplessness in the face of historical forces and processes through the Hazens' son, Sam, who declares that losing a leg in the war will be "worth it" if he can convince those belonging to his parents' generation and social class of their failure to protect freedom.

Once America has gone to war, the focus shifts from plays that urge and justify involvement to those documenting engagement in the war effort, both by those who go abroad to fight and by those left behind. Works appearing while the fighting goes on, even when written by well-established dramatists, however sincerely felt, tend to be little more than patriotic tracts in their intention and appeal. Moss Hart's *Winged Victory: The Air Force Play* (1943), with a cast of 75-plus nonspeaking extras and locales from the Midwest to the South Pacific, is as much pageant as drama, a stage documentary about wartime bonding and tearing asunder during training and battle. First performed by more than 300 soldiers and their wives before reaching Broadway, the theatrical enterprise of mounting the show as a benefit for Army Emergency Relief itself becomes analogous to the united effort of the airmen in battle. Initially, the men cover over their fear of war by talking "about it like kids going to a wonderful party." The subversion of sexual consummation—one of the flyers has his furlough cancelled on his wedding day—which is a staple of these plays, brings their sacrifice home to the audience while elevating the shared pain of the women who must wait. The soldiers' growing camaraderie and commitment helps see them through separation from children, many of them born while the fathers are continents away, and loss of best buddies. Predictable as drama, *Winged Victory* rapidly descends to a sermonette for war as a learning experience and an opportunity to remake the world into a place that transcends nationalism: war teaches that no boundaries exist in the sky, and the world is too small, and too many live in ignorance and hunger for there to be artificial divisions on earth.

Maxwell Anderson, who with Laurence Stallings had written *What Price Glory?* (1924), one of the most famous of American war plays, handles actions and themes virtually identical to Hart's but on a constricted, more personal level in *The Eve of St. Mark* (1942), produced by 75 theaters around the country before reaching New York. Taking its title from a legend about a virgin who stands at the church door and sees all those, including her lover, who will die that year pass before her, the work tells of another relationship left sexually unconsummated because of war. Notable for two expressionistic dream scenes (one in verse) that suggest a kind of mental telepathy between the soldier overseas and his mother and his fiancée back home, *Eve of St. Mark* sets the selfish will to live and love against the desire to fulfill one's patriotic duty and risk all to help usher in a new and better world. The woman left behind comes to accept the man's victory over self-interest as a symbolic marriage and the reason why she must "honor him at the sacred altar" even after his death; his mother understands that letting him go off to fight a war whose morality is never at issue is a proof of her selfless love and sacrifice for a higher cause. She and her husband, in fact, willingly send all their sons off to the war effort.

Once the fighting is over, American dramatists, even in plays about the war, apparently feel less constrained and thus able to present it more critically. Thomas Heggen and Joshua Logan's *Mister Roberts* (1948), a hugely successful comedy tinged with seriousness that starred Henry Fonda and ran for 1157 performances, satirizes a fanatical commanding officer explicitly likened to the totalitarian leaders arrayed against America and its allies. The Captain runs his Navy cargo ship like a petty tyrant, meting out punishments for minor infractions such as appearing on deck in the Pacific heat without a shirt (shades of General George Patton). His chief antagonist, Lieutenant (jg) Douglas Roberts, accuses the Captain of being everything he "joined to fight against" in almost the exact same words the radio announcer on V-E Day uses to describe "our enemies: the forces of ambition, cruelty, arrogance, and stupidity. . . . a malignant growth!" Roberts's own symbolic act of war lies in throwing overboard the Captain's prized palm tree, what he calls a "malignant growth" just like the Captain. When Roberts succeeds in getting the ship assigned to a liberty port, the individual sailors for the first time bond together into a crew; they reemphasize the power that emerges from having a common cause—egalitarianism in rebellion against authoritarianism—when they present Roberts with a handmade medallion, the "Order of the palm . . . for action against the enemy, above and beyond the call of duty." And Roberts's example lives on when his successor, Ensign Pulver, throws the Captain's two new palm trees overboard for cancelling the ship's evening movie.

If America defeats one enemy, and the crew and its junior officers get the best of another, Roberts overcomes still a third. Dissatisfied with his limited involvement in the war effort and believing that "anyone who doesn't fight is only half-alive," he receives a transfer to combat duty on a destroyer. But where once he thought this would signal an escape from "tedium" and "apathy" and "monotony," he understands that "the most terrible enemy of this war is the boredom" that follows one everywhere and that requires constant vigilance. When Roberts is killed, it ironically happens not while he is manning the guns but while drinking coffee in the wardroom as a Japanese suicide plane hits. In deromanticizing death in war, Heggen and Logan simultaneously give new value to all the seemingly nonheroic acts of those in the audience who feel they somehow missed the chance to prove themselves in battle.

In the 1954 stage adaptation of his novel *The Caine Mutiny Court-Martial*, again featuring Henry Fonda for a run of 415 performances, Herman Wouk casts a more serious look at a naval commander whose actions exceed the proper exercise of his authority. Set within the framework of a courtroom melodrama so that the theater audience tacitly become the observers until the brief didactic final scene that thematically upends much that has come before, *Caine Mutiny* focuses as much on counsel for the defense Lieutenant Barney Greenwald as it does on Lieutenant Commander Philip Queeg, who has had charges brought against his subordinate, Lieutenant Stephen Maryk, for relieving the commander of his duties while at sea in the midst of a typhoon. Queeg, another obsessive disciplinarian meticulous about the smallest details such as shirt tails hanging out, encounters troubling charges of cowardice—the sailors have nicknamed him "Old Yellowstain"—as well as of violation of regulations for erasing the log book. Wouk's psychological profile of Queeg explains his naval career as a compensation for paranoia that manifests itself in "rigidity of personality, feelings of persecution, unreasonable suspicion, withdrawal from reality, perfectionist anxiety . . . and an obsessive sense of self-righteousness."

Although Greenwald successfully defends Maryk, having to establish Queeg's mental incompetence and thus ruin his career tears the lawyer apart. For Greenwald refuses to brand all officers "stupid sadists," upholds the "principle of respect for command," and believes that challenging Queeg's authority resulted in pulling a minesweeper from the South Pacific "when it was most needed." Himself the victim of racial slurs—his former law school classmate and attorney for the prosecution accuses him of "shyster tactics"—Greenwald considers Queeg a hero for fighting to save Jews like his mother: "They're cooking us down to soap over there. They think we're vermin and should be exterminated and our corpses turned into something useful." Wouk's *Caine Mutiny* becomes, then, a morally confused and subtly reactionary work: arguing that the need to protect the ethnic outsider justifies questionable, even illegal, actions, Greenwald insinuates that, in time of war, those in authority are free to abrogate basic rights with impunity and that all their orders must be carried out even if wrong. Yet isn't that the very same justification that the war criminals will put forward at their trials? Apparently, in the age of McCarthy, to criticize even excesses of the defenders of freedom becomes somehow anti-American, and the liberal intellectuals, those whom Grenwald sees as "up on Proust 'n' *Finnegans Wake* 'n' all," immediately become suspect villains.

A more extended examination of bigotry among American fighting men appears in Arthur Laurents's *Home of the Brave* (1945), where racist slurs against the Japanese enemy as "squints" and "slant-eyed bastards" echo those directed at Private Peter Coney, called a "lousy yellow Jew bastard." Prefiguring a work like Peter Shaffer's *Equus* (1973), Laurents employs a heavily expressionistic form as Coney, under the guidance of an army doctor/psychiatrist, is gradually led to abreact, or relive, the circumstances surrounding a psychosomatic paralysis. The victim of anti-Semitism from a young age, when he overheard taunts of "dirty shenies" and suffered beatings by schoolmates for observing the Jewish holy days, Coney feels betrayed by his best buddy Finch, himself taunted as a "kike lover," when Finch barely catches himself saying "you lousy yellow— jerk." Though non-Jews in America are hardly ever thought of as gentiles—and so stigmatized as a group for being so—Coney has always been stigmatized as outsider; as Arthur Miller would declare in *Incident at Vichy* (1964), "Each man has his Jew; it is the other." Rather remarkably, the doctor judges Coney responsible for victimizing himself by allowing his "sensitivity" to his difference to become "a disease."

Feeling "glad" when Finch is shot because Finch "hated him for being a Jew," Coney's guilt causes a sudden paralysis that prevents his walking away from the dead Finch. He only experiences a cure when another soldier, who has lost an arm and will thus suffer discrimination as "a stinking cripple," makes Coney realize that every soldier experiences the same relief in surviving when others die. Differentness on any level, physical or psychological or moral, is a burden to be eschewed; nondiscriminating sameness is the sacred American ideal: "Everybody's different—but underneath we're all guys." Yet this movement toward an erasure of difference actually evades the problem of Jewishness, or of any racial otherness. Acceptance into the American community would seem to demand loss of individuality and hiding of diversity, which underlines one of the flaws of a supposedly egalitarian society.

The final horror of anti-Semitism in the Holocaust reaches the American stage in Frances Goodrich and Albert Hackett's 1956 Pulitzer Prize dramatization of *The Diary of Anne Frank*. Not that either the original or the play itself centers on the extermination camps; in fact, Goodrich and Hackett submerge the issue of race far beneath the surface. True, when the Frank family in hiding tear the mandatory Stars of David—marks of Cain forced upon innocent scapegoats—from their clothing, the outline remains, an indelible mark because race is not subject to erasure. Yet race is simultaneously, as Jean Renoir proposes in his classic antiwar film *Grand Illusion* (1937), an artificial divider employed to excuse brutalization in the cause of nationalism.

Anne Frank teaches how people not only endure but prevail over dehumanization through linking their individual fate to the spirit of community that arises even among strangers in times of fear. The play testifies to the inability of any external force to imprison the mind and spirit, while demonstrating how inhuman conditions can nonetheless lead to inhumane actions and self-generated victimization. As Anne's father, Otto, who, in a frame original to the play discovers his daughter's diary after her gassing, warns at one contentious point during their isolation: "We don't need the Nazis to destroy us. We're destroying ourselves." Essentially, however, *Anne Frank* is a rite of passage play; Anne's extraordinary circumstances hasten her process of individuation and moral development as young women and author. Writing her diary supplies a means of gaining immortality through leaving a record behind; the act of artistic creation affords a way of understanding the Holocaust, of seeing suffering and death as "part of a great pattern," even possibly a prelude to transcendence. A play more of uplift than of anger, faithful to Anne's original *Diary*, it calms rather than enrages. The narrator of the outer frame (Otto Frank) functions as a moral chorus, interpreting the inner narrator (Anne herself) and urging the audience to regard the work of art (the *Diary* itself) as somehow ameliorating the horror of the extermination camps.

The plays of the postwar period raise the issue of how the powers that liberate differ from the powers that oppress. An army on foreign soil, even if it has come to free a people from tyranny, is still an occupation force, an outside group with the strength to dominate and impose its values and culture on the natives, and so the new wielders of authority cannot help but be suspect. The American liberators of Sicily in Paul Osborn's stage adaptation of John Hersey's novel *A Bell for Adano* (1944) must, in fact, contend with the widespread impression that Americans are "barbarians" and "savages . . . worse than the Germans," who will treat the "little people" no differently from Mussolini and the local "crooks" who formerly ran city hall. The American Major Joppolo is even addressed as "Duce" when he obeys his superior's orders to keep the much-needed food carts from entering the village; granted, he does this against his better judgment, for he desires nothing less than to demonstrate that democracy is government as servant rather than master of those governed. To make recompense, Joppolo eventually secures a replacement bell for the one that Mussolini, robbing the townspeople of their "spirit" and "meaning," commandeered to make rifle barrels.

Himself a first-generation American whose parents emigrated from another small Italian town, Joppolo looks favorably upon soldiers of diverse ethnic heritages, many of whom still speak the language of the countries they invade, joined together as a prefiguration and promise of what the United States might become. The army can provide an example of pluralism in action; at home, America's diversity could be its strength. Yet amidst the euphoria of crushing foreign tyranny overhangs an uneasy awareness of how, once back in the States, these men will almost inevitably divide along race, class, and ethnic lines.

John Patrick's *Teahouse of the August Moon*, a fairy tale for adults adapted from Vern Sneider's novel and winner of the Pulitzer for drama in 1954, takes a deeply critical stance against the rectitude of imposing democracy on a nation subdued by outside force. The play's Brechtian narrator, Sakini, who acts as interpreter for the occupation army on Okinawa, judges the current subjugation as only the most recent in a series perpetrated for more than six centuries "by Chinese pirates . . . English missionaries . . . Japanese war lords . . . American marines." *Teahouse* documents the attempts of the American military to introduce technology, capitalism, and democratic rule, even if to accomplish this requires that "every one" of the natives be shot, into a culture more interested in beauty than materialism and utility. Colonel Purdy, the stereotype of the bullying officer, errs when he dispatches Captain Fisby, a former humanities teacher, to implement social and economic changes. Though Fisby possesses enough ingenuity and good old American get-up-and-go to see the local sweet-potato brandy as a source of immense profit, he chooses instead to nurture the native crafts such as vase painting, for, as one of the artisans remarks, no one can "take pride in work of machine."

Fisby encourages the natives to construct an exquisitely simple teahouse as a site for the ritual ceremony, rather than the school called for by the army manual; when the military conquerors who prize productivity over beauty order it dismantled, the sounds of its destruction harken back to the ax blows felling the trees at the end of Chekhov's *The Cherry Orchard*. The cultural difference of Japan is further symbolized by Lotus Blossom; at first rejecting her because, in his cultural insularity, Fisby equates the geisha with a prostitute, he later altruistically renounces her because racial prejudice back in the States would ensure her rejection. Fisby, however, still embraces the Oriental ideal of inner serenity that arises from a "gracious acceptance." Emphasizing the civilizing role of art, Sakini explicitly becomes an illusionist at the play's close; after the teahouse is reassembled, he "snaps fingers and the August moon is magically turned on in the sky." The teahouse becomes a theater within the theater; the place works its magic upon those who enter it in the same manner that the narrator/artist/illusionist pulls the audience momentarily away from a life driven by pragmatism into the world of art. Yet at the very end Sakini, as a Brechtian commentator, pointedly insists that any chance for coexistence and communication between two cultures is obliterated when an excess of missionary zeal requires that the native culture become totally subservient to the cultural hegemony of its foreign oppressor.

Playing Politics

If America's mission abroad while the war is in progress goes largely unquestioned on stage, not so the government and citizens at home. The characteristic ideas and outlook of a group of what might be termed political plays appearing between the end of World War II and 1960 are implicitly grounded in a political ideology that stretches back through Emerson and Thoreau—who, in "On Civil Disobedience" pointedly challenged, "Why does government mistrust its wise minority?"—to

Alexis de Tocqueville and John Stuart Mill. Prizing freedom and individual conscience, these thinkers all understood that political power and moral right do not necessarily coincide. Since the ambitious who govern are susceptible to corruption, and since the vast majority of the governed may be apathetic, these social thinkers express a radical, iconoclastic skepticism of a majority rule that may be intolerant of the minority in its midst, enforcing conformity in thought and action, a fear that became a reality during the McCarthy period. Majority rule, if not enlightened by intellect and culture, may mean, in short, that mediocrity rules and that the charismatic leader who tries to point the way to reform may be stigmatized as a rebel and an outsider.

Robert Anderson recognizes that those who have served in the war with a clarity of mission and want to extend that idealism to public office risk disillusionment and cynicism. In *Come Marching Home* (1946), a former college teacher and writer, John Bosworth, arrives home from World War II to a hero's welcome orchestrated by the media-aware yet corrupt State Senator Crawford, only to find himself reluctantly pitted against Crawford in the next election as a replacement for a candidate killed in an accident. No longer believing, as his father taught him, that one could bring about Candide's "best of all possible worlds" through winning a local election, Bosworth would prefer to retreat with his wife into their own private world, secure from disappointment and negativism. Despite threats of bodily harm and smear tactics over his father's unscrupulous business deals and his own radicalism in college, Bosworth enters the fray at the behest of his mentor, who argues that he might counteract "all the rottenness, stupidity and greed that runs riot in this country regardless of what some poor little guy may do on a beachhead in Sicily, Italy, France, or Iwo Jima."

Bosworth discovers that the electorate, jaded by the past ineffectuality of their officials, is "sound asleep," actually contributing to the corruption through their complacency. Terming himself "a pillar of society" in an allusion to the title of Ibsen's drama, he risks, like Dr. Stockmann in another Ibsen play, *Enemy of the People*, becoming an arrogant elitist who regards the mass of humanity with disdain. The conflict assumes a sharper focus over the question of the limits, if any, of one's social responsibility. When the party withdraws its support on election eve, Bosworth must choose between retreating from the political arena or waging a campaign as an independent. In opting for the latter course, following Mill's and Ibsen's "aristocrats" he adopts the messianic role of prophet. Nevertheless, as Ibsen well realized, the possibility remains that

Bosworth will continue to be a "patriot out of season," always marching one step ahead of the benighted majority. (An undiscriminating majority feeling the need for social change might, of course, be duped rather than served by another type of arrogant politician. This is strikingly seen through Willie Stark, the populist turned demagogue, in Robert Penn Warren's 1959 stage adaptation, largely shorn of its philosophical musings, of one of the great American political novels, *All the King's Men*.)

The same year as Anderson's *Come Marching Home*, Howard Lindsay and Russel Crouse wrote *State of the Union*, loosely based on Wendell Willkie's campaign for the presidency, in order "to stir the conscience of the individual citizen . . . to say certain things but to do so amusingly." Too often, Lindsay and Crouse intimate, the majority of voters are "lazy . . . ignorant . . . prejudiced people" who allow themselves to become pawns of the lawmakers, who, in turn, increasingly consider politics on a par with sports. As the kingmaker James Conover announces in one of the metaphor's earliest appearances in American theater: "In this country, we play politics and to play politics you have to play ball."

This mildest of comedies of manners (awarded the Pulitzer Prize for 1946) examines, in part, the role of the woman behind the political animal. The word "union" in its title refers to both the public and private arenas; the point of contention between Grant and Mary Matthews is sometimes the political contest, but is just as often "the other woman," a newspaper publisher named Kay Thorndike, with the romance plot almost superseding the political. Mary, bemoaning the fate of the politician's wife long before it became fashionable to do so, tries to keep the charismatic Grant's "big man" ego complex in check. Burdened by a "streak of decency" that insulates him from the seamier side of politics, he maintains belief in the best instincts of the American public, refusing to prey on either the emerging Cold War hatred of the Russians or on the easy solution of lower taxes. In the play's somewhat jingoistic ending, Grant, marriage not only intact but even strengthened, refuses to "play ball" as a candidate and so settles into the role of citizen gadfly. This underscores the playwright's message that if a society wishes to be truly democratic, no one of its citizens can hide from responsibility in an apolitical stance.

Gore Vidal's *The Best Man* (1960), also set during a political convention, focuses as well on two leading contenders for their party's presidential nomination and whether they will descend to smear tactics, using rumors of former mental instability and innuendos of homosexual conduct to destroy each other's chances. As Vidal writes almost prophetically in his "Notes," he intends to "demonstrate how, in our confused age, morality means, simply, sex found out. To most Americans, cheating, character assassination, hypocrisy, self-seeking are taken for granted as the way things are." What gives *Best Man* greater texture than a work like *State of the Union*, which it resembles most nearly in plot, is the characters' willingness to engage in ethical discussions touching on the ends of their actions rather than simply focusing on political shenanigans.

Fighting for the nomination are Secretary of State William Russell—somewhat akin to Adlai Stevenson, Democratic nominee in 1952 and again in 1956—who decries both the tendency of "people in a democracy . . . to think they have less to fear from a stupid man than from an intelligent one" and also the image-mongering media who foist off on the electorate a "product [that is] sometimes . . . a fake"; and Senator Joe Cantwell, a ruthless "end justifies the means" appeaser. Russell, the liberal humanist man of conscience being sucked into compromise and corruption merely by wanting the power that would come with the presidency, refuses to stoop to his opponent's tactics and use the available testimony to libel Cantwell's private life. Yet he cannot allow a man who utterly lacks any "sense of right or wrong" to become president, and so he throws his support behind another contender, clearly not "the best man," who is then assured of the nomination, while he himself retreats completely from public life. A sense of defeat pervades Vidal's political arena, where the intellectually astute and morally committed likely never come out winners, and this from a writer who himself ran twice, albeit unsuccessfully, for elective office.

Although Loring Mandel professes that his 1961 dramatization of Allen Drury's Pulitzer novel, *Advise and Consent*, is "personal, not political," it becomes in many ways the ultimate Cold War play, in which homosexuality is regarded as next to treason. Those who preach appeasement with the Russians are the real villains, although what Vidal said about "morality [being] sex found out" applies here as well, since compounding the evil of the appeasers are their scurrilous antihomosexual attacks. A pragmatically amoral president ("a lie is a perfectly ethical instrument of government," he believes) dying, symbolically, of cancer, nominates as secretary of state a man who believes that because the Russians have America's "back to the wall in power, prestige, and technology" since winning the space race, we must "give [up] something . . . before our position gets even weaker." The nominee lies under oath about his membership years earlier in a communist cell, rationalizing that he "has atoned" and is committed to serve. His strongest Senate supporter is even more of an appeaser, proclaiming he "would rather crawl on his knees to Moscow than perish under a thermonuclear bomb." To ensure that the nomination is approved, the senator steals from the office of the committee chair, Brig Anderson, evidence of a brief homosexual liaison Brig had in Hawaii during the war.

It would be easy to oppose the nominee for his wishy-washiness over the Russians; Brig chooses to oppose him instead for his lying and expediency in being a party to bribery and blackmail. Although he feels neither "regret [n]or guilt" over acting on his vulnerability in responding to the "first personal touch in three years" during an army experience that tended to dehumanize and depersonalize the individual, Brig commits suicide rather than "bend and be silent" about the nominee's unsuitability. In the play's final moment, the vice president breaks a tie vote, saying "no" to the nominee, as word comes that the Russians have landed on the moon. *Advise and Consent* appears to cut two ways with its audiences: it enshrines the Cold War politics of one-upmanship, while paying lip service to gay rights—though after his one indiscretion Brig became safely heterosexual. In the world of *Advise and Consent*, it is apparently perfectly all right to be measuredly progay, but not to be prodetente, even temperately so.

Posing the Woman Question

A highly popular comedy from immediately after the war—and one sufficiently resonant to be revived in London in the early 1970s under the direction of dramatist Tom Stoppard and filmed anew in the early 1990s—bridges the two categories of plays discussed thus far and introduces a feminist note as well. Garson Kanin's *Born Yesterday* (1946) tells a Pygmalion and Galatea tale, with the woman transformed so far beyond the expectations of the person who arranges for her tutoring that she ironically bests him. Set in Washington, D.C., the seat of political power, the play addresses a Shavian theme: the necessity for reason and intelligence to exercise control over money and muscle. Harry Brock, a scrap metal war profiteer, represents the new robber barons and captains of industry whose political influence reaches into the Congress, here in the person of Senator Hedges, who follows the "common practice" of being bought. Devoid of any sense of civic responsibility, these profiteers make a mockery of the free enterprise system, creating a dog-eat-dog society. Their amorality—Kanin pointedly uses lyrics from Cole Porter's "Anything Goes" to conclude act 1—breeds a "don't care-ism" that infiltrates all areas of American life; when personal selfishness becomes legitimized on such a large scale, it becomes equivalent to fascism, the enemy supposedly defeated during the war.

Brock, desiring a veneer of education and refinement for his spunky mistress, Billie Dawn, captivatingly played by Judy Holliday for 1642 performances of the play, enlists the aid of Paul Verrall, a columnist for the *New Republic* who has written "The Yellowing Democratic Manifesto" to argue that the "rules and ideals and—principles and hopes on which the United States is based" have been largely ignored of late. When people get "wiser" and understand that by government should be meant a "few million people" and not a machine that thrives on influence peddling, then there will follow "a revolution." This indeed happens when Billie becomes educated and gets the goods on the abusive Brock, who has covered over illegal dealings by putting financial holdings in her name. With Verrall to guide and inspire her, Billie reads and reads, which awakens her curiosity, stimulates her imagination, and develops her independence. Real power resides in the knowledge that comes from the printed word, so much so that Brock, feeling threatened, destroys her books in an obvious allusion to the Nazi book burnings. But in this play about sexual politics and empowerment, a "Big Fascist" like Brock cannot prevent Billie's e(wo)mancipation: "You don't own me. Nobody can own anybody," she proclaims, asserting that only the ignorant need ever submit to being truly powerless.

One of the commanding motifs of classic American literature has been a continuing tension between the individual and society: between personal rights, freedoms, and endeavors on the one hand and community needs, repressions, and sanctions on the other; between empowerment to be oneself and perceived powerlessness at the hands of a patriarchal system. The plays discussed here suggest that although the war may have united Americans in a commonality of spirit and made them willing to submit to authority to prevent anarchy, the people were never fully comfortable in denying adequate space for individualism; even such authoritarianism as inevitably comes with rank in battle seems inimical to the egalitarian ideal. The personal integrity of those in power, both in the military and in government, is suspect, for their ambition to "rule" within what purports to be a democratic structure makes them neglect, or even forget, the call to personal moral integrity and the communitarian ideal. Furthermore, the hegemonic culture, attempting to mask over or erase differences, fails to respond adequately to the realities of racial, ethnic, class, and gender divisions. Sameness as a goal in the areas of thought and political belief, upheld as a strength against the enemy without, ironically may have exposed the nation to such enemies as victimization and discrimination from within.

2

Eugene O'Neill:
''Faithful Realism''
with a Poet's Touch

In a famous passage of reverie late in Eugene O'Neill's *Long Day's Journey into Night* (1956), Edmund, a portrait of the author as a young artist, lyrically recounts for his matinee-idol father, James Tyrone, a transcendent moment he experienced while at sea. When the elder Tyrone responds by proclaiming that "there's the makings of a poet in you all right," Edmund rejects the compliment, insisting on the incommensurateness between his vision and the seeming paucity of his language: "I couldn't touch what I tried to tell you just now. I just stammered. That's the best I'll ever do I mean, if I live. Well, it will be faithful realism, at least." Edmund/O'Neill did, of course, survive his 1912 bout with consumption to become, within less than 25 years, America's first major playwright and its only dramatist to be awarded the Nobel Prize for literature.

When he received that honor in 1936, O'Neill paid tribute to August Strindberg, the Swedish dramatist whom he had long acknowledged as his master. More than 10 years earlier, in "Strindberg and Our Theatre," O'Neill had attempted to define the Scandinavian playwright's achievement as "the precursor of all modernity in our present theater" by coining the phrase " 'behind-life' plays" to designate Strindberg's radically new form. Rejecting as outmoded those works which simply held "the family Kodak up to ill-nature," O'Neill saw Strindberg as breaking free from the bounds of naturalism through bringing expressionism into the drama, creating what the young disciple would describe as " 'super-naturalism.' "[1] In his perceptiveness about Strindberg's dramatic strategies for revealing the states of mind and soul of his characters, O'Neill hit upon the integration of realism with expressionistic techniques that would later become one of the hallmarks of classic American drama in such plays as Williams's *A Streetcar Named Desire* and Miller's *Death of a Salesman.*

O'Neill's own productivity during the two decades beginning around 1915 would itself be characterized by a tremendous urge to experiment with dramatic styles and hybrid forms. He would espouse naturalism in the early one-act sea plays, as well as in *Beyond the Horizon* (1920), *Anna Christie* (1921), and *Desire under the Elms* (1924). He would venture into expressionism with *The Emperor Jones* (1920), *The Hairy Ape* (1922), and *All God's Chillun Got Wings* (1924). He would employ the masked drama in *The Great God Brown* (1926), the interior monologue in *Strange Interlude* (1928), and the split personality in *Days without End* (1934). He would recast classical mythology by setting a Greek trilogy in Civil War America in *Mourning Becomes Electra* (1931). No matter the form, throughout all these works and those that would follow there recurs an emphasis on striving for a sense of belonging, of oneness or at-homeness with the self, with the family or community, with nature, and with the force that rules nature; the word "home," in fact, became a leitmotif in *Desire under the Elms*, just as it would be in *Long Day's Journey into Night*. In a justly famous and widely quoted 1928 letter to theater critic George Jean Nathan, O'Neill claimed that the dramatist "must have [as his] big subject . . . The death of the old God and the failure of Science and Materialism to give any satisfying new one for the surviving primitive religious instinct to find a meaning for life in, and to comfort its fears of death with." For almost a dozen years, from the mid-1930s to the mid-1940s, O'Neill would fall silent on the stage, only to reappear briefly just after World War II, and then be absent again for a decade until his triumphant reemergence in the mid-1950s, first on the Swedish stage and then on the American, three years after his death in 1953. Yet during that period of public silence, he was privately agonizing over the works that would come to be considered as among his greatest ever. Largely stripped of experimentation, they are written in Edmund's mode of "faithful realism," adumbrated by touches of the "poet" whom Tyrone foresaw.

The Cycle Plays

As early as 1934, O'Neill had begun pondering an ambitious cycle of plays under the collective title "A Tale of Possessors Self-Dispossessed." What was at first projected to be four or five plays grew to seven and then nine and finally eleven works that would trace "the material, psychological, and spiritual history" of an American family over nearly a century and a half. O'Neill's emphasis in the cycle would be to show how greed for material prosperity sapped the spirit and true wealth of the nation, making a mockery of the American dream. The United States had become, O'Neill would say, "the greatest failure the world has ever seen" because it did not have "sense enough" to realize that the key to happiness lay in the biblical injunction, "For what shall it profit a man if he shall gain the whole world and lose his own soul?"

The only play from the projected cycle completed to O'Neill's satisfaction during his lifetime was *A Touch of the Poet,* worked at on and off between 1935 and 1942. The fact that the play has seen only one major New York production, with Helen Hayes in 1958, a year after its world premiere in Stockholm, has perhaps prevented its being recognized as a pivotal work for the later O'Neill. Yet *Poet* highlights important thematic patterns that will recur over and over again in this last burst of creativity until O'Neill's debilitating physical condition essentially forced him to stop composing after 1943. These motifs center on the nature of love, the possibility of living life without illusion, the dissolution of personality in a succession of masks or roles, and the primacy of art and the artist's vocation.

Set in a no-longer-prosperous tavern a few miles outside Boston, *Touch of the Poet* takes place on 27 July 1828, the anniversary of the glorious Battle of Talavera, at which Major Cornelius "Con" Melody, Irish immigrant turned barkeep, was commended for bravery by the Duke of Wellington. Melody, who has separated himself socially and politically from the Jacksonian Democrat Irish riff-raff in the town, is, as his sobriquet "Con" indicates, a poseur who adopts a succession of masks. In "Memoranda on Masks," a seminal essay written for the *American Specta-*

tor in 1932, and one of the few items he ever wrote (except for his voluminous correspondence) other than his plays, O'Neill proposes the philosophical basis for what he calls a *"Dogma for the new masked drama. One's outer life passes in a solitude haunted by the masks of others; one's inner life passes in a solitude hounded by the masks of oneself."* This universal tendency to resist being known by others and even by the self through adopting a succession of masks poses a strategic problem for the playwright who must discover new methods for "unmasking" the "inner drama . . . of souls," for "express[ing] those profound hidden conflicts of the mind which the probings of psychology continue to disclose to us." One element of O'Neill's genius as a dramatist is his ability to accomplish that goal of dramatizing interiority through largely visual or gestural means.

The most prominent element in O'Neill's set description for *Poet* is the "large mirror" on the left wall of the tavern's dining room. From a visual perspective, the four most highly theatrical moments in the play occur when, once in each act, Con Melody stares at his reflection in the mirror, becoming his own audience; it is as if the tavern were a stage, the mirror's frame a proscenium, and the actor and viewer were one. The fact that the reflection, the person reflected, and the person looking at the reflection are one and the same only underscores the fragmentation and dissociation of personality and raises Pirandellian questions. Can the mirror ever give back the truth by going beneath the surface to reveal the reality, or does it simply confirm the mask or reflection? Is there, finally, any unitary self beneath the mask to affirm?

In the first instance in act 1, Con, overseen by his contemptuous daughter, Sara, finds reassurance through the mirror's image of himself as "an officer and a gentleman," supported by a recitation of Byron's disdainful lines ("I stood / Among them, but not of them"). O'Neill repeats the imagistic pattern in act 2, but now with the Yankee wife and mother Deborah Harford as Con's audience. By the third instance, Con appears in costume wearing his soldier's dress uniform, as he strikes his "arrogant, Byronic pose" before the Harford family lawyer. By the last act, Con has killed the Major's prop, his cherished mare, and does a "vulgar burlesque" of his earlier pose, now assuming an exaggerated "mocking brogue" of the Irish shebeen keeper ancestry that he has heretofore denied. These visually symbolic moments force one to think about the moral consequences of illusion for a modernist writer such as O'Neill: Does any real self or "I" exist to be discovered, or is the self simply a fluid succession of roles or masks and life a matter of playacting? Isn't Con simply moving from one equally false illusion (the heroic Major) to another (the thieving innkeeper), as was true of O'Neill characters as far back as Yank Smith in *The Hairy Ape*, who progressed from an illusion of belonging, to a condition of not belonging, and then ultimately to another illusion of belonging?

Con has always found unquestioning support in his illusions, and will continue to find it, from his wife, Nora, for that is how she defines the nature of her love for him. Although "ashamed" of Nora's peasant background, Con escaped the loneliness of one-night stands with local whores and married the pretty if pregnant Nora before going off to war. For her part, Nora must have been attracted by the prospect of rising socially, marrying the handsome man who lived in the castle that his newly gentrified father, who had started out as "a thievin' shebeen keeper," bought with money bilked out of tenants and borrowers. Now Con, who dissociates himself publicly from the lower-class Irish Catholics in the Massachusetts town in favor of the more aristocratic Protestant Yankees, never lets Nora forget her peasant roots; she, moreover, can never forget the Catholic faith she guiltily left behind to marry Con.

In short, her condition is one of servitude (the title of one of O'Neill's apprentice plays) and differs little from several other instances of ethnic and class oppression: immigrant peasants by Yankee landowners, Irish by English, Catholics by an authoritarian Roman church. Nora will make herself into a drudge so that Con can maintain his pretense of high station. She will endlessly forgive and excuse his insults and abuse, blaming them on his drinking, and even encourage him in his illusions of social superiority, perhaps so she can rationalize away her own oppressed condition by feeling superior. Nora refuses, however, to consider her service as slavery; rather, it becomes the source of her honor, her love for Con being what sustains her. Yet that, perhaps, is simply her own illusion to make her station in life bearable. And her refusal to ever criticize or find fault with Con may, in fact, render her love for him destructive rather than creative in its impact.

Sara, in her love for Simon Harford, son of a Yankee business-man, refuses to be totally her mother's daughter. The concept of loving so that "you can't call your soul your own anymore" carries ominous connotations, especially given the verbal echo later in Mary Tyrone's admission in *Long Day's Journey into Night* of having lost control of her soul through her addiction, and hardly suits Sara's plans for rising socially and materially in the world. Although at times she pays lip service to the notion of a woman's finding her sole definition of self in love for a man, she ultimately acts more pragmatically; she will not let her heart rule her head. She will love, but she will not be so much a slave to love that she relinquishes her power. Thus, she would, if necessary, agree to her father's plot of seducing Simon, whose honor would then trap him into marrying her. And she will, as Con predicts, eventually root out Simon's Thoreauvian dream of escaping from the corruptions of society into the pristine woods and there becoming a poet, though Simon's dream, dependent on a myth of innocence that retains little connection with the realities of people's lives, is itself an illusion. The American myth of a recoverable Edenic state available by moving into the wilderness has (to borrow F. Scott Fitzgerald's formulation) "receded before us" in O'Neill; the new American experience is one of materialistic greed and aggressive competition, one that ultimately victimizes society's underclass and destroys the sensitive artist figure.

Sara, who herself embodies something of the poseur in masking her real motives, vacillates in her attitude toward Con's illusions, at times wanting him to wake "from his lies and mad dreams . . . to face the truth of himself," while at other times feeling agony over the fear that he will permanently throw off his pose of "Major." When the "requiem" is finally played for the dead gentleman/soldier, Sara "mourn[s]" his loss, since Con's illusions fed her own and gave her faith in rising above her station. Nora says that "love" alone will now need to sustain Sara, but her love will be grievously tainted by the lust for power, as shown in *More Stately Mansions*, the sequel to *A Touch of the Poet*, set some years after Sara and Simon have married.

Although O'Neill called *More Stately Mansions* (1939) "Unfinished Work" and requested that the typescript be destroyed after his death, it reached production, translated into Swedish and extensively cut, in Stockholm in 1962; five years later Jose Quintero directed the American premiere, with even further cuts, first in Los Angeles and then in New York in 1967, starring Ingrid Bergman and Colleen Dewhurst. In act 3, a triumphant Sara, who out of greed has willingly turned herself into a sexual object, using her body as a commodity with which to buy power over her husband, assumes much the same assured stance before the mirror that Con had in *Poet*. Yet the first mirror the audience sees in scene 1 of *Mansions* during Con's offstage wake is "a cracked mirror hanging askew," which reveals how potentially false and distorted the image reflected might be. To gain material and psychological power, Sara must, like the two other central characters in the play, dispossess her better self. From the perspective of the two women, Sara and her mother-in-law, Deborah, *Mansions* is a battle to control the husband-lover-son, and O'Neill's almost sculptural arrangement of characters on stage underscores the debilitating, smothering nature of the two women's embrace in act 4 that dispossess Simon of his true self. This bears out Travis Bogard's statement concerning one important aspect of the "Possessors" cycle, that it "was to show woman as destroyer,"[2] a theme so prevalent in many of the dramatist's earlier plays. From the perspective of Simon, the battle is between an idealistic ideology and artistic vocation on the one hand and, on the other, the equally powerful pull to satisfy latent Oedipal longings and become a little boy once again. At first a believer in a Rousseauistic, classless society in which human nature is uncorrupted, Simon eventually does a complete aboutface: men must be as the times are, and so he pursues power without scruple, for to win is good, to lose bad. Claiming art's incompatibility with competitiveness, he burns the manuscript of the sociopolitical tract he has been writing (just as O'Neill would one day do with the notes and drafts for his aborted cycle) and devotes himself to profiteering in the slave trade.

On both sides, that of the women and that of the son-husband, the drive is toward securing happiness, but in O'Neill that is at best an elusive and misdirected goal, especially if unmerited or selfish. As Simon remarks to his mother when she recounts a fairy tale with a surprisingly grim ending, "I would still like to discover if you could possibly imagine a happy ending to that tale." Happy endings in O'Neill are either more than characters should hope for, or if they ever do arrive, are unconventional. In the epilogue to *Mansion*, Sara and Simon, released from the pull of greed, have left the fine house and are ensconced in a cabin in the woods, somewhat unconvincingly satisfied to be back working the land, although Sara still wants the "American promise" of material success to be available to their four sons. The final scene of the play proper ends more compellingly, with Deborah choosing to entomb herself in the octagonal summerhouse (its arched door painted the same Chinese lacquer red as was used at Tao House, where O'Neill wrote his last works) in her formal garden that tames and distorts nature.

The summerhouse seems to be equated with the mind, and entering it with a retreat into interiority, solipsism, and ultimately madness. Deborah, who conducts "insane, interminable dialogues with self," has long escaped through her romantic imagination into the world of dreams, recurrently one in which she is Napoleon's mistress. She vacillates between her desire to lose herself totally in the dream and to maintain contact with external reality. Her final, willed entrance into the summerhouse should be seen, however, as an expiatory rite, designed to atone for her grasping possession of Simon. Realizing that she must free Simon from his obsession with her, she acts out of love when she shoves him away from the door and prevents his entering with her, since for the son that would be a journey back to the womb-now-become-tomb. Having earned the opportunity to save him by, for once in her life, putting another ahead of the self, Deborah appears "happy" and "blessed" in her complete withdrawal from reality. Whether that happiness is real or is simply feigned in order to "set [Simon] free" remains ambiguous; for Deborah might, as does Hickey through his pose of insanity in *The Iceman Cometh*, be playacting in order to salvifically restore others. Verbal patterns in *Mansions* also point the way toward *Iceman*: Neither life, which "just stammers haltingly to an unintelligible end," nor death, "a meaningless ceasing to breathe," has meaning, and "when the bride or bridegroom cometh, we are kissing Death." Yet Deborah's final act of enclosure in the summerhouse perhaps finds its nearest parallel in Mary Tyrone's retreat to the past in a *Long Day's Journey into Night*, in a drug-induced fog of forgetfulness in which she, too, gives up the writer/son.

"Pipe Dreams" and the Right Kind of Pity

The American poet, critic, and composer Ned Rorem once commented that, in contrast to much of the theatrical work emanating from Europe in the postwar years, there exists an "intellectual tameness" about most American drama; and there is certainly some truth in this assertion that the strong suit of most American plays is not the philosophical viewpoints they espouse. It is to be found, rather, in the variety of their theatrical styles and techniques and in the immediacy of the emotional impact exerted upon audiences. O'Neill himself, in fact, in assessing his career in a letter dated 1944, asserted that his own "most valuable contribution as an *American* dramatist" was that he "awakened the world to the fact adult American drama existed, beyond pure theatrical entertainment" that could be "criticized as art, like works of the best European playwrights." And if there is any single American drama that belies Rorem's assertion and supports O'Neill's own it is surely *The Iceman Cometh* (1946), the densest and most richly philosophical of O'Neill's works; little wonder that it has been a favorite with European critics, exhibiting as it does a full share of the thematic complexity associated with some of the Continental philosophers turned playwrights such as Sartre and Camus.

At the time of *Iceman*'s composition, O'Neill was in a bleak frame of mind. His letters make apparent just what a state of depression the threat of World War II plunged him into, so that he could barely summon up the will and energy to write. To various correspondents he confided that he "had sunk deeper and deeper into a profound pessimistic lethargy" during "these times when nothing seems of less importance than whether another play is produced or not produced, or written, or not written, for that matter!"

Unsuccessful during its first showing in New York, *Iceman*'s 1956 revival at the Circle in the Square, directed by José Quintero, with Jason Robards, Jr., as Hickey, inaugurated the O'Neill renaissance on the American stage. The inhabitants of Harry Hope's run-down saloon, based partly on characters O'Neill knew at The Hell Hole and Jimmy the Priest's in New York in 1915, are a microcosm of society's down-and-outers, awaiting the arrival of the salesman Theodore Hickman, known as Hickey, who will help them celebrate Hope's birthday. For them, the bar furnishes a warm haven, a kind of supportive, nurturing womb; yet it is also, as the verbal imagery indicates, a kind of tomb, a "morgue" filled with "corpses" and "stiffs" when the drink does not have its desired effect of blinding these people to reality. O'Neill uses drinking (and falling off to sleep) strategically as a way of effecting entrances and exits, so to speak, of his large cast of main and supporting characters without always having to move them on and off the stage. For the characters themselves, drink may cancel inhibitions, increase candor, help nostalgically recall the past, or bring about oblivion, thereby hiding them from the truth. The minor or choral voices all share in a similar pattern: once idealistic, they have all seen the defeat of those ideals and retreated to a world of illusion or "pipe dreams," from which they claim they will awake and face the truth and begin living their lives again "tomorrow," as indicated by the name of one of them, Jimmy Tomorrow.

Hickey comes unto them as a type of evangelist, preaching a doctrine that calls for destroying illusions in favor of living with the truth. Yet the essence of the gospel of this salesman as con man is nihilism; his brand of salvation, instead of bringing peace to this misbegotten lot that recognizes its illusions for what they are and causes no harm to others by living in illusion, actually brings death. The effect on Harry Hope, with his multiple or layered pipedreams, is illustrative. For 20 years, ever since his wife Bessie's death, Harry has stayed inside; this former ward boss and small-time politico claims that nobody ever played him for a sucker, that he loved Bessie dearly, and that he lost all ambition when she died, but that eventually he will go out again. Yet he no more than leaves the safety of the saloon before he hurries back, distraught. He will never again venture out, just as he did not really love Bessie. Now the liquor has lost its desired effect, and he can no longer retreat to his illusions. Hickey is the Iceman (or Death) of O'Neill's title, which blends the sacred with the profane, its biblical allusion to Christ as the bridegroom yoked with a bawdy reference to an adulterous lover who is breathing hard but has not yet reached orgasm.

Hope's confession is paralleled by those of others about the women in their lives. Women at first glance seem to be marginalized in this play; the only ones who appear on stage are subsidiary characters, the three whores, Cora, Margie, and Pearl. And yet, the important unseen characters, much talked about, are all women. Jimmy Tomorrow, for example, confesses that it was not his wife Marjorie's adultery that drove him to drink, but his drinking that led her to unfaithfulness. The most important of these offstage women is Evelyn, Hickey's wife, whose story becomes central to the play. Once again, the confession is a gradual peeling back of layers. When Hickey tells the stunned group that Evelyn has died, he claims that being released from the marriage has freed him from the need to drink and brought him peace, a happiness he wants to share with the habituees by showing them what Evelyn's pipedream did to their marriage. (Significantly, the last word of each of the first three long acts is "happy," which may be O'Neill's signal that the notion human beings can ever be happy constitutes the worst illusion of all.)

Evelyn was, like Nora in *Poet*, an unfailingly supportive and devoted wife. When Hickey returned from his frequent debauches, she always forgave him, never held him to account, always took him back. That may, in fact, have been her need. But such an uncritical love only served to increase his guilt. When Hickey admits that he killed his wife, he claims to have done it as a proof of his love, so that she could no longer be hurt by his drunken infidelities and the perpetual need to forgive him. Yet that constant forgiveness proved demeaning to him, making him "feel like a skunk." Her love became intolerable, because it produced guilt in the loved one for his inability to love equally in return. Inadvertently, his true attitude toward Evelyn as a "damned bitch" comes out, though he tries immediately to retract it. When he perceives the effect his confession has on the others, he claims that he was insane at the time of Evelyn's murder; whether he makes that claim for himself, because his guilt is too much for him to bear, or whether he does it for the others, so that they can retreat contentedly to their illusions once more, remains ambiguous. And if he does it for the others, the question becomes whether this is the "right kind" of pity or the wrong, as Evelyn's was.

The other arrival at Harry Hope's, this time a complete outsider, is Don Parritt, who, like Hickey, comes with a need to confess what he has done to the central woman in his life. Indeed, the connection between the two men is masterfully indicated by the counterpoint in their dialogue, with Don oftentimes responding as if Hickey had spoken for him. The manner in which they handle guilt, however, differs. Hickey, perhaps bluffing insanity, seems to need understanding, whereas Don demands that another judge him so that expiation can follow; in order to forgive himself, he requires that someone else mete out the punishment. If Hickey might be seen as an inverted Christ, bringing a salvation that is no salvation, Don is a Judas figure, having betrayed his activist mother, Rosa, to the government authorities.

As with Hickey, Don's pipedream of why he squealed on the radicals is many layered, so he only gradually confesses the actual reason. He begins by rationalizing that the radical movement was itself only a pipedream; then he claims to have gone to the authorities out of patriotic duty, then for money to spend on tarts. Finally, he backs off from his protestations that he still loves his mother to an admission that he really hated her for not attending to him fully during years when she had other men, and for making all his decisions for him. He comes to Harry Hope's for judgment, specifically approaching Larry Slade, who had been his mother's lover and thus functions as a father figure; O'Neill even leaves open the possibility that Larry may be Don's biological father.

Larry, the only character who remains on stage during the entire course of *Iceman*, may well be O'Neill's most subtle and complex creation. Larry's destructive pipedream is to think of himself as "the Old Foolosopher" who has safely ascended the grandstand from which he can watch life with detachment. Unaware that this is a pipedream, Larry claims to be through with pity, through with the movement and Rosa, waiting to welcome the comfortable sleep of death. Hickey, though, understands that Larry's seeing all sides of every question has actually paralyzed him into inactivity.

Hickey serves as a catalyst for Larry, forcing him to take action; that Hickey can exert a positive rather than a destructive impact on Larry is, though, more the measure of Larry's greater inner strength, as contrasted with that of the other inhabitants at Hope's. In essence, Hickey insists that Larry not act toward Don in the way that Evelyn had always acted toward him, for to do that means offering the "wrong kind of pity," the kind that might make the giver happier but serves only to make the receiver feel guiltier. Larry must stop fooling himself that the movement and Rosa no longer matter to him; that he somehow remains disconnected from the destiny of others; that he longs for, rather than fears, death. At great personal cost to himself, Larry becomes the demanding father/god and provides Parritt with the judgment essential if he is ever to feel forgiven, sentencing him to take the jump off the fire escape. Such submission to the demands of a harsh patriarch as a prelude to atonement forms a recurring motif, and evidence of a residue of Puritanism, in O'Neill, from Desire under the Elms, through Mourning Becomes Electra, to Iceman.

Larry, meanwhile, has freely chosen commitment, to a cause and to life itself, over noncommitment or detachment. That need for demonstrating a willed commitment to others, along with a focus on the destructive force of an uncritical love, are as much Iceman's central themes as is O'Neill's emphasis that ordinarily "humankind cannot bear very much reality" and so must take refuge in the safe and many times harmless harbor of illusion. Larry can admit to being Hickey's "only real convert to death" precisely because he becomes the only inhabitant at Hope's who from now on will live totally without illusion. He understands that it truly is an illusion to believe that disinterestedness and retreat can solve human problems (perhaps a reflection of O'Neill's growing pessimism about isolationism as a legitimate stance in the face of historic evil). Whereas formerly Larry had looked forward to dying submissively as an escape from the human condition, only now is he really ready to accept death by recognizing it as a feared part of life. If O'Neill in Touch of the Poet intimated that life is tragic because the self is ultimately unknowable, in Iceman he appears to be suggesting that life is tragic because the great majority of humankind find it bearable only when they do not look at the truth. In his next play, the deeply autobiographical Long Day's Journey into Night, he will propose that life's tragedy resides in the fact that most people come to knowledge about themselves too late to affect any change.

The Autobiographical Plays

Although it may not possess the thematic density of Iceman Cometh, O'Neill's intensely autobiographical Long Day's Journey into Night is generally considered his greatest work, for its consummate skill in language, characterization, and symbolic motifs, for its raw emotional power—recollected, if not in tranquility, at least with acceptance—and for its ability to move audiences. The dramatist himself thought it his "best play." In many ways, on the surface it remains a simple play, telling of one summative day and night in the lives of four family members, and yet it is extraordinarily profound. O'Neill underwent considerable agony composing "this play of old sorrow, written in tears and blood," dredging up his own ghosts from the past; it was a cathartic experience, analogous to the plunges into personal and familial darkness that he always demanded of the characters in his works. When he completed it on 22 July 1941, he dedicated it in "gratitude" and "love" to his wife, Carlotta, on their twelfth anniversary: "A sadly inappropriate gift, it would seem, for a day celebrating happiness. But you will understand. I mean it as a tribute to your love and tenderness which gave me the faith in love that enabled me to face my dead at last and write this play—write it with deep pity and understanding and forgiveness for *all* the four haunted Tyrones." When the play, first seen in Stockholm, was produced in the United States in 1956 with Frederic March, Florence Eldridge, Jason Robards, Jr., and Bradford Dillman, it posthumously won O'Neill his fourth Pulitzer Prize for drama—the others had been for *Beyond the Horizon*, *Anna Christie*, and *Strange Interlude*.

Each of the four Tyrones, along with being the object of bitter accusations and recriminations by the others, is experiencing what might be called, in the broadest sense, a crisis in faith tied to a failure in vocation. Their admission of this sense of failure accounts for the central forward action of the play; this, in turn, gives rise to the work's confessional structure, complete with extended monologues, hastened under the influence of artificial stimuli like drugs and drink. All other significant action has happened in the past; O'Neill's biographer, Louis Sheaffer, refers to "The Past" in *Journey* as "an unseen presence looming over all and constituting in effect a sixth member of the household."[3]

As Mary Tyrone says, moreover, in a line echoed and re-echoed in O'Neill's later works (and indebted perhaps to Ibsen's recurrent emphasis on the moral connection between past and present and the way that the former can poison the latter): "the past is the present isn't it? We all try to lie out of that but life won't let us." The visual and aural conjunction between the words "lie" and "life," which Nina pointed to specifically in *Strange Interlude*, underlines the importance of the life lie, the thing that protects one from the truth, for O'Neill's characters.

The situation of James Tyrone, Sr., the play's pater familias, represents O'Neill's final handling of the tension between the poet and the businessman that goes as far back in his work as the early play, "Fog"

David Hay's set for the original Broadway production of *Long Day's Journey into Night. Courtesy of the Collection of American Literature, Beineke Rare Book and Manuscript Library, Yale University.*

(1917). Overly conscious of the fine line separating economic security from the poorhouse ever since his father deserted the family and left the young son to help support his mother and siblings, James has become obsessed with saving for the future and is miserly in his ways, though not with money for drink or land speculation; he has been particularly cheap with medical care, first for his wife and now for his younger son. The drive for the dollar led him, most disastrously of all, to give up a career as a Shakespearean actor, praised even by costar Edwin Booth, for fame and great fortune as a matinee idol in *The Count of Monte Cristo*. In short, he sold out his artistry for profit. Retrospectively, he looks back and wonders, in a passage similar to the overall theme of O'Neill's aborted cycle on America's decline into materialism, "What was it I hoped to buy that was worth it?"

If James chose a glamorous career as popular performer in preference to a fulfilling vocation as a serious actor, his older son Jamie suffers from never having pursued any calling. Unlike his father, he is a nonartist, who has held odd jobs in the theater as bit actor and jack-of-all-trades. Without any vocation to anchor him, he experiences a general sense of malaise and has become cynical and jealous, even developing a Mephisto-phelian kind of sneer. At least, however, he lives without illusions about himself; quoting from Dowson, he admits his name is "might have been." Believing that it was his brother's birth that addicted their mother to morphine, he has always been vindictive and destructive toward Edmund, confessing that he wants him "to fail." Yet, most important, for his younger brother's sake he risks losing Edmund's love in order to warn him against the concerted threat that Jamie poses to his well-being in hoping he will fail in everything he attempts. His confession, then, is an act of both hatred and love. These are the poles between which these characters continually fluctuate, as was made especially clear in Sidney Lumet's stunning film version of the play, as they advance and retreat from one another, embrace and push away or revile.

The Tyrones' younger son, Edmund, the incipient artist, finds himself groping toward his vocation as a poet. Now a fledgling writer on an inconsequential local paper, he has lost the sense of purpose and belonging he felt when he had shipped out to sea and experienced a transcendental, near-mystical union in what was an epiphanic moment, a poet's lifting of the veil of appearance to plumb the reality beneath. In what might be a biblical allusion to the passage from Paul in *1 Corinthians* about seeing face to face rather than through a glass darkly, Edmund speaks ecstatically of penetrating the secret: "Then the moment of ecstatic freedom came. The peace, the end of the quest, the last harbor, the joy of belonging to a fulfillment beyond man's lousy, pitiful, greedy fears and hopes and dreams! . . . Like a saint's vision of beatitude. Like the veil of things as they seem drawn back by an unseen hand. For a second you see—and seeing the secret, are the secret. For a second there is meaning! The hand lets the veil fall and you are alone, lost in the fog again." At the same time, however, he knows of the intractability of this experience to language, of the ineffectuality of the word to incarnate the vision, or at least doubts his own facility with such words, claiming he could only "stammer" in "the native eloquence of us fog people." The fog, a perva-sive symbol in the play, might be the human condition of life deprived of the art that pierces through the appearances. Yet the fog also symbolizes death, for the sea, functioning as the desideratum of Edmund's death wish, holds promise of escape and loss as well as of ecstatic union: "The fog and the sea seemed part of each other. It was like walking on the bottom of the sea. As if I had drowned long ago. As if I was a ghost belonging to the fog, and the fog was the ghost of the sea. It felt damned peaceful to be nothing more than a ghost within a ghost."

The fog serves as the mother Mary's symbol, too. She finds the fog, which can hide one from oneself, comforting, and the foghorn, which beckons one back to an unwanted reality, a threat. The fog becomes analogous to the morphine that she uses to dull all the pain and retreat from the present into the past: from aging, evidenced by white hair and arthritic hands; from guilty memories, over leaving her sons to go on the road with her actor husband, and thus perhaps being responsible for their son Eugene's death (the dramatist gave his own name to the dead boy); from shame over having found surcease from physical pain in morphine; from regret over having given up a vocation as a concert pianist or a nun to marry James Tyrone. As an Irish Catholic among Yankee Protestants, Mary feels marginalized from any social circle, lacking female companionship except for the servant girl, Cathleen. She went from being her father's daughter to being her husband's wife without ever developing an identity of her own, and without finding the home she hoped to acquire. The curse of the romantic imagination that made her fall prey to the matinee idol deflected her from pursuing those earlier dreams of fulfillment in either art as a pianist or religion as a nun; so her real betrayal occurred much earlier than her addiction.

All the men in her life have somehow failed her, from the father who gave her away to the husband who left her lonely within marriage to the lost sons who either died or are dying or are debauched, so much so that she distrusts any God whose gender is male. Imitating the iconography of the Virgin to whom she prays for forgiveness, Mary's final entrance finds her wearing a sky-blue nightdress, but trailing the wedding dress that she wore for her marriage to James Tyrone. At the same time, the elaborate lace gown serves as a reminder of the dress she would have worn as a bride of Christ on the day she professed her vows as a nun— just as the newspaper clipping that Tyrone has saved about his performances with Booth in Shakespeare recalls the might-have-beens of his foreshortened career as a classical actor. The morphine, however, is powerless to return Mary back all the way to the time of innocence; instead, she ends suspended, frozen in that moment when happiness turned into pain: "But then I met your father and was so happy for a time."

Mary, who in moments of lucidity admits to being a "lying dope fiend," articulates O'Neill's peculiarly American notion of determinism, which positions human beings as both fated and free, or, perhaps more accurately, as free and then fated by the results of exercising that very freedom. Talking about "things happen[ing]" so that it finally becomes "too late" for substantive change, Mary speaks of making small choices and then no "longer being able to call your soul your own." It is a philosophy of diminishing possibilities: each significant choice entails automatically halving all of one's future choices; to choose A over B is not only to reject B, but to lose as well all the options that having chosen B instead of A would have offered. So although at every moment free to choose, by choice one seals the past and, paradoxically, closes doors on the future. For the three older Tyrones, the past has become the present to such a degree that the opportunity for creative change no longer exists. In this play of loss and regret, of knowledge gained too late, only for Edmund can the future still potentially open out through art.

O'Neill's final play, *A Moon for the Misbegotten*, which closed before it ever reached New York in its initial 1947 production, but played triumphantly on Broadway in the 1970s with Colleen Dewhurst and Jason Robards, Jr., under José Quintero's direction, is also a summative play. In its satirical jabs at Harder, the Standard Oil man and neighboring landowner of the Hogan family who had earlier been the brunt of a joke in *Long Day's Journey into Night* and is ridiculed again here for his social snobbery and pretension, it recalls the socialist/anarchist sentiments of such O'Neill radical juvenalia in verse as "Fratricide" (1914). In its imagery of the brooding, nourishing mother and obsession with the Oedipal conflict, as well as in the pattern of sons leaving to find freedom from the hard lot of the father, it harkens back to *Desire under the Elms*. In its movement toward forgiveness and, all passion finally spent, resting in peace and happiness, it replicates a dominant movement in *Strange Interlude*. In its father-daughter dynamic, it parallels *A Touch of the Poet*. While several of O'Neill's late plays develop the motifs of masking, acting, and role playing, *Moon for the Misbegotten* brings these issues to the foreground, making them emphatic; among the most frequently recurring words in the play are "plotting," "acting," "taletelling," and "gameplaying," or variations thereof.

Since the play values character over action, much of it is talk, but talk and storytelling of a very high order, calling upon O'Neill's reserves of Irish humor in a way that hardly any of his earlier works do. One of the plots is almost farcical, the other deeper, richer, and more subtle. On one very basic level, the plot of the play is itself a plot, as Phil Hogan and his daughter, Josie, contrive to stay on the land they have farmed by preventing James Tyrone, Jr. (Jim), from selling the property to Harder, who will evict them straightaway. Hogan, long a widower, would sorely miss Josie's company were she to marry, and so feels some ambivalence toward Jim. Yet he sees this as Josie's chance not just to better herself and secure their tenancy on the land but also as an opportunity to find happiness and save Jim from self-destructive drunkenness. So he and Josie will join in a scheme to trick Jim if it appears that he will go back on his word; Josie will even, if necessary, play the whore to get him into bed and secure the necessary papers about their rights. But this is at best a subsidiary plot, even more so than Sara's union with Simon in *Touch of the Poet*.

If some critics speak of *The Iceman Cometh* as O'Neill's "anti-mother play," *Moon for the Misbegotten* might be considered as a work that alternates between mother-as-failure and mother-as-saviour. The failed mother, at least in the eyes of Jim Tyrone, is the mother who deserted him by dying. The Oedipal bond between them might be seen as an extreme formulation of one of the central, long-standing myths in O'Neill, that of the need to belong to something or someone outside of the self. Yet this bond has prevented Jim from entering into any "clean" relationship with another woman, since that would defile his love for his mother. Thus by now he is well practiced in adopting the mask of the cynic as a protection against the possibility of romantic love. When he lets down his guard and his feelings for Josie inadvertently or unconsciously break through, he must immediately pull back from them, claiming as an excuse that if he permitted expression of them he would "poison" her with his own cynicism as well.

Moon for the Misbegotten shares with such other late O'Neill works as *The Iceman Cometh* and *Long Day's Journey into Night* a confessional structure, with Jim as penitent come to Josie as priest(ess). Once again, as with Mary Tyrone in *Long Day's Journey into Night*, who will address only the Blessed Virgin with her pleas for renewed faith, Jim can only approach the warm and understanding mother-god: having failed his mother, he must seek forgiveness through the mother surrogate. When his mother lay dying, he had fallen again into drunkenness and believed that she saw and was hurt by it as she moved in and out of consciousness. And so, as Hickey had with Evelyn, Jim rationalizes that his mother is better off dead, not having to live with knowledge of his failure. On the train, when he is bringing her body back east from California for burial, he continues his debauchery by sleeping with a whore, attributing his actions to grief over his mother's death. Finally, though, he admits the true source of his guilt: through his actions he was getting revenge on his mother for deserting him by dying.

The elemental and physically oversized Josie, to whom Jim turns for forgiveness, is the last in a long line of Earth Mother figures in

O'Neill, beginning as far back as Abbie in *Desire under the Elms* and Cybel in *The Great God Brown*. Josie, too, has been a poseur, surrounding herself with a carefully created myth of whoreishness, both to perpetuate an illusion of attractiveness to the opposite sex and, at the same time, to protect herself from being taken advantage of by those who do not want her for herself. Like Jim, she must constantly be on guard lest her mask drop. Although she believes in the power of love to make things different for herself and Jim, she is reticent to admit her affection since she thinks he could only be ashamed of her in comparison with his Broadway ladies. Yet when Jim's love for her reveals itself, she responds with an expression of faith in his word that he would never renege on his promise to the Hogans, and then confesses the fact of her virginity to him. That, however, raises for him the spector of the taboo, and Jim falls to treating her lustfully.

At this point Josie makes the most important choice in the play, one that justifies not only seeing her as protagonist but regarding *Moon for the Misbegotten* as the final enshrining, indeed deifying, of the compassionate and forgiving mother, as opposed to the hard and unforgiving father/god. Josie, recognizing Jim's guilt over his lust, does not hate him for it. Instead, at great expense to herself, she will proffer him the greatest love of allowing him to rest in her arms, a love that will cost her precisely because it is nonsexual. As Michael Manheim writes, "O'Neill asserts the child at the mother's breast as the sole still unquestionable model of authentic human love, without which the universe seems endless and terrifying indeed."[4] Because of her willing sacrifice of sexuality—which always seems to taint physical love for O'Neill, who appears never to have escaped completely from a Puritan strain—Jim will rest in peace for this one night. When he awakes, moreover, Josie will tell a lie for his sake, trying to convince him that he had not acted brutally toward her, though he can never forget that he did. The comparable attempt at mutuality on his part, at doing *for* Josie, comes in his protestation of his love for her as he leaves, which he "stammers out," but then it must be remembered that in O'Neill "stammering" is "native eloquence," containing a touch of the poet's vision within it.

The religious iconography and central symbolic image of *Moon for the Misbegotten* is that of the Pieta, not, however, of Jim lying across Josie's lap but of Jim lying in a position of rebirth between Josie's legs, head upon her breast. As she claims, the Virgin has borne "a dead child in the night, and the dawn still finds her a virgin." Just as the Blessed Virgin needed to accept her role as Virgin Mother, bringing into the world a son who must die, so must Josie "bear" a son only to see him leave. Though she can forgive Jim as his mother's surrogate, she knows that he can never forget; as he has said earlier, the past happens over and over again. So the only release from the "bum racket" of life into some semblance of peace comes through death, a never-ending sleep that Josie prays will come to Jim soon. The visual stage image at the end, as in *Long Day's Journey into Night*, is of a mother alone; Josie's isolation, however, is a consciously chosen condition, sacrificing any hope for sexual consummation with Jim to his final union with peace and happiness in death. O'Neill has stripped down his final play to an emphasis almost wholly on characters united under the light of the moon, traditionally associated both with the female goddess of love and with the light of the imagination. From one perspective, it might be said there are just two actors and a stage light. In this last long, for O'Neill almost minimalist, play, less is more. An almost sculptural image tells his tale of two people who come to possess themselves in a fullness of compassion and forgiveness heartbreakingly won.

An Answer to the Absurd

If O'Neill's first substantial efforts at drama were the brief sea plays for the Provincetown Players, beginning in the 1915–16 season, late in his dramatic activity he returned to the one-act form. Although his intention was to write a cycle, with the overall title "By Way of Obit," O'Neill completed only one of these short plays, *Hughie*, eventually performed in 1965, more than 20 years after its composition, with the consummate, quintessential O'Neillian Jason Robards, Jr., in the starring role. Not only its one-act form but also *Hughie's* experimental nature hark back to O'Neill's early days as a playwright. O'Neill described his intended technical innovation in a 1942 letter to George Jean Nathan: "the main character talks about a person who has died to a person who does little but listen. Via this monologue you get a complete picture of the person who has died—his or her whole life story—but just as complete a picture of the life and character of the narrator. And you also get, by another means—a use of stage directions, mostly—an insight into the whole life of the person who does little but listen." Here O'Neill seems intent on testing the boundaries of drama as performed on stage to explore to what extent a character's stream-of-consciousness can be conveyed solely through gestures and expression. The general critical position is that *Hughie* defies full representation in the theater, where the text as O'Neill conceived it must somehow always remain incomplete; some even charge that O'Neill, by never intending that the first-person thoughts contained in the stage directions would be heard by the audience (either though direct address or in recorded voice overs), actually evaded his responsibility as far as the stage is concerned. From one perspective, then, *Hughie* is an antiplay, exposing the limitations of the dramatic form itself.

In the study, however, where it can be more fully realized by being imagined in the theater of the mind, *Hughie* seems most like a short story that blends dialogue with both first- and third-person narrative. Charlie Hughes, the new, withdrawn night desk-clerk in a run-down Broadway hotel, does his best to shut himself off from the incessant talk of Erie Smith, a small-time gambler and sport just back from a drunk and down on his luck, by directing his thoughts to other things, including the city sounds that impinge upon his consciousness: garbage cans, an El train, a taxi, a cop on his beat, a streetcar, an ambulance, a fire engine. These noises are welcome, because they chart the passing of time, however slow, and the promise of release.

The other inhabitant of the hotel lobby, Erie Smith, is, like Con Melody, another of O'Neill's characters who has turned his life into a performance. As Christopher Bigsby notes in *Modern American Drama, 1945–1990*, in O'Neill's last plays "the characters are all self-conscious performers seeking protection in the artifice of theater, playing roles that will deflect the pain of the real. . . . To perform is to be."[5] As a teller of tales, Erie demands the presence of an audience, not only to assuage a longing for companionship but also to confirm the romanticized image he creates of himself. He has a self that he desperately needs to sell, and when there is no attentive listener to appreciate and buoy up the self as he (re)creates it through language, then he falls into something akin to despair, as signaled when he stops twirling his room key. Charlie, at first uninterested, gradually takes on the traits of the dead Hughie, moving out of his shell when he finally prompts Erie to regale him with stories about the glamorous Arnold Rothstein. Once again, O'Neill's emphasis, as it had been in *Moon for the Misbegotten*, rests on mutuality; these two men give each other a reality by engaging the other. They come together not only in their penny ante gambling but, finally, in their shared perception that life is "a goddammed racket."

Visually, O'Neill calls attention early in *Hughie* to the clock on the wall, to time passing, to entropy; verbally, he reiterates the word "nothing" or some variation of it, particularly in the description of Charlie, which is handled by negatives, by saying what he is not. Again, as Bigsby remarks, "*Hughie* works on the principle of absence" (25). The recurrent emphasis on night and silence links with death and mortality, with the hotel lobby even described as a kind of morgue. So the play might be seen as akin philosophically to absurdist drama, especially with Beckett's *Waiting for Godot*, in which the characters also play games to give them the impression they exist and discover their own reality by engaging the other. If Godot will never come, at least Didi and Gogot (whose combined names provide the letters necessary to spell "Godot") have each other; perhaps that mutually shared pain is the most that can be hoped for in Beckett, or in much of the later O'Neill.

Increasingly, critics have come to situate O'Neill's "modernism" as evidenced in the last plays within the framework (in Bigsby's words) of "an absurdist vision" and the "reality of entropy" or a "process of unbecoming."[6] At the center of the plays lie two gapping absences: of a god who gives meaning; and of a unitary conception of self. As Bogard comments, O'Neill came to "agree with Nietzsche that men live in a godless world" (415); so for the dramatist, neither "the old God" nor "the new gods" any longer fulfill their chief function of alleviating fear and comforting humankind in the face of death. Even though death might prove, ironically, to be the final sought-after belonging, foreshadowed in the rare moment of mystic vision and union, the certainty of that transcendence must remain forever hidden.

In light of this, the individual attempting to find some (re)assurance can only flee, as in Albee, to a succession of illusion upon illusion: to masks, to role playing, to tale telling, to creative narrative. Yet even when such imaginative constructs attain the level of art, they may be futile gropings, except in those extraordinary fusions between artist and vision and vision and audience. And all of these retreats into illusion generally prove solipsistic or isolating endeavors, resulting in fragmentation of identity, disintegration of the ego, and loss of "true self," unless they somehow break through to and are shared with the "other." So mutuality, as between Larry Slade and Don Parritt in *The Iceman Cometh*, Josie Hogan and James Tyrone in *Moon for the Misbegotten*, or Charlie Hughes and Erie Smith in *Hughie*, becomes for O'Neill the final value. Larry's recognition of Parritt's need for expiation must demonstrate itself in the passing of judgment; Josie's response to Jim's need shows itself in the offer of forgiveness—hers seems the better way, though it is the person on the receiving end of the compassion who determines the nature of the gift. Yet in each case, the commitment to mutuality requires sacrifice on the part of the giver. Communion between individuals cannot be bought cheaply, or without pain, for O'Neill's misbegotten souls.

Lillian Hellman:
The Conscience of the Culture

As a number of commentators over the years have noted, the single remark by Lillian Hellman that is most likely to be remembered comes not from any of her dozen plays or four volumes of memoirs but from her May 1952 testimony before the House Un-American Activities Committee. Determined not to contribute to the Cold War paranoia sweeping the country by naming names and thus ruining the reputations of others who might at one time have been communist sympathizers, she declared: "I cannot and will not cut my conscience to fit this year's fashions."

The high moral tone of her utterance was indicative of Hellman's stance throughout her half-century career as a writer, both endearing her to friends and providing fodder for enemies. Just as her play of a decade earlier, *The Searching Wind* (1944), had condemned the liberals' failure to respond adequately to the fascist threat abroad in the late 1930s, she now took a radical stand against what she regarded as a cowardly and dangerous backing away by the intelligentsia from the concerted threat to individual liberty at home. In fact, along with Hellman's recurrent theme about the contest between the power of love and the power of money, one of the dominant motifs in her works for the stage charts the decline of the ideals of liberal humanism, particularly as evidenced in the coexistence of culture with evil: how is it that highly civilized societies not only countenance but actually become complicitous in inhuman acts?

Southern Moralist

Hellman shares this interest in the fate of culture and art as it is threatened by commerce and power with such other twentieth-century writers as Bernard Shaw in *Heartbreak House* and E. M. Forster in *Howards End.* As a Southern Jewish Woman Playwright, Hellman would appear to be thrice the outsider; yet to some degree or other she defies or transcends each of these categories. Born in New Orleans in 1905, she spent six months of each year of her girlhood in that city, the other half in New York, where the family had moved when she was six. As she explained to an interviewer in 1975, "I came from a family . . . who had been Southerners for a great many generations"[1] (the families on both sides had emigrated from Germany in the second quarter of the nineteenth century).

To her Southern background she always attributed being "brought up to believe we had a right to think as we pleased, go our own, possibly strange ways."[2] If her mother's solidly middle-class Alabama family had exploited African-Americans, her father, she reports, had actually stood up to whites who were abusing a black woman; during her own lifetime, Hellman's closest emotional attachments to other women would be with two black women who were more like family to her than servants, Sophronia and Helen, lovingly recalled in her first volume of memoirs, *An Unfinished Woman* (1969). Furthermore, as Kenneth Holditch has suggested, "the dichotomies that concern her—the old landed gentry versus the *nouveaux riches,* the Old South traditions versus the New South movement, Agrarianism versus industrialism, a code of honor versus the new amorality—are inextricably linked to the milieu of the region."[3]

One of her father Max's epithets for the young Lillian was "the first Jewish nun on Prytania Street." Hellman, however, was never a practicing Jew and would write only one play featuring Jewish characters, and that at the end of her theater career—Holditch calls her "one of the

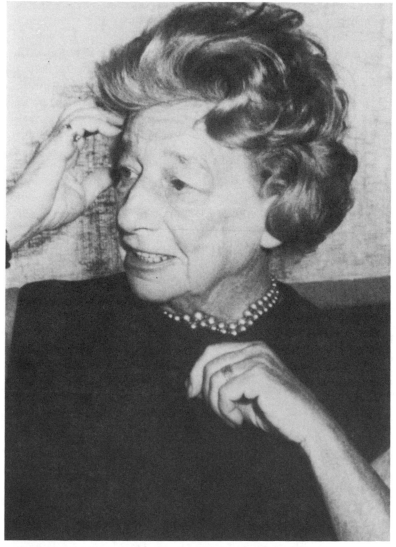

Lillian Hellman in the early 1970s. *Photographer unknown. By kind permission of Rita Wade and the Estate of Lillian Hellman.*

least Jewish of all Jewish authors" (15); nevertheless, she still felt "very glad I was born a Jew. Whether brought up as one or not, somewhere in the background there was the gift of being born a Jew" (*Conversations, Hellman*, 291). If nothing else, her ethnic heritage made her peculiarly sensitive about being vulnerable to silencing or persecution by a repressive authoritarianism; in 1940, she said: "I am a writer and I am also a Jew. . . . I want . . . to be able to go on saying that I am a Jew without being afraid of being called names or end in a prison camp or be forbidden to walk down the street at night."[4] Such statements notwithstanding, some critics have found her ethic more Christian, perhaps Calvinistic, than Jewish and conclude, though not very convincingly, that "her pervasive anti-middle class bias" and her denigration of "self-serving . . . narrow personal ambition" is "not only un-Jewish but ultimately anti-Jewish."[5]

Hellman herself always bristled at the designation as "America's most important woman dramatist," considering it discriminatory, even demeaning. Not that she lacked sympathy for the feminist movement, although as she writes in *Unfinished Woman*, "By the time I grew up the fight for the emancipation of women, their rights under the law, in the office, in bed, was stale stuff."[6] Consequently, as becomes apparent in the plays, she saw the woman question almost wholly in economic terms: "I don't think it's of any great moment who carries out the garbage. I think it is important that people be economically equal. So that if somebody feels like walking out, there's a way for her to earn a living rather than suffering through a whole lifetime because she can't" (*Conversations, Hellman*, 205). It is thus not surprising to discover that Hellman considered Brecht's *Mother Courage* the great play of her time. What classification, then, if one must be found, most appropriately describes her? Throughout most all her life, Hellman remained a respected member of the liberal eastern, progressive literary establishment. Those among the group that has come to be known as the New York intellectuals who would demur from that judgment do so on the basis of her continuing to be an apologist for Stalinism long after his atrocities became known. By the time of her death in 1984, the only category that could begin to approximate her protean reputation might be something on the order of "American person of letters."

Hellman's first postwar play, *Another Part of the Forest* (1946), was intended as the second part of a trilogy (the third segment was never written) following the career of Regina Hubbard Giddens, who made her initial appearance in the dramatist's last play before the war, and still her most widely known, *The Little Foxes* (1939). The action in *Forest*, which takes its name from an oft-used stage direction in Renaissance drama, occurs in 1880, taking up the life of the Hubbard clan 20 years earlier than in *Foxes*. *Foxes* had focused partly on the responses of two southern women to their societally conditioned dependency on men. By that play's end, Regina, for whom financial power had become a substitute for sex, has triumphed economically over both her husband and brothers, in a kind of gleeful revenge for having years before been dispossessed and betrayed by her own father. Meanwhile, her neurotic sister-in-law, Birdie, has retreated through alcohol into a nostalgic remembrance of a southern past that never was. *Foxes*, which received two highly publicized New York revivals—one in 1967, directed by Mike Nichols at Lincoln Center, the other in 1981, starring Elizabeth Taylor on Broadway— might be seen as the paradigmatic Hellman play: an extraordinarily well-made melodrama. The same characteristics are true of *Forest*.

In her 1942 introduction to the Modern Library edition of *Six Plays*, Hellman provides her fullest response to frequent criticisms of well-madeness and melodrama, as well as offering a justification for her habitual moral summing-up. If the well-made play is one "whose effects are contrived, whose threads are knit tighter than the threads in life," she finds no objection so long as the plays "convince you, or partly convince you, [for] then the dislike of their being well-made makes little sense." If melodrama "[b]y definition . . . is a violent dramatic piece, with a happy ending," Hellman only judges it pernicious when "it uses its violence for no purpose, to point no moral, to say nothing, in say-nothing's worst sense." Finally, she confesses to being "a moral writer, often too moral a writer, and I cannot avoid, it seems, that last summing-up. I think that is only a mistake when it fails to achieve its purpose, and I would rather make the attempt, and fail, then fail to make the attempt."[7]

Although most commentators see Ibsen's presence rather than Chekhov's in the plays Hellman wrote before *The Autumn Garden* (1951), something of a Chekhovian influence, in subject matter if not in technique and tone, is already apparent in *Little Foxes* and *Another Part of the Forest*. Both works are partly swan songs for a cultured, genteel way of life, now dying out only to be replaced by a more pragmatic and utilitarian business model, one careless of people, whose prime value resides in their being negotiable commodities. These plays reenact the Chekhovian tension between culture and business, perhaps best encapsulated in the contents found in the safety deposit box of Regina's husband, Horace Giddens, in *Foxes*: along with the bonds and securities are baby shoes, a cameo, a violin piece, some poems and schoolbooks. In *Forest*, the Hubbard home, a southern Greek Revival mansion, gives the appearance of a seat of culture and learning. The family's patriarch, Marcus, calls frequently upon Aristotle as a source of inspiration and ethics, though the principles cited jar badly with his actions; even his much-touted appreciation for music turns out to be something of a sham. Marcus's supposed love of culture and the arts proves only a thin veneer covering over venality and immorality.

On the other hand, Lionnet, the Bagtry family estate built on the institution of slavery, is falling into ruin because of the family's inability to adapt to the post–Civil War economy. The Bagtrys are represented by a sister and brother: by Birdie, a somewhat faded and woebegone lover of music, with her impractical dreams of Lionnet's restoration through a loan from Marcus, and John, a sentimental believer in the lost war as the only time he was "good" and "happy," whom Regina considers as a potential mate. Both Bagtrys are adrift in a romantization of things past, John so much so that he will head to Brazil to fight against the abolition of slavery in order to maintain his commitment to a former, if now dishonored, "way of life."

The two Hubbard sons suggest a coarsening even of Marcus. The dissolute Oscar, who rides with the Ku Klux Klan on its raids and lynchings, loses the social-climbing whore he plans on marrying when she realizes he will never control the family money. The older, Ben, who confesses to having no interest in the arts and finds the Greek Revival house too "delicate" and "swell" for his bourgeois tastes, displaces and unmans his father through swindling and blackmail. Once in control of his father's assets, he can take advantage of opportunities since "things are opening up" to new money. What Robert Brustein noted in his eulogy at Hellman's funeral about money as "usually the hidden extra character of her plays, often the most important one"[8] bears directly on *Forest*. During the War, Marcus bled his home by profiteering from running the blockade; worse than that, the Union soldiers followed him back across the lines and massacred 27 southern boys, including John Bagtry's twin. Marcus rationalized his actions by claiming southerners "deserved to lose their war and their world," because the South stood in the way of historical progress.

The favorite child, daughter Regina, for whom Marcus harbors incestuous longings (he dislikes any man who courts her and turns glum when she is away), has him wound around her finger, receiving assurances, until Ben decides otherwise, that she can go north to Chicago where she plans to meet and marry Bagtry. The rural, agrarian South is on the decline, while the industrialized, urbanized North is on the rise; the garden is being displaced by the city. Possessed, as Gale Austin comments, of a "painful self-awareness . . . of her subjugation,"[9] Regina must finally capitulate to the ascendant Ben, deserting her father, whose chair the elder son assumes. Regina, despite her earlier determination not to marry for money, will be traded in marriage to Horace Giddens to bring his holdings into the family; she must sacrifice erotic fulfillment if she desires to satisfy her ambition. Love and economic power seem inimical in this family, which measures the worth of everything by a quantitative rather than qualitative weight. In the play's final image, Regina chooses to sit near Ben, completely ignoring her father who, now stripped of his financial independence, has become worthless to her. The close of *Forest* thus forms a diptych with that of *Foxes*, where Regina's newly empowered daughter, Alexandra, predicts her mother's perpetual loneliness as a woman despite Regina's having triumphed financially over Ben.

There ordinarily exists a marked division between the good and the evil in Hellman's plays, and in this regard *Forest* fulfills the expectation. Marcus's wife, Lavinia, is an outsider, descendant of a lower-class family from the "piney woods," whose grandmother taught her to read and write. Convinced she has lived in sin for decades by knowing the secret of Marcus's lying and cheating, Lavinia forms her closest attachment with the servant Coralee, whom she accompanies to the black church; only on the periphery of her society can Lavinia feel at home. In Ibsenite fashion, the play gradually reveals that Lavinia witnessed the secret of Marcus's behavior: by bribery he bought his "innocence" from suspicion of having deliberately led the Union soldiers to the southerners, an action Lavinia witnessed and recorded in her Bible. Rejecting an ameliorative interpretation of the biblical passage about the poor being always with us as a justification for doing nothing to help them, she desires now to make amends by teaching the poor from whom she sprang.

Hellman's valorization of this brutalized, slightly fanatical woman, almost blessed in her derangement, indicates the depth of this dark satire on a society that delights in bartering human beings, whether they be daughters or servants, for economic gain. As Hellman remarks in the section titled "Theatre" in *Pentimento* (1970), she intended, evidently without success, that the tone of the later play be a corrective, clarifying an attitude toward the characters in *Little Foxes* that had gone largely misunderstood: "I had meant the first play as a kind of satire. I tried to

do that in *Another Part of the Forest*, but what I thought funny or
outrageous the critics thought straight stuff; what I thought was bite
they thought sad, touching, or plotty and melodramatic."[10] Becoming a
daughter of Chekhov, whom she describes in the introduction to his
Selected Letters as a "tolerant man [who] gave pity where it was due" but
also "a tough, unsentimental man with a tough mind,"[11] along with the
disciple of Ibsen she had always been, Hellman found herself facing some
of the same sentimentalizing tendencies by critics that the Russian master
suffered at the hands of his early interpreters.

Hellman's Adaptations and the McCarthy Period

Before she wrote another original play, Hellman turned to adaptation,
something she would do four times during the second half of her playwriting career. To her mind the process of literary adaptation must involve
making the other writer's work her own: "I changed the plays a fair
amount," she explains, "so they became in a sense in part mine at
least" (*Conversations, Hellman*, 121). A central issue in discussing the
adaptations revolves around what might have attracted Hellman to the
original works in the first place. Hellman's adaptation of Emmanual
Robles's *Montserrat*, which opened under the dramatist's own direction
in 1949 to indifferent reviews and ran for only 65 performances, joins
Watch on the Rhine (1941) and *The Searching Wind* as collectively her
most overtly political plays. In retrospect, *Montserrat* bears an uncanny
similarity in its handling of material and tone to the later political plays
of Harold Pinter, such as *Mountain Language* (1988) and *One for the
Road* (1984), that dissect the capriciousness and brutality of totalitarian
regimes in which power, viciously exercised, elevates itself as the only
right.

   Montserrat centers on events during Simon Bolivar's insurrection
against the Spanish occupation army in Venezuela in 1812. The authority
against which the radicals fight claims a triple allegiance to God, King,
and Country, a kind of unholy trinity of the ecclesiastical, political, and
military powers. Within the Spanish ranks is Montserrat, who supports
the revolutionary force led by Bolivar when it becomes clear that the
colonial power's claim of God's sanction is being called upon to justify
turning the country into a slaughterhouse. Instead of subjecting Montserrat himself to torture in order to discover Bolivar's whereabouts, his

Excellency's henchman, Izquierdo, who has already led the massacre of a thousand prisoners, indiscriminately pulls six people off the street to be summarily executed if Montserrat does not talk. The six, including a merchant, a mother, an artist, and an actor, form a microcosm of society, representing different social strata and attitudes toward political repression. Despite their differences, they share a conviction of having done nothing wrong and of wondering what all this has to do with them; the priest, who supports the Spanish occupation by arguing that they are "guilty of nothing but innocence," of the "crime [of] having been born," makes their fate a Beckettian one that might be linked as well to the rounding up of victims during the Holocaust.

Montserrat himself must choose between his devotion to Bolivar's cause and his responsibility to six people who will be murdered because of his intransigence in the name of right. What sanction does he have to make these people, most of whom are uninvolved and dispassionate, if not openly opposed to the cause, become martyrs for the people? Should the individual be a sacrificial scapegoat for the community? One of the six thinks so, and she keeps Montserrat from wavering until Bolivar has time to group the revolutionaries around him for his next advance. Another of the minor characters, Zavala, embodies a position that, given Hellman's blacklisting from Hollywood screenwriting in the late 1940s and early 1950s and her interrogation by the House Un-American Affairs Committee, seems prescient for the playwright herself. Zavala draws a line of conscience that he will not violate; he "reserves a space for what we will not do" under pressure from any government, even one to which he otherwise remains loyal. Equally as callous as Izquierdo is the ruler, the oblivious Excellency, who remains unseen, but whose beautiful piano playing echoes periodically from offstage. His music sounds while murders in his name take place. Once again in Hellman, culture and art have failed to humanize; instead, they coexist with evil.

Carl Rollyson's comment that "after *Montserrat*, [Hellman] would write an entirely different kind of play, one that was removed from politics and from the fiery atmosphere of her best-known stage work,"[12] fails to be precisely accurate when taking into account her 1955 adaptation of Jean Anouilh's treatment of St. Joan in *The Lark*. By "scal[ing] down the play, cut[ting] the comparisons to the World War II German invasion of France and the tributes to the French spirit" (*Pentimento*, 202), Hellman helped underscore the analogy between Joan and her inquisitors on the one hand and the suspected Communists and the House investigating committee on the other. Hellman condemned the whole McCarthy era as a "shameless period" in American history; the responsibility fell not only to the witch hunters and Red baiters who actively hounded and persecuted others but also to the moral failure of the silent, self-serving liberals, even Leftists, who stood passively by. In her memoir about the period, *Scoundrel Time* (1976), her severest critics find a revisionist reading in the worst sense of that word, that is, fraught with untruths. Hellman writes that she "had, up to the late 1940's, believed that the educated, the intellectual, lived by what they claimed to believe: freedom of thought and speech, the right of each man to his own convictions, a more than implied promise, therefore, of aid to those who might be persecuted. But only a very few raised a finger when McCarthy and the boys appeared" (40). Addie's line from *Little Foxes* can serve as a gloss on their failure: "There are people who eat the earth . . . I think it ain't right to stand and watch them do it."

Hellman does not exonerate herself from blame on at least two counts. First, she admits to having been blind to "the sins of Stalin Communism . . . that for a long time I mistakenly denied" (*Scoundrel Time*, 40). Second, she sees that her tactic when called to testify before the House committee in May 1952 was motivated in part by her fear of going to jail; the strategy outlined in her famous letter to the committee, whereby she would not plead the Fifth Amendment and would waive the privilege against self-incrimination but only on the condition that the committee not ask her about others, prevented her from being held in contempt, as Arthur Miller and others who refused to name names were. Her letter, which through a clever maneuver by her lawyer was released to the press during her testimony, thus putting the committee on the defensive and winning the day for Hellman, proclaims her commitment to the American and Christian ideals of duty, truth, loyalty, honor, and decency that preclude her bringing "bad trouble to people who, in my past associations with them, were completely innocent of any talk or any action that was disloyal or subversive" (*Scoundrel Time*, 93).

Even more immediately than *The Lark*, the 1952 revival of her first hit *The Children's Hour* (1934) assumed an added dimension under Hellman's own direction—along with such other plays as Miller's *The Crucible* and Robert Anderson's *Tea and Sympathy*—in the context of the excesses of anticommunist fervor during the Cold War. *The Children's Hour*, in which a malicious accusation of lesbianism results in the suicide of one woman, who comes to recognize the truth of her sexual orientation, and in the broken engagement and financial ruin of her partner in running a girl's boarding school, shows the destructive power of guilt by innuendo and insinuation. Charges of "unnatural" acts and any deviation from the heterosexist society's norms create fear tantamount to the threat of communist infiltration. Some commentators on Hellman's early works, such as those who take offense at the portrayal of the unhappy lesbian in *The Children's Hour,* tend to be unsure of her commitment to the feminist cause. Perhaps a contributory factor in this suspicion was Hellman's own independence; she was always able to inhabit what Virginia Woolf saw as essential, "a room of one's own," and so was never denied control over her life/texts solely because she was a woman, but only for her perceived political radicalism during the Hollywood blacklisting. Yet *The Lark,* along with offering a response to authoritarian suppression, provides evidence of Hellman's protofeminism in the appeal of Joan, who "was history's first modern career girl, wise, unattractive in what she knew about the handling of men, straight out of a woman's magazine" (*Pentimento,* 202).

The setting of *The Lark* is the least realistic of all Hellman's plays and its structure the most complex, with its fluid handling of time including jumps and fast forwards, its mix of narrative segments with dramatic scenes, and its gestures toward metatheatricalism in numerous comments about playing out roles. It considers the individual's responsibility to be true to her conscience and the need to accept the contradictions in flawed humanity. Joan embodies the power of the individual to energize the society, and the right, nay, the absolute duty, to disobey an established order that would thwart the minority in its midst; part of the "insolent breed," she "will not denounce" what she is and has done. Just as Hellman could not "cut [her] conscience to fit this year's fashions," so, too, "when something is black [Joan] cannot say it is white." Embodying a humanistic credo of courage and intelligence, Joan decenters God in favor of man, who is "a miracle" not despite but precisely because of his admixture of good and evil, angelic and animal. When she temporarily recants the truth under pressure from the inquisitors, Joan understands that all she has done is to "[eat] the dirt of lies" in order to secure "a few years of unworthy life." Although Hellman could discover in Montserrat and Joan two heroes to add to her own Kurt Muller from *Watch on the Rhine,* her ironic vision has always been a sober, even a dark one. In her libretto for the comic operetta *Candide* a year later, any embrace of extremism—even idealism, optimism, utopianism—is faulted, and every creed, such as that which Pangloss passes on to his pupil, is almost as empty as the untrustworthy Polonius's maxims in *Hamlet,* and therefore suspect. Personal, moral conduct remains as the final value.

The Chekhovian Plays

In her major works for the theater from 1950 on, Hellman evidences a shift in style away from the Ibsenite dramas of the 1930s and 1940s; as William Wright notes, "she had been hounded by the critics into other styles: the Chekhovian *The Autumn Garden*, then the Williamsish *Toys in the Attic* and finally the Albeeish *My Mother, My Father and Me*" (292–93). As has already been noticed, the Chekhovian motif of the dying out of an older, more genteel culture to be superseded by a newer, more vulgar and brutish order, the replacement of art by pragmatic business, had been a focus as far back as *Little Foxes* and *Another Part of the Forest*. But now, with *Autumn Garden* (1951), Hellman pens one of the most Chekhovian of all American plays in its reduction of outward plot, its wistful, elegiac tone of loss, and its handling of an ensemble cast. As Wright argues, Hellman is still more judgmental, less lyrical, and less humorous than Chekhov (236); yet in *Garden*, emotion is conveyed more by subtext than by action, and visual symbolism of place and objects carries, as it does in Chekhov, more of the drama's meaning.

Hellman also calls *Autumn Garden* her "best work": "*The Autumn Garden* is my favorite play of my own. I don't know why except that I think I said more of what I felt in *Autumn Garden* than I ever said before or afterwards. I think it's the most mature play I ever wrote. . . . It was me being all I knew at the minute rather than me being only a certain part of what I knew at the minute" (*Conversations, Hellman,* 175). *The Autumn Garden* also signals a new thematic direction for Hellman in its consideration of time and change, a thematic focus that resurfaces in the last book she published before her death, the fourth and in many ways most intriguing volume of memoirs, *Maybe: A Story* (1980). As a Proustian meditation on time and memory, *Maybe* places greater emphasis than the earlier play on the relativity of truth, the unknowability even of the self, and the impact of time's passage on forgetting and remembering. It should perhaps be considered as Hellman's apologia for deviating from the exact truth in her imaginative reconstructions of the past. A reflective passage from *Maybe* comes close to encapsulating the central perception of *Autumn Garden*: "The piles and bundles and ribbons and rags turn into years, and then the years are gone. . . . So much of what you had counted on as a solid wall of convictions now seems on bad nights, or in sickness, or just weakness, no longer made of much that can be leaned against. It is then that one can barely place oneself in time. All that you would swear had been, can only be found again if you have the energy to dig hard enough, and that is hard on the feet and the back, and sometimes you are frightened that near an edge is nothing."[13]

The Autumn Garden occurs along the Gulf Coast in a somewhat "shrunk and shabby" boarding house that was once "*the* great summer mansion." The time is September 1949, and what is being harvested are the lives of a large number of mostly middle-aged characters. The leitmotifs in this drama of lost chances and dashed dreams are aging, waste, emptiness, boredom, ennui, the kind of atmosphere in which people, for want of anything better to do, hurt one another emotionally and psychologically. The enemies are time's passing and the inability to reconcile fiction with fact, desire with act. As is usual in Chekhov, too, a number of real or putative triangles or sexual dalliances take place that configure the large cast and keep them sorted out for the audience.

Constance Tuckerman, the owner of the house, had long ago been the object of the portrait painter Nick Denery's attentions; Nick now returns for a visit along with his wife, Nina. Among the summer vacationers are a couple whose marriage is tottering toward dissolution, General Benjamin Griggs and his wife, Rose, whom Nick makes plans to pursue, as well as Ned Crossman, whose friendship with Constance has never eventuated in marriage. Living with Constance is her niece from Europe, Sophie, now engaged to Frederick, a mama's boy being used for financial gain by the homosexual novelist Payson; the old Europe/new America motif hinted at in the Sophie/Frederick relationship adds a Jamesian touch to this southern drawing room. Sophie, the displaced outsider who takes control of her own future in a way that the others do not, forms the moral center of the play. After the drunken Nick places himself in a compromising position with her, she insists on terming Nick and Nina's pay-off exactly what it is, "blackmail," for if it were anything else, then she would need to feel either gratitude for charity or humiliation at being bought off.

The play's central visual symbols are two portraits of Constance by Nick. The first was painted 23 years ago, finished the day before he left to study in Paris and enter into a marriage that provides Constance with vicarious happiness over what she erroneously imagines to be his happy union. Constance desires to stop time and only remember herself as she was "in the picture upstairs," for, as Sophie says, love comes "once" and never again for well-bred ladies like Constance. Nick, on the other hand, thinks he can erase the intervening years, partly by doing a new portrait of Constance, unglamorous in a cheap housedress, that he can exhibit publicly next to the old. Constance, finding it difficult to admit her regret over a life that has not been "good and full and happy," fears that people will laugh with pity over the changes they see in her between then and now. Nick, too, is aware of wearing down and coming to hate himself, but Hellman does not intend that any pity be generated for this "petty sensualist" and venal philanderer. A failed artist, really only "a gifted amateur" who has not completed a new painting in the past 12 years and who uses the ruse of his artistry as an opportunity for flirtation and an entree into liaisons, Nick meddles in the lives of the other summer visitors in order to generate some excitement in his own; as his wife, Nina, pointedly chides him, "Have you ever tried leaving things alone?"

Constance realizes that she mistakenly made "a shabby man into the kind of hero who would come back some day all happy and shining" and fears that now she will "be alone forever. . . . such a waste." Her failure, a universal one, is that of having lied to herself. When she asks Ned Crossman to marry her, he responds that it is now too late, as he is no longer in love with her. Once her love for him might have made him "different," but now he deliberately wastes his life away in drink. Griggs considers Ned's choice of the kind of man he has become preferable to his own chance wasting of his life. He wants to begin again, without his childlike wife, who is so unlike his more serious mother, but will compassionately remain with her in a marriage empty of affection.

In the only passage from Hellman's work that her long-time companion, Dashiell Hammett, completely rewrote (though he frequently made suggestions for revisions), Griggs voices the central thematic statement. It is instructive to compare Hellman's original with Hammett's more nuanced version: Hellman's draft emphasizes that the opportunity for decisive change, available early in life, suddenly becomes severely delimited because of the succession of previous choices one has made. In her original, similar in idea to both O'Neill's *Long Day's Journey into Night* and Albee's *A Delicate Balance* (1967), she reflects soberly on the intersection between past decisions or indecisions and present possibility: "There are no minutes of great decision. Only a series of little ones coming out of the past. You don't suddenly turn around—because it's too damn late, and you've let it go too long" (quoted in Rollyson, 300). Hammett's version offers a somewhat more existentialist point of view, expressing the way in which the succession of choices one must continually make finally creates, and thus determines, what one becomes, the content of one's character: "So at any given moment you're only the sum of your life up to then. . . . the turning point in your life, the someday you've counted on when you'd suddenly wipe out your past mistakes, do the work you'd never done, think the way you never thought, have what you'd never had—it just doesn't come suddenly. You've trained yourself for it while you waited—or you've let it all run past you and frittered yourself away." In *Autumn Garden*, Hellman's characters have frittered their lives away, as did many of Chekhov's. As Ned remarks, in a verbal echo of a line from *Uncle Vanya*, "they'll all be gone soon," and all that one will be left with is the self he or she has made.

In another almost equally Chekhovian American play of a few seasons later, the similarly titled *In a Summer House* (1953), Jane Bowles focuses on three mother/daughter pairs to explore the trauma of one daughter's separation from her beloved yet controlling mother as she grows from adolescent to adult and changes from single to married, moving reluctantly from the womblike gazebo to the marriage bed. As in Hellman's play, psychologically debilitating regret over the past and fear of loneliness and loss potentially result in paralyzing stasis, were it not for the possibility of escape offered to Hellman's Sophie and to Bowles's Molly.

Toys in the Attic (1960), Hellman's last original play, proved one of her greatest theatrical successes. Starring Maureen Stapleton and Jason Robards, Jr., it ran for 556 performances on Broadway, winning Hellman her second New York Drama Critics Circle Award (the first had been for *Watch on the Rhine*). If she had turned to her mother's family, the Newhouses of Alabama, to find models for characters in *Little Foxes* and *Another Part of the Forest*, with *Toys* she turned instead to her father's; as she recounts in *Maybe*, "Without question, both my aunts [Hannah and Jenny] were in love with their brother" (80). She knew, though, in drafting the play, that the character based on her father, Max, would never be the focus: "I can write about men, but I can't write a play that centers on a man. I've got to . . . make it about the women around him, his sisters, his bride, her mother" (*Pentimento*, 206).

The two spinster Berniers sisters—Anna, 42, and Carrie, 38—have literally lived for their brother; their certainty of his need for and dependency on them has been the raison d'être for their existence. Now that Julian has left, married the much younger Lily, and gone to Chicago, the family home that once seemed to Anna "an old tomb" now impresses her as having grown bigger "as people left it." The opening dialogue insists upon the ubiquity of loneliness, as the enervated Carrie compares the monied old ladies with the "lonely" dead in the cemetery. In relationships in this house, emotional feelings have remained unspoken; they have been defined, instead, in the transaction of money and material goods, in a confusion of love with things. Nor have any of the relationships been generative; even Julian is impotent with his bride when they come back to visit under the ancestral roof. After his marriage, Anna and Carrie continue to proffer Julian financial support as a means of maintaining his dependency on them. As Anna says with some desperation, "You are our life"; they have invested themselves wholly in someone else.

Julian, however, has brought off a lucrative business deal without their help and, basking in his newly discovered self-respect and sense of improvement, he now attempts to break free from his condition of subservience by giving them things, including a paid-off mortgage, tickets for a long-postponed European trip, and, most tellingly, jewelry and negligees, until they are sated. Yet when he resigns Carrie's job for her he goes too far, forcing Anna and Carrie to reassess the game they have been playing with him all along. Once the status quo is upset, truth telling follows. Anna realizes that without Julian's needing them, "the poor house came down," and she seeks to put the blame on her sister for his decision to go away again. She accuses Carrie of having always wanted Julian to sleep with her, and says that his awareness of "her lust" will drive him permanently away. Carrie, whom the servantman Gus once characterized as having "kept [her] vagina in the icebox," does, indeed, beg her brother to stay, trying to bribe him with the promise of playing a piano concert for him. She fears old age and the sight of gray hairs in the mirror. For her part, Anna is distraught as well; some need had made her take her mother's children as her own, and now she fears that with Julian's leaving she will never have his children to grow old around.

Hellman suggests that, as was true of her own aunts, "all women living together take on what we think of as male and female roles," but these are sometimes "a rather puzzling mix-about" (*Pentimento*, 12). Here, although Anna appears to be in control, Carrie actually called the tunes for their life together. Without Julian, all that lies in wait for these two sisters is the death they vividly remember seeing their own mother face. While they fooled themselves that Julian was dependent on them, it was really they who depended on him. They needed to be needed, and when that need evaporates, their lives are empty. This is the finish of romance, of daydream, of fantasy for them. As objects who had lives only in the eyes of their brother, they sublimated their need to be loved into an obsession to love. As Caroline Heilbrun might say of them, "the old story of woman's destiny . . . does not give way to another story for women, a quest plot" for self-definition and determination,[14] because of their being fixated in total dependency on Julian. The relationship among the three siblings was in fact a codependency, a destructive union in which controlling behavior is a clinging dependency and power and powerlessness are confused.

Although his two sisters are themselves unable to do anything to keep Julian with them, Lily accomplishes it for them. Unsure of her sexual desirability and believing that Julian only married her because her mother paid him to, Lily wounds herself physically to gain his attention. Fearing that Julian's dealings with the mixed race Charlotte Warkins are sexual rather than purely financial, Lily informs Charlotte's husband, Cyrus, about Julian's meeting with his wife. After Cyrus's thugs attack Julian and Charlotte, Julian returns wounded and bleeding; feeling defeated, he reenters the house, to remain there with his wife and sisters. Rollyson explains the play's title, *Toys in the Attic*, in the following manner: "The drama is Freudian and surely influenced by [Hellman's] own psychoanalysis, by her own probing of the unconscious—the attic of memories—for the toys, the seemingly little playthings that end up making the patterns of our lives" (379). It seems possible, as well, that Hellman might have had Ibsen's *A Doll House* in mind. In that drama, Torvald treats Nora as his plaything, making her economically and, he believes, ethically dependent upon her, just as her children are her little dolls; she escapes that role and begins to define herself as an individual by leaving the house and slamming the door behind her. In Hellman's play, the characters all remain emotional children, having never grown out of their immature relationships. Change and development frighten rather than excite and challenge. They retreat back into the house, closing the door behind them, secure yet psychologically infantile in the tangled web of codependency they have spun over the years to keep them from facing their diminishing present and eventual death.

Farewell to the Theater

For her last foray in the theatre, Hellman adapted Burt Blechman's novel *How Much?* to the stage in 1963 as *My Mother, My Father and Me*. The most Jewish of all her plays, it begins as a family farce reminiscent of Kaufman and Hart's wacky *You Can't Take It With You* (1937), but then shifts in tone to something akin to Odet's *Awake and Sing!* (1936), even ending, as that work does, with the grandparent giving advice and support, both moral and financial, to the grandson. Hellman felt, in fact, that part of the reason for her play's lack of success and speedy departure from Broadway after just 17 performances may have been the change in "tone midway from farce to drama and that, for reasons I still do not understand, cannot be done in the theatre" (*Pentimento*, 209). As Wright accurately suggests, Hellman's choice as her "targets for fun [of] the American mom, teenage *angst* and consumerism" (292) link the work to Albee's *American Dream* (1960). Replete with enough racial and ethnic stereotypes to offend almost everyone, the play seems like a preview of the popular television sitcom *All in the Family*. Hellman's family, although not drawn as cartoon characters in the manner of Ionesco as is Albee's, exhibits the same tendency to commodify relationships.

The play is structured as a family narrative, dictated by Berney, the son, who is trying to find himself. Having become disenchanted with music, he dabbles in painting and photography, though he thinks he will finally go to medical school to discover himself there. His sentimentalism over the plight of African-Americans makes him want to go out and raise up the downtrodden, just as when he was a youngster he had wanted to save the Indians. As the play ends, however, he is making his livelihood simulating Native American music, though this appears little different from what some Indians themselves do when they exploit their heritage by reducing it to entertainment and souvenirs for white tourists. Hellman thus poses the problem of how one can preserve and transmit culture without commercialism and commodification, without reductionism and victimization.

Although content to be financially dependent on her husband, Berney's mother, Rose, feels it permissible to deny her husband sexually since he is not rich. She is an inveterate consumer, indiscriminately bringing home a mink hat, silver coffee service, a bird in a cage, girdles, ice skates, and Meissen china; the world is one big fire sale to her. When her mother needs to be put into a nursing home, Rose goes to bed with the proprietor in return for better accommodations at lower cost. Her husband, whose shoe business is faltering without a war in progress to help the market, joins with the doctor to produce "The Honor Death Shoe," a cheap model that can be used for burial purposes. If the apocalypse does not come for civilization (as it does not in Albee's play), this is still an apocalyptic vision of American family life and of the death of the liberal humanistic ideal. The play's blackly comic tone might be seen as a bold departure for Hellman, though the strongly felt moral viewpoint she upholds is consistent with that in her earlier works. Here, however, she attacks just too many targets too superficially.

After the failure of *My Mother, My Father and Me*, Hellman left playwriting behind and turned to her highly successful memoirs. In one interview she declares, "I see nothing wrong with saying that you're tired of one form and want to try another. I believe that's what happened to me. The theater . . . never held any great glamour for me. . . . I didn't start out as a playwright. . . . Most playwrights stay with it too long. I'm glad I changed forms" (*Conversations, Hellman*, 289–90). Moreover, Hellman is aware that hers was always essentially a verbal rather than a visual gift: "I don't basically have a theater imagination in spite of the fact I have a very decent theater technique" (*Pentimento*, 279). By her own stringently critical assessment, "The plays aren't as good as I'd remembered. . . . they're too on the nose—too airless. I pounded at things too much. They'll have a minor place in the end, the plays, but no complaints about that. A minor place is a good place" (Feibleman, 65).

Throughout her career, Hellman remained her own woman, using the stage, however impersonal the plays might seem at times, to impress on audiences her personal belief in the Hemingwayesque virtues of courage, honesty, loyalty, and decency, as well as to set forth certain strongly felt convictions: that economic dependency constricts individual freedom, that excessive materialism infects emotional relationships and the culture at large, that an idle romanticizing of the past together with the passage of time diminish the possibilities for fulfillment and change. With the four volumes of memoirs, a long and lively narrative based on the text of her own life rather than that of her characters took center stage. Hellman, by recreating and reimaging herself, joined the memorable portrait gallery of Regina Hubbard Giddens, Constance Tuckerman, and Carrie Berniers. More so than the plays, the memoirs and the portrait of Hellman enshrined in them must be judged for their truth to art rather than fidelity to life.

4

Arthur Miller: Fathers and Sons, Society and the Self

The plays from the first period of Arthur Miller's career—beginning with the Hopgood award-winning apprentice works of the 1930s written when he was a student at the University of Michigan and moving through *The Man Who Had All the Luck* in 1944 to *A View from the Bridge* in 1956—are shaped by two of the defining events in the dramatist's life: the Depression of the 1930s, when he witnessed his father's fortune crumble, and the McCarthy witch hunt of the 1950s, when he was found in contempt, though never imprisoned, for refusing to name names of communist sympathizers. Of the first, Miller would later write in his autobiography, *Timebends: A Life* (1987): "The Depression was only incidentally a matter of money. Rather, it was a moral catastrophe, a violent revelation of the hypocrisies behind the facade of American society."[1] Of the latter, he would say: "The overwhelmingly significant truth, I thought, as I still do, was the artist-hating brutality of the Committee and its envy of its victims' power to attract public attention and to make big money at it besides" (*Timebends*, 242). What links these two events, the first economic, the second political, is their undermining of what

Miller sees as every individual's inherent need "to evaluate himself justly" and to have others confirm that judgment. Both of these outside forces threaten the individual's dignity and sense of self-worth and forestall any attempt to inscribe his or her name in the family and in the society, in short, on history—or, as Miller phrases it in the introduction to his *Collected Plays*, the "need to leave a thumbprint somewhere on the world."[2]

Some version of Eddie Carbone's cry from *Bridge*, "I want my name," insistently threads itself throughout Miller's works, for the honor that attaches to one's name is nothing more nor less than the material outward sign of the essential inward person. If, as Miller claims in "The Family in Modern Drama," the "subject of all great plays" is how man takes "the outside world," which is "an alien place,"[3] and makes of it a home, then this feeling of at-homeness can only result when the individual inscribes himself or herself on that world truly, when the inscription reflects and accords with one's assessment of oneself.

Success, Morality, and the Judgment of History

This tension between self and image adumbrates Miller's first New York play, the somewhat ponderous and plodding *Man Who Had All the Luck*, which ran for only five performances in 1944. In it, David Frieber, the man with the luck, demands that some logical connection exists between what he does and the good that comes to him, that responsibility for one's actions and the reward (or, alternatively, punishment) somehow mesh. David refuses to accept one of the other character's reading of humankind as completely at the mercy of external forces: "A man is a jelly fish laying [*sic*] on the beach. A wave comes along and pulls him back into the sea, and he floats a while on a million currents he can't even feel, and he's back on the beach again never knowing why." Instead, David demands justice, "a good reason for everything": "If people don't receive according to what they deserve inside them we're living in a madhouse," he claims. If human worth is not part of the equation of success, then all order and rationality seem gone from the universe; if things come from luck, rather than goodness, then David will be just "a wreck, a broken dwarf crawling under the sky, waiting for what will hit him next."

So when good things happen to David—the death by accident of Andrew Falk, who had stood between his daughter, Hester, and David;

the soaring of his financial position through an auto mechanics shop, a farm, a quarry—David wonders whether he is "good enough to deserve" all these things or is simply being poised for a sudden plummeting. Believing it preferable that the bad that is bound to come ("everybody carries a curse") descend and then free him from future doubt, David lets his imagination of disaster run berserk. He will test fortune first by putting all his resources into a mink farm; then by thinking that if only his and Hester's much-wanted baby would die "all else would be safe"; and finally by deliberately allowing all the fish in another business venture to die so that he can live free of the fear of catastrophe, all to verify that individual responsibility is paramount.

The link between moral character and success that David and several later Miller protagonists either worry over or sometimes prefer to ignore may find its most potent analysis in sociologist Max Weber's treatise, *The Protestant Ethic and the Spirit of Capitalism* (1905), which examines the relationship between material success and providential blessing, wealth being an outward manifestation of one's "state of grace" and "sign of election." Capitalistic enterprise, even "pecuniary interests," is, therefore, not only justified but also "morally enjoined"; if "acquisition" by the bourgeois businessman and "labor" by the workman, each deemed a "calling" or vocation, lead to wealth, then that wealth should be regarded as "a sign of God's blessing." Such a belief can be, in Weber's words, "a powerful lever" in support of the capitalist ideal. Yet this same ethic that glorifies success remains open to debasement, for the "pursuit of wealth, stripped of ethical meaning, takes on the character of sport," leading to accumulating wealth as a justification for questionable actions in the intensely competitive, dog-eat-dog world of American society.

Imagery of business competition as sport pervades Miller's first success, *All My Sons* (1947), which received the nod for the Drama Critics' Award over O'Neill's *Iceman Cometh*. The story of a businessman, Joe Keller, who knowingly sends out faulty airplane parts during wartime, resulting in the deaths of numerous flyers, and who then lets his partner, George Deaver, be the fall guy, *All My Sons* inaugurates Miller's emphasis on the web that unites the individual and the social milieu: as Miller writes in his essay, "The Shadow of the Gods," "society is inside of man and man is inside of society" (*Theater Essays*, 185). No act exists in isolation, and no action can be without its consequences. To demonstrate this connection between an action in the past and its effects in the present, between guilty choice and moral retribution, Miller adopts the linear form of the realistic, Ibsenite, well-made social problem play, complete with its studied plotting to manipulate audience emotion and its building of suspense until the revelation of a secret from the past, in this instance a letter confirming not only that the Kellers' older son, Larry, died in the war but that he actually killed himself when he learned about his father's crime.

In what the set designer Mordecai Gorelik calls a "graveyard play," Larry's presence has been felt from the very first moments through visual stage symbolism, both in the tree that was planted to commemorate his missing in action and that blew down in the wind the night before the action begins, as well as in the slight mounding of earth visible in the yard. Larry's mother, Kate, refuses to accept his death, for she intuits that to let him go would be to name Joe guilty and to shake her faith in God, who would not let a son be killed by his father as recompense for the father's guilt. Neither can she countenance that Ann Deaver, the business partner's daughter and once Larry's fiancée, has now become engaged to marry Larry's younger bookish brother, Chris, himself torn between the image and the reality of his father, between idealistic goals and compromising choices.

A decided strain of anti-intellectualism runs through Joe Keller, who feels inadequate in the face of younger men better educated than he; rather than a thinker, he considers himself a doer. Like so many parents in American drama, Keller rationalizes that he acts only with his family in mind; "the whole shootin' match," he claims, is all "for [his] sons." The father believes he can buy his sons' respect through material means, love becoming a kind of commodity. Furthermore, his image for the business world comes uncomfortably close to the stereotypical picture of war. His surviving son, Chris, however, claims to be ashamed of money and rejects the business ethic, at least in part, if the "loot" is covered in "blood"; any profit that comes from war is tainted. Though Chris's high ideals cause some others, such as the Kellers' neighbor Sue Bayliss, to object that he presents a holier-than-thou image impossible to emulate, in practice Chris has actually been compromising by receiving money from the plant; the self-righteousness and moral superiority of Miller's spokespersons can sometimes prove a hard pill for other characters, and even audiences, to swallow.

The image of blood becomes a central one in *All My Sons*, not just the blood of the dead flyers that stains the profit, but also the image of the blood line between the generations. Joe Keller believes that the biological connection between himself and his sons is primary, that to be creator and provider for his sons is the sole measure of value. Chris rejects this, arguing that fatherhood cannot be just a matter of biology or blood; it involves an ethical dimension as well. Fathering, in Miller, becomes a test of one's moral integrity, a way to full humanity; viewed from that perspective, Larry and Chris prove better fathers to the men under their command than Joe is to them. Moreover, sons demand that the father must be an ethical or moral example for them. As Miller also suggests in his essay "The Shadow of the Gods," the parents become godlike; the father's power equates with that of the moral law. And so Chris, and society, must judge Joe Keller not simply on the basis of how good a material provider he has been for his family. When Joe Keller says that if there is anything "bigger than family" he will put a bullet through himself, he foreshadows the close of the play. Chris leads him to acknowledge that his former perspective was myopic, that indeed there remains always a responsibility to the larger community. Those dead pilots were "all [his] sons." As one of the characters in Miller's recent play *The Ride Down Mt. Morgan* (1991) remarks when pushed to define the bottom line of human obligation, "There are other people."

Yet in Miller, the survivor bears a responsibility. Here the son who forces the father to the bar of justice for having failed to live up to a moral ideal is himself left to face guilt associated with the other's death. What right has the son to judge so harshly? In the family, must the son always "kill" the father in the process of individuating himself and establishing his own moral stature? In a society, must the rebellious question and continually challenge and even usurp the authority in power in order to rejuvenate the social order? When Kate Keller pleads with Chris that now he must "live," she seems unaware of the irony, of this burden that the morally mature and active carry with them for having lived by a value system that runs counter to the status quo, and that has resulted in the punishment of the father for his limited ethical and social vision. *All My Sons* is perhaps, then, not as tidily closed as its well-made form leads an audience to expect.

What the playwright terms this "theme of survivor guilt" (*Timebends*, 522) continues to be a compelling motif in Miller, particularly in such later works dealing with the Holocaust as the television script *Playing for Time* (1980), where the art of the orchestra members (performed for an audience half of whom are condemned to death while the other half are morally repugnant in their conduct but still love music) protects them from annihilation in the death camps; or in the dramatic fable *Incident at Vichy* (1964), where the Jew who escapes and lives shares the burden for the death of the Gentile who willingly gives him his pass to freedom and dies. As is true for Chris Keller, living is never bought easily; in *Vichy*, the survivor might be said to deserve his special grace only because he decides not to act vengefully toward the wife he has stopped loving. Even in the Pulitzer-Prize-winning *Death of a Salesman* (1949), Miller's greatest success with audiences and critics, another idealistic surviving son, Biff Loman, must carry with him the knowledge that his father, Willy, from however limited a perspective, sacrificed himself so that his son could live and prosper. Miller might almost be said, in both *All My Sons* and *Death of a Salesman*, to be as interested in the response of the sons as he is in the fate of the fathers.

Miller's Revisioning of the American Dream

In its initial production, *Death of a Salesman* starred Lee J. Cobb and played for 742 performances on Broadway. Since then, it has seen frequent revivals, including one featuring an all-black cast; its most recent appearance on Broadway (1984) featured Dustin Hoffman and John Malkovich. When Miller originally conceived *Death of a Salesman*, he called it "The Inside of His Head" and thought in terms of confronting the audience with the image of a phrenological skull on a drop curtain that would then open up to reveal the stage. Even though he eventually jettisoned this concept, he retained the intention of showing Willy Loman's way of thinking, his mind in disintegration really, as he assesses himself and moves toward his decision to commit suicide. The desired effect was to demonstrate how everything, past and present, memory and fact, dream and reality, exists together simultaneously within an individual; then and now would be seen as contemporal. In Miller's first draft, the setting consisted simply of a series of platforms; actually, as the play's director Elia Kazan reports in his autobiography, *A Life* (1988), it was the designer, Jo Mielziner (who had earlier designed *The Glass Menagerie* [1944] and *A Streetcar Named Desire* [1947]), who conceived of the salesman's skeletal house, with the two scrims: one with a leaf motif in a bright yellow green to create the patina of a nostalgically recalled idyllic past that perhaps never existed; the other with a towering apartment building motif in a searing orange to indicate the reality of an encroaching urbanized and mechanistic world. When the action occurs in the past, the characters are to move freely, even onto the forestage, without observing the house's imaginary wall lines; in present time, how-

Study sketch by Jo Mielziner for set design of *Death of a Salesman*. *Estate of Jo Mielziner, used by permission, Theater Arts Collection, Harry Ransom Humanities Research Center, The University of Texas at Austin.*

ever, except during the "Requiem" at the end, they are to honor the implied divisions. The distinction between the present reality and the past as recalled would be underscored by sound as well as lighting, with the faraway flute music associated with Willy Loman's father heard during the moments of idyllic reverie.

Although *Death of a Salesman* upholds the Ibsenite mold in that it moves toward the revelation of a secret, its structure is not linear in the sense that expository passages gradually supply necessary information about the past during the ongoing action. Instead, the past as remembered in Willy's mind is dramatized through something very like acted-out soliloquies that illustrate rather than simply tell. Nor did Miller intend that these segments from the past be regarded as flashbacks; what he sought was "a mobile concurrency of past and present." That fluidity would be achieved partly by events organized and arranged through something resembling free association, with a word or an image setting off a memory from the past, such as Linda's torn stockings segueing into the silk hose Willy gives to the other woman. Because the play is an attempt to objectify or externalize the inner experience, and because that inner experience sometimes assumes a dreamlike, hallucinatory, or nightmarish aura, the result is something close to the "subjective truth" arrived at through expressionism.

Willy Loman is falling apart physically, mentally, and emotionally because of the disparity between the powerful dream of what might have been, perhaps accessible only to his disturbed imagination, and the reality of what his life has become. In his determination not to be a little man, Willy was driven by two ideals, the first to be number one, the second to do something for his sons. As a salesman, Willy's self-image requires support from outside himself; he needs to sell himself to others in order to sell himself to himself. When others begin to doubt the self-image, so, too, does Willy, becoming alienated from himself. Actually, two deaths of a salesman are observed in this play; the other came to Dave Singleman, who died in his velvet slippers on a train and whose funeral attracted hundreds. Willy fails to understand, however, the significance of this other salesman's last name: if he, Willy, is "low" man or common man, Singleman achieved something out of the ordinary, making him the exception rather than the rule. But then Willy's heroes have always been, as Thomas Porter describes them in *Myth in Modern American Drama*,[4] the supreme egotists who, from Ben Franklin and Horatio Alger through the robber barons to their debasement in Dale Carnegie and Willy's own brother, Ben, pursue the American Dream of rags-to-riches self-reliance. For them, money means happiness and success equals grace; to lack either is to fail, or even be damned, in the eyes of the all-holy system and its adherents.

Anxious about his own material failure after years of plodding work, Willy is disturbed as well over the way his two sons, Biff and Happy, have turned out, because it seems to reflect back on him and indicate a lack of proper respect by them. Willy, as the good father, had always tried to achieve things for his sons, both to live again through them and to earn their love. Like Shakespeare's Lear, however, Willy measures the giving and receiving of love through material tokens. So immaterial things, such as moral standards, are devalued, justifying petty thievery and cheating as a means to get ahead, as if success were due his sons simply because they are the Loman boys. Miller, in fact, might well have titled the play "Father and Sons" because of the extraordinary number of biological or surrogate paternity relationships in it.

Willy felt disconnected from his own father, the peddler who left to ply his craft across country, and so remains unsure of how to parent; Willy's older brother, Ben, whose success story in Alaska and the diamond mines of Africa may be merely romantic mythologizing on Willy's part, functions partly as a substitute father to Willy, attempting to inspire self-determination through capitalist enterprise; Willy's neighbor Charley, and even his former boss's son, Howard, though younger than himself, both offer Willy counsel and advice. Biff's brother Happy assumes the father's role as arbiter of morality when he initiates Biff into the life of women and wine. Meanwhile, Charley and his son, Bernard, the no-nonsense, nondreamers, seem to effortlessly achieve conspicuous success and rise to greater heights through each generation within the system that defeats Willy, as if to demonstrate, according to Christopher Bigsby, "that a full-hearted commitment to capitalism is not incompatible with humane values" (Bigsby 1992, 88).

With this focus on fathers and sons, the role of women within the play is reduced to a marginalized one. Except for Linda Loman, the others are all women simply used by the men as release from the tension or loneliness of trying to secure a niche in life (Willy's woman in Boston), or as proof of prowess and compensation for limited success (Happy's compulsive conquests of his boss's women). Linda, dutiful housewife and drudge, supports Willy in his illusions and, perhaps unwittingly, helps foster his deceit; to her, love means never criticizing, even when loving criticism would be the only means that might help jar Willy out of his self-imposed blindness. Miller, in acknowledging "a more sinister side to [his] women characters," himself comments that "they . . . protect [the men's] mistakes in crazy ways. They are forced to do that. So the females are victims as well."[5]

And yet by portraying woman as the marginalized "other," Miller may be pushing home his point that the feminine values of nurturing and compassion have been shoved aside in favor of masculine aggressive-ness; as he remarks, "the system of love is the opposite of the law of success" (Collected Plays, 36). This absence, or at best imbalance, contri-butes inevitably to a deficiency in the pursuit of the American Dream, brought about partly because the fathers fail to instill proper expansive values in their sons, settling instead on a narrow ethic of competition as measure of the man. Traditionally, the family has afforded such a compelling arena for American dramatists precisely because, in a pluralis-tic society, it functions as the primary site for the development of moral consciousness and codes of behavior.

Although Biff concludes, and with some justification, that Willy "had the wrong dream," a "phoney dream" that he should "burn," it might be more accurate to say that his whole-souled pursuit of an unobtainable goal led him to rationalize flawed values. Yet if Willy instilled distorted values in his sons, they failed him as well by breaking the bond of connection with him through all their little acts of desertion (again, shades of Lear's children), culminating in the restaurant scene where they leave him alone and befuddled to go off with their pick-ups for the night. Years before, Biff had also walked out on his father when he discovered him in a Boston hotel with another woman, because of the father's failure to measure up to the son's image of moral authority that a father must uphold. From that moment on, Biff's potential for self-definition and success—according to Willy's terms at least—though never as great as his athletic glory in high school seemed to promise, diminished. Willy attributes Biff's apparent failure in life to his desiring to punish his father out of "spite"; closer to the truth is Biff's rejection of being shaped in the mold his father desires. Biff dreams instead of a romanticized, Thoreauvian retreat back to nature, of working with his hands somewhere away from the competitive urban rat race from which he feels alienated. Significantly, the inclination appears to spring from his grandfather, an artisan who made and peddled flutes in the West. Willy likewise suffers from some unsatisfied romantic longing for a link with a sustaining Nature, as is most poignantly recalled when he tries to plant the carrot seeds by moonlight in the "boxed in" concrete jungle that has displaced the garden once surrounding the house.

Motivated to buy back Biff's respect and earn his "worship," Willy commits suicide to provide the insurance money that he thinks will finally allow Biff "to be magnificent." As Lyman muses in *Mt. Morgan*, is not insurance an attempt at "buying immortality . . . reaching up out of the grave to pay the bills, to remind people of your love?" Yet Willy does not understand Biff at all. Once again, he thinks in terms of reciprocity, of commodity exchange, not understanding that he already "owns" Biff's love without sacrificing himself on the cross of money, a sacrifice that can cause Biff nothing but guilt. So if *Death of a Salesman* rehearses the story of Willy's disintegration, it is no less the play of the son's maturation, of finding an identity that corresponds to his desires rather than parental expectations. Admitting he "stole [him]self out of every good job since high school," Biff refuses to shift the blame for his failure onto his father; he does believe, nevertheless, that Willy filled him too "full of hot air" and smugness, holding out as possible an unlimited level of achievement never really open to them or to most individuals. Though he does not argue with others' assessment of his father as a hard-working, "unappreciated prince," at the same time, he rejects the pie-in-the-sky belief that they will ever ascend to "number one." One confirmation of Biff's growth in self-knowledge comes through contrast with the deficiency of his brother Happy's delusions. A tall-tale teller like his father and a morally unscrupulous go-getter, in the face of all evidence to the contrary, Happy clutches at the illusion of success being just around the corner.

Although Biff claims that "no one will feel pity" for Willy if he commits suicide, that probably does not accurately gauge the audience's reaction. Willy is, of course, partly society's victim—forced into a mode of action that says that in America material success matters above all else—and partly victim of himself—unable to recognize the limitations of the dream that drives and finally devours him, unable to see that, like the unlimited possibility symbolized by the green light on Daisy's dock in Fitzgerald's *The Great Gatsby*, "the orgiastic future . . . year by year [has] recede[d] before us." Though Willy's own limited insight prevents his ever coming to self-knowledge (he is, like Lear, a man "who but slenderly knew himself"), there does remain a sense of waste and loss at his death. For who would claim that living always and everywhere without any dream is preferable to living with a dream, however misguided? Is it better "to walk away" and "ring up zero"? Willy chooses to die, leaving behind what he always wanted and had, though he never realized it because he searched for proof of it in the wrong places: the love of his son Biff.

If Biff's maturation process removes the focus from the father and shifts it temporarily to the son, the "Requiem," with its eulogies by Charley and Linda, restores the emphasis on Willy. Yet the play's closing lines, "We're free," literally referring to the mortgage on the house ironically just paid off, raises the issue of freedom versus limitation: to what extent can Biff ever be free of the baggage of past generations, of the weight of responsibility that his father sacrificed himself so that he might live? To what extent can anyone ever be totally free of the dream that, once debased, proves as destructive now as it was once empowering? Through the story of Willy Loman, Miller has also penned an elegy for America's touted egalitarian ideal. It was intended to be, in Miller's own words, "a time bomb . . . under the bullshit of capitalism, this pseudo life that thought to touch the clouds by standing on top of a refrigerator, waving a paid-up mortgage at the moon, victorious at last" (*Timebends*, 184).

Miller's Idea of Tragedy

In his essay commemorating the play's first anniversary, "The *Salesman* Has a Birthday," Miller states: "the tragedy of Willy Loman is that he gave his life, or sold it, in order to justify the waste of it" (*Theater Essays*, 15), which intimates that he refused to countenance his position as a nobody. Although the contention among critics over Willy Loman's status as a tragic hero likely will never be satisfactorily resolved, indisputably Miller's discussion of that issue in "Tragedy and the Common Man," which appeared a month after *Death of a Salesman* premiered, is the most famous critical document ever written by an American dramatist. In his *Poetics*, the oldest systematic exploration of the topic, Aristotle posited that the tragic protagonist is a character of noble birth, neither wholly good nor wholly bad, who, through some error in judgment, brings about his own downfall, effecting a catharsis of pity and fear in the audience. In his essay, Miller attempts, first, to establish that the tragic possibility has no inherent connection to one's social station at birth but remains the right of every individual by virtue of a common humanness shared by all. He then takes Aristotle's notion of the *hamartia*, or error in judgment, what has come to be called "the tragic flaw," and inverts it.

For Miller, being flawed, since it is nothing more nor less than man's "inherent unwillingness to remain passive in the face of what he conceives to be a challenge to his dignity, his image of his rightful status," evidences not something negative and thus to be avoided; rather, it exists as something positive, to be embraced. The great majority of people, satisfied to passively "accept their lot without active retaliation," and refusing to act upon "the total compulsion to evaluate [themselves] justly," remain flawless and so are not fit subjects for tragedy. Furthermore, heroic action, demanding freedom and dignity and challenging the social environment that would deny these rights, transcends a purely psychiatric or sociological view of life; once undertaken, such action "demonstrates the indestructible will of man to achieve his humanity," thereby speaking to man's "perfectibility," his refusal to be cowed or made little (*Theater Essays*, 3–7). Miller's perspective on tragedy, then, is a concomitant of the individual's insistence on rightly inscribing his or her name on history.

The Autonomy of Human Conscience

Before writing another original play after *Salesman*, Miller set his pen to adapting a work by his chief dramatic influence, the Norwegian social playwright Henrik Ibsen. His forebear's positing of a moral connection between the past and the present seems to have particularly fascinated Miller. Not only did Ibsen excel at masterful exposition, at revealing what happened before the play opened that makes the current action accessible, a feat Miller calls the "biggest single dramatic problem" facing any playwright, he also brought to drama the "fascinating interplay of cause and effect that have long been a part of the novel," rendering the stage "the place for ideas, for philosophies," of great appeal to Miller because of his aim to "entertain [audiences] with his brain as well as his heart" (*Theater Essays*, 17).

Working on *An Enemy of the People* (1950), originally written by Ibsen back in 1882, apparently helped crystallize Miller's thinking about the dilemma of the morally aware and committed citizen who sees his community embarking on an immoral social position. The protagonist, Dr. Thomas Stockmann, moves out of the private arena of the family and into the public realm as he reveals that the waters by which the town hopes to secure its economic advancement are polluted and putrid; the miraculous spring on which the town's economy is to depend is actually a pesthole. For his refusal to compromise on his truthfulness, Stockmann finds himself pitted against various factions and branded a criminal. As Miller comments in his foreword, *Enemy* raises the "central theme of our social life today. . . . whether the democratic guarantees protecting political minorities . . . [should] be set aside in time of crisis" (*Theater Essays*, 17).

Ibsen's original work appears imbued with the ideas of John Stuart Mill from *On Liberty* (1859), which weighs the rights of the enlightened minority in the face of recalcitrant majority opinion. While prizing individual conscience and character, Mill sensed that majority rule may mean that mediocrity rules; he suspected that collective rule by the majority levels everything down to a kind of uniformity, an average that prevents the exceptional from flowering except when a society is willing to permit and nurture an indispensable aristocracy of thought and character. "No government," he claims, "by a democracy or a numerous aristocracy, either in its political acts or in the opinions, qualities, and tone of mind which it fosters, ever did or could rise above mediocrity, except in so far as the Many have let themselves be guided (which in their best times they have always done) by the counsels and influence of a more highly gifted and instructed One or Few."

Stockmann's brother, Peter, the town's mayor, puts the expediency of the many before the integrity of the one. Peter subordinates the individual to the state, believing in submission to the authority that oversees the general welfare. Civic power is to be used to protect old ideas from being challenged and to ensure uniformity of belief; freedom of inquiry and expression are to be limited "if the proper line is crossed." The liberal newspaper editor Hovstad would seem to be diametrically opposed to Peter in his dislike of bureaucracy and his belief that the underdog must have his say in governing, for the social contract ideally encourages the ability, intelligence, and self-respect of the citizenry. And yet, Hovstad temporizes: the newspaper cannot buck public opinion, added to which is the practical matter of higher taxes to clean up the springs. Liberals like Hovstad, in fact, fail because, unwilling to adopt the truly revolutionary stance of a Mill (or an Ibsen or Miller), they still idolize the authority of majority rule over the moral weight of the oftentimes more enlightened minority.

Dr. Stockmann as an idealist naively and mistakenly thinks that people will always side with the truth, even when doing so threatens their material well-being. The poisoned springs are, however, only a symbol of the larger poison of intolerance within the body politic—just as the faulty airplane parts in *All My Sons* signify a failure of the capitalist system that places money over integrity. Dr. Stockmann assumes a missionary role in inculcating the belief, again as in *All My Sons*, of a larger responsibility, so that the community would be made broader, more civilized. Whereas his older daughter, the teacher Petra, is Ibsen's "Clear-eyed hope for the future," the Doctor's wife falls prey to being tempted by the practicality of a Joe Keller, if not of instigating immorality at least of tolerating injustice for the sake of the family's well-being. Yet in Miller the family unit is never the supreme social entity.

Ultimately, Dr. Stockmann must become "a revolutionist" against the age-old lie that the majority, as he observes, "always has the right on its side when, in fact, it is always wrong." Following Mill's notion of an intellectual moral elite, the Doctor argues that "one must know the truth before the many can know it," so to be the people's (in the sense of the majority's) enemy is not to be flawed. As Neil Carson remarks, in Miller's plays "the moment of awareness is always a preparation for the moment of choice."[6] Although Miller sides with Stockmann in his insistence that morality consists in a belief that is acted upon—that to be right one must do right—he, though probably to a lesser degree than Ibsen before him, might take pause at Stockmann's messianic complex, in which he compares himself with Christ and Galileo. For his mission perhaps veers over into madness, as he vows to save as "sacred relics" the rocks that the masses throw through his windows. In light of the hysterical witch hunt to ferret out those with dissenting political views soon to overtake America, Miller can retrieve a final irony from Stockmann's decision to go to America where there is "more room to hide." The playwright's comment that *Enemy of the People* glorifies "the need, if not the holy right, to resist the pressure to conform" (*Theater Essays*, 16), makes it very much the forerunner of the central thrust in Miller's next original play.

For the historical situation and incidents in *The Crucible* (1953), his most often revived work, Miller goes back to the 1692 witchcraft trials in Salem, Massachusetts; he even intersperses within his printed text long narrative passages setting forth the factual background. Although the intention of these extradramatic segments may have been to validate Miller's veracity in recreating the past, the issue of his objectivity never became central in discussions of the play. What did, instead, assume center stage was the apparent analogy between the witch hunt and the tactics of the congressional committees searching out communist sympathizers and fellow travelers during the House Un-American Activities Committee and McCarthy hearings, although a too-insistent emphasis on the analogy may in fact have limited the play's appeal for its initial audience. In the way that both episodes in American history played on the hysteria and paranoia of the many in order to incriminate the few, and on the phenomenon of a society's need to create scapegoats to bear its repressed guilt and insecurities, the parallels are not difficult to find. Miller himself admits that he regarded the McCarthy hearings as "profoundly ritualistic, a surreal spiritual transaction that connected Washington to Salem." Bigsby cautions against being misled into finding too exact a parallel between the two historical events, and certainly the play's continuing power as drama transcends one's knowledge of the early 1950s; Bigsby suggests further that just as telling an analogy might be found in the wartime persecution of the Jews, a subject that Miller would later handle openly in both *Incident at Vichy* and *Playing for Time*. In fact, although his early novel *Focus* (1945) examines anti-Semitic persecution, Miller refrains from becoming an explicitly Jewish dramatist (in the vein, for example, of Clifford Odets) until his works from the mid-1960s on.

The political/social climate of the 1950s notwithstanding, *The Crucible* continues Miller's probing examination of the individual in relationship to a repressive, tyrannical society, this time asking, and re-asking, in light of *Enemy of the People*, several key questions: How are moral values arrived at? What is the place of secular law in the equation? Can a lie under oath ever be a moral truth? Where does final authority ultimately reside? Although Miller zeroes in on the trial of one man, John Proctor, he begins with the largest unit, in this instance the Puritan theocracy that feels threatened by apparent consorting with the devil, moving afterward to the family unit disrupted by adultery. The discovery before the play opens of several girls, including the daughter and niece of the town minister, Reverend Parris, dancing naked in the forest during a black mass orchestrated by the West Indian woman, Tituba, starts the chain of events. To deflect guilt from themselves, the girls, led by Abigail Williams, begin naming names of those who have supposedly sold their souls to Satan. Battle lines become drawn, based on property disputes, on attitudes toward the materialism of Parris, and on questions of strict adherence to religious observances.

The theocracy can only survive, in fact, through the willingness of the community members to submit their individual intellect and will to the higher authority of the state-church that, as Bigsby says, requires "a singular reading of the world, a reality constituted by those who claim to possess or interpret the word" (Bigsby 1992, 96). For some, such strict, unquestioning obedience is appealing because freedom seems burden-some; John Proctor is not one of those. He and some others realize that the Puritan patriarchy coerces obedience through exercising the tyranny of power rather than the law of love. Among those accused by Abigail, who had an affair with John before the play opens, is John's wife, Eliza-beth, now pregnant with their third child; thus images of generativity amongst the stern naysaying community are associated with the Proctors: the baby, the freshly plowed earth, the flowers.

To substantiate Elizabeth's claims to truthfulness when she denies consorting with the devil, John tells the Court that she will surely not lie if asked whether he had been a lecher, something to which he has already confessed unbeknownst to her. But she does lie, out of love for him, out of feeling responsibility for having been a cold wife after the birth of their last child, and out of a belief that she cannot sit, unlike Chris in *All My Sons* or Biff in *Death of a Salesman*, in judgment upon another. Only John can judge himself, only he can find the "shred of goodness" within himself, which is the step he must take before he can go to his death. For Abigail has pointed the finger at him as in Satan's grip, too. Aware, however, of his sexual failure, he names himself too guilty to go to death, "mounting the saint's gibbet" with all those completely innocent of the trumped-up charges in a society where "the accuser [is] always holy now."

In the final act of the play, John makes a series of decisions, some of them reversing earlier ones, manifesting the existential nature of Miller's *Crucible*—as Jean Paul Sartre, who wrote the French adaptation, seemed to intuit. To simplify, the existentialists take as a given the fact that one *is*, but one becomes *what* one is—that is, one's essence—by the choices one makes and the consequences of those choices. When John confesses to his sin of lechery, he does it both to alleviate his guilt and to save his wife, since he trusts the Court will see Abigail's vindictiveness in her charges. When he signs the confession to being in the devil's ploy, he does so both because he deems himself unworthy to die a saint's death and because he refuses to name and incriminate others—which is what Miller himself and many of those called to testify before the House Un-American Activities Committee also refused to do. Is to withhold names to be less than truthful, and so to lie? Or does it, like Elizabeth's lie, become a moral truth?

John, however, only moments later, tears up his confession (much as St. Joan had) when he realizes it will be made public and taken as evidence that he claims others to be in Satan's power, thus blackening their good names. Yet he also destroys the written "lie" because, though it would save his life, it would ruin his good name and that of his family. In the words of the poet Robert Lowell, John Proctor finds within himself the "lovely peculiar power to choose life and die." He must answer only to himself: human conscience is the final authority, autonomous in all things. Even the law must, in fact, be violated when it comes into conflict with the dictates of a rightly formed conscience, for when conscience is inviolable, law can never be supreme. Miller himself delineates "the real and inner theme" of *The Crucible* as "the handing over of conscience to another, be it woman, the state, or a terror, and the realization that with conscience goes the person, the soul immortal, and the name" (*Collected Plays*, 47).

The representatives of the law, civil in the person of Judges Danforth and Hathorne, religious in the persons of the Reverends Parris and Hale, are unwilling to make the authoritarian institutions they represent, state and church, subservient to the individual. (The theologian Hale does eventually see the obsession and excesses for what they are and tries to distance himself from the evil being done in the name of right; his conflict may be even more subtle than that of the chief protagonist.) In response to those who found his judges too villainous, Miller's comment that, if he had to do it over again, he would make them even more evil because absolute evil does indeed exist, appears to lend added credence to Bigsby's reading the Holocaust behind *The Crucible*. Proctor, because he finally "refuses to remain passive" in the face of a "threat to his personal dignity" that would rob him of his name and his self-respect and his innocence, fulfills Miller's criteria for the tragic hero even more unquestioningly than does Willy Loman. At certain points, *The Crucible* approaches the Shakespearean in tone, though productions face the danger of treating the material so ponderously and reverentially as to lessen its fiercely human impact.

The Community of Common Men

Arthur Miller rounds off the first decade of his professional playwriting career with what began as two lengthy one-acts. A *Memory of Two Mondays*, while not actually a "memory play" in its structure as *Death of a Salesman* is, must yet have been as close to his personal experience as any of Miller's first half-dozen plays, for it focuses on a young man in the 1930s as he prepares to leave a factory job to matriculate at the university. As such, it highlights the recurrent tension in Miller's work (and in much of modern American drama) between the intellectual and the working man—a variant of the poet-artist/businessman conflict evident in O'Neill. On one level, A *Memory of Two Mondays*, which Miller terms an exercise in "abstract realism" for its handling of time wherein days and seasons effortlessly fade into one another, is a fanfare or paean for the common worker, celebrating the camaraderie and community that result from bonding together. The warehouse setting, though "dirty and chaotic," is actually "a little world, a home to which . . . these people like to come," but still a world not devoid of mean-spiritedness and petty ethnic prejudice; and the working men form a microcosm of different nationalities and temperaments and talents, something like the cross-section of the populace one finds in the proletarian social plays of Elmer Rice and Clifford Odets during the late 1920s and 1930s.

Yet the shipping room is, at the same time, severely restrictive, a closed-off space. Miller plays up the contrast between the limited world within and the expansive universe without through two characters: 18-year-old Bert, his protagonist, who brings the daily *New York Times* and *War and Peace* with him to work, and 40-year-old Kenneth, an immigrant

Irishman full of romantic yearnings and an appreciation for poetry (a "useless occupation in Ireland"), who bemoans that there exist few readers anymore of works like "O Captain, My Captain," Whitman being the classic American poet closest to Miller in viewpoint. In a symbolic moment, Kenneth, for whom war and death await (the play is set at the time of Hitler's coming to power) takes "one swipe" at the grimy windows and magically "all of them are flooded with . . . a little of God's light"; suddenly, the garden outdoors is visible, but then, with mythic overtones of loss, it turns to winter. Such ambivalences and ambiguities help prevent the play from becoming just another wistful story of growing up.

Bert, with some sadness, sees the implacability of time; these people, who will be "ghostly figures" he shall remember, will age and die "like a subway emptying." To leave the familiar factory to pursue an education means dislocation; at the same time, however, it is proof that one's class need not determine and condemn one to a preordained existence. If growth entails loss as well as gain, if Bert never again will be totally *of* these people no matter how much he might be from them, he understands that he "can't stop time"; the individual is part of a larger sociohistorical process. Through the stage/world metaphor that adumbrates the close of A *Memory of Two Mondays*, it is almost as if Bert is "moved" by some higher force to make "an exit."

Perhaps even more than *The Crucible*, Miller's A *View from the Bridge*, which began as a one-act play in free verse but was expanded to full-length for its London production in 1956, provides a testament to the savagery of the McCarthy years, as it focuses on branding someone as "other" and on betraying the outsider to the authorities. If, in Hitler's Germany, homosexuals were as stigmatized and hunted down as Jews, in postwar America, being a homosexual was often as suspect as being soft on communism; in fact, the two were sometimes conflated. And so in A *View from the Bridge*, which explodes gender stereotyping and lays bare its deficiencies, Miller explores how the supposedly patriotic act of reporting an illegal alien to the authorities can be used as a cover for antihomosexual fear and prejudice, no matter how unsubstantiated the rumors are by fact; as Gerald Weales suggests, being an informer is a lesser stigma than being a sexual deviant.[7]

The "view" in the play's title connotes the perspective taken by the narrator, the lawyer Alfieri, as he retrospectively filters the tale of Eddie Carbone, a longshoreman in Brooklyn's Red Hook district, while the "bridge" pinpoints the narrator's role as conduit between play and audience. The distanced and sometimes cryptic Alfieri blends functions of the chorus from classical theater with those of the Stage Manager from Thornton Wilder's free-ranging experimental pieces: he sets the scene, introduces characters and events, and positions the happenings in past time, fostering a sense of powerlessness and inevitability, as the action "run[s] its bloody course"; he becomes actor/participant in the story; he serves as advisor and conscience to the central character, cajoling and warning Eddie as he rushes to his destiny; and he helps raise the tale to the level of myth, editorializing and moralizing for the audience. In this last capacity, Alfieri serves as spokesperson for one of the types of law and justice that come into conflict in the play. As a lawyer, Alfieri upholds the system of codified laws that form the foundation of civilized society, though he does propose that these ordinances are grounded in a natural law sanctioned by a divine justice. Yet, as Miller makes clear in the play, there exists a more primitive tribal justice of "blood law" based on codes of behavior that predate any written laws, and it is on this elemental level of passionate response to perceived threats to one's dignity that the action proceeds.

Inverting the Phaedra-Hippolytus myth that O'Neill had updated in *Desire under the Elms*, Eddie Carbone's impulsive passions bring him into opposition with moral and social imperatives springing from community taboos against incest and homosexuality. Eddie, whose marriage to Beatrice has become distant physically, rationalizes his incestuous feelings for her niece, Catherine, who lives with them, by employing the vocabulary of the overly protective, and later well-intentioned if possessive, father. Thinking of her as either still his "baby" or as a virginal "madonna," he criticizes her short skirts and high heels and "wavy" walk as too seductive, dislikes her boyfriends, and worries over her safety should she move away and go to work. Alfieri and Beatrice both caution Eddie against his refusal to recognize the excessive love that defies "nature" and warn him to "let [Catherine] go."

When Beatrice's cousins Marco and Rudolpho arrive illegally from Italy to hide in the Carbone apartment, Eddie's jealousy manifests itself over the flirtation and then growing affection between Catherine and Rudolpho, whom Eddie sees as trying to "steal" his niece. Eddie claims that the blond and slightly effeminate Rudolpho, with the "wacky hair like a chorus girl" who sings—a favorite song is "Paper Doll," which speaks tellingly of possessiveness—cooks, and sews, gives him the "heeby-jeebies," whereas Marco "acts like a man." Feeling threatened over the loss of Catherine to Rudolpho, and trying to convince his wife and niece that the boy only wants to marry so he can stay legally in America, Eddie attempts to bolster his position with a show of machismo, ridiculing Rudolpho and making him stagger under the blows from a boxing "lesson," to which Marco reacts by challenging and bettering Eddie's strength, thereby openly humiliating him.

Eddie's final challenge to Rudolpho's masculinity, and a proof for many critics of Eddie's latent homosexuality, occurs when Eddie first kisses his niece and then Rudolpho on the lips, as if to prove "the guy ain't right" because he does not "put up a manly fight." In David Savran's recent reading of Miller's canon, "*Bridge* demonstrates how the fear of effeminacy slides into homophobic panic, which, almost inevitably, slides into homosexual desire. It documents the difficulty in Miller's work of separating erotic fascination from erotic dread and of the extraordinary anxiety produced by a man's confrontation with the Other, the feminine within."[8]

Unable to prevent the wedding, Eddie sees snitching on Marco and Rudolpho to the immigration authorities as his last resort. After Marco spits in his face, Eddie demands a public show of "respect" and honor to his name; in the street fight during the play's final moments, Marco stabs Eddie to death. Alfieri eulogizes Eddie as an embodiment of "something perversely pure," as someone "who allowed himself to be wholly known." If this rather lame choral comment seems somewhat hollow and unconvincing to audiences, it is perhaps because it tries to confine Eddie within rational categories that can hardly encompass the unruly passions that essentially define who and what he is, that were somehow larger than him, and that he lacked the wherewithal to handle, let alone understand. In his impulsive actions and defiance of logic rests his mystery.

Reminiscent of the "Requiem" that serves as a coda to *Death of a Salesman* in its attempt to reduce to a concrete explanation what has essentially been an imaginative perception and construction of character, the close of A *View from the Bridge* might be unsettling for other reasons to audiences and readers of the plays from the first half of Miller's career. Seemingly, the ideal of conduct has always been precisely delineated, an absolute sorting out of moral categories, of right from wrong. As Miller, terming himself an "impatient moralist," observes in *Timebends*, "to me the idea of the law was the ultimate social reality, in the sense that physical principles are the scientist's ground—the final appeal to order, to reason, and to justice. In some primal layer Law in God's thought" (584). And yet these rational categories can hardly contain such protean characters as a Willy or a Proctor or an Eddie, who are ruled finally by some elemental need to express a vision more ethically pure and imaginative than an uncomprehending society is willing to countenance; in fact, in setting up the autonomy of human conscience as the final arbiter, Miller holds for a relativism that is resistant to any absolute categories and sometimes even at odds with his own strident moralism.

Ultimately, in Miller, the authoritative pronouncements and mores of the father/social construct must be subservient to the son, and only the individual who achieves full selfhood through a revolutionary questioning and challenging of conformity and the status quo can be truly successful in inscribing his or her name on history. To temporize or compromise, to "settle for half" as Alfieri counsels may be preferable or to "walk away" as others suggested Willy should do, is exactly what Miller's heroes must refuse to do. That refusal is what defines them; it is, moreover, also what makes them, especially Willy and Eddie, resistant to—because they are larger than—the kinds of summing up that the choral characters, such as Charley and Linda in *Death of a Salesman* and Alfieri in *A View from the Bridge*, speaking for Miller, attempt. They refuse to be bound by the very moralizing that constitutes one of Miller's hallmarks as a dramatist.

5

William Inge:
The Terms of Diminishment

I n "The Tiny Closet," one of several short plays from the early 1950s, William Inge writes about a genteel and fastidious middle-aged man, Mr. Newbold, who harbors a secret. Occupant of a room in a midwestern, Victorian-style boarding house, he insists upon his right to have "*some* place, just some little place, that's completely private," a space that he can "call my own, my very own," and so forbids his landlady to unlock the door to his tiny closet. But she and a neighbor lady, suspicious that any man so unnaturally prim and tidy as Mr. Newbold must be "a *spy*, or a criminal, or a lunatic," invade his privacy only to discover a cache of elaborate women's hats that he designs and makes. For this they broadcast him as "a freak," undermine his pride, and utterly shatter his ability to dress up, pose, and "create some image of beauty," reducing him to a sobbing, "hopeless child." Although "The Tiny Closet" might be seen as Inge's response to the tactics of the House Un-American Activities Committee, it can serve as a more generalized condemnation of the bigotry and prejudice of those who curtail the freedom of others by castigating difference and marginalizing as outsiders all those who dare diverge from societal norms.

Inge, born in Independence, Kansas, in 1913 (he died by his own hand 60 years later), is rightfully considered the first and probably still, with the possible exception of Missourian Lanford Wilson, the most significant dramatizer of the Midwest. As Jordan Miller notes, "The Midwest of Inge's plays is the great middle ground" whose inhabitants are "easily recognized for their very common nature," but while "relying heavily on regional quality, [Inge] succeeded in transcending it almost completely."[1] Inge is never simply an apologist for the Midwest; rather than sentimentally distort the area and its people, he regularly criticizes its narrowness and provincialism, even its meanness. As Tennessee Williams, whose *Glass Menagerie* (1944) solidified Inge's own decision to pursue a playwriting career, would note after witnessing the phenomenon of his protégé having four hit plays in little more than a half dozen years, "the true and wonderful talent [of Inge] is for offering first, the general surface of common American life, and then not ripping but quietly dropping the veil that keeps you from seeing yourself as you are."[2]

Through the title of "The Tiny Closet" Inge may be alluding to his own homosexuality, which, as small-town high school English teacher in the late 1930s, he needed to keep veiled and about which he never reached a satisfactory accommodation or acceptance. He dramatizes the pain of his sexual orientation most personally in another short work from the same period, "The Boy in the Basement." Spencer Scranton, a small-town mortician whose life seems depressingly limited to "One dead body after another," is the only child of a "regal-looking" yet prudish and repressed mother. Trying to motivate Spencer's father to be more ambitious, her constant needling has instead reduced him to infantile dependency and "mumbling inarticulateness"; now an invalid confined to a chair, he "sit[s] like a discarded bridegroom." Spencer can only uncloset his homosexuality when he flees the mother-dominated home for the gay bars in the big city, yet a temporary escape from her condemnatory attitudes ends with Spencer's return to emotional and psychological dependency.

When Joker, the young delivery boy whom Spencer adores chastely and unbeknownst to anyone but himself, drowns during some horseplay on a picnic, Spencer must express his sense of bereavement alone, in the private space of the funeral home's basement preparation room, through the gestures of "rub[bing] one soft hand warmly over the boy's chest as though it were precious metal" and "pick[ing] up one of the boy's hands and kissing it warmly." Society's intolerance, which demands that some types of love be hidden away, has denied Spencer the full expression of his humanness; the audience understands that Spencer is participating symbolically in his own funeral rite as much as Joker's. While recognizing the dysfunctional Scranton family as uncomfortably close to "the popular stereotype schema of the homosexual situation," Georges Sarrotte proposes that "Boy in the Basement" is the "nucleus of Inge's work as a whole," calling Spencer the "prototype of all the frustrated female characters" who form the centerpieces of Inge's plays.[3]

Inge's Circumscribed Females

The "frustrated" women of his two works that frame the 1950s—Inge's first success, *Come Back, Little Sheba* (1950), and his first failure, *A Loss of Roses* (1959)—share names strikingly alike, Lola and Lila. In the foreword to the later play, whose action Inge "purposely set[s] in the Depression because [he] feel[s] that underneath our inflated prosperity today, there is a serious depression which we are struggling not to face," the dramatist claims to have "adopt[ed] during the last ten years . . . an existentialist view . . . that man can only hope for an individual peace in the world"; Inge's appropriation here of the term "existentialist," unlike Lorraine Hansberry's, is a casual one, not really borne out in his characters by any awareness of how their choices determine what they become. In *A Loss of Roses* itself, the voice of the tent-show evangelist rails against "[t]he depression of the heart, the drought of the soul, the deflation of the spirit [that] is the worst Depression of all." It is this psychological and emotional depression, caused by an awareness of diminishment and the necessity to come to terms with it, that pervades the lives of Lola and Doc Delaney in *Come Back, Little Sheba*—strikingly performed by Shirley Booth and Sidney Blackmer—who both mourn their lost youth.

Lola, now 40 and frumpy, was once the beauty queen of her senior high school class. When Lola, daughter of a strict, possessive father who kept tight reins on her for fear she would be violated, got pregnant at 18 by Doc, the first boy she had any "fun" with, her father forbid her ever to enter the house again. After they married and their baby girl died, Doc never allowed Lola to go to work. Denied the chance to be either mother or career woman, she has become a careless housekeeper who spends her empty days in self-pity, sublimating unfulfilled sexual needs by devouring candy, listening "transfixed" to the radio soap opera "Taboo," and eyeing the "husky" milkman who invites her to feel his flexed muscles. Doc's life history is no less drawn according to the classic textbook scenario: a mama's boy of some financial means who idolized women as "beautiful angels," he courted Lola prudishly for a year before he dared tremblingly kiss her; after marriage, he gives up dreams of ever being a "real" doctor to become a chiropractor. His money slips away, he becomes an alcoholic ("Most alcoholics are disappointed men," Doc rationalizes), he turns away from Lola sexually, finally expressing his suppressed hatred for what he perceives to be Lola's part in his failure by verbally and physically abusing her.

Admittedly, Inge displays a tendency to make the backgrounds of his characters too predictable, to overdistribute the sociopsychological details of their upbringing. And yet, these affectingly familiar characters are drawn with such compassion for their weaknesses that audiences immediately recognize and care about them, and so what might at first seem a deficiency—in that his characters seldom reveal the fascinating ambiguities associated with classic stage creations—becomes instead a hallmark of Inge's dramaturgy. What director Elia Kazan finds true of *Splendor in the Grass*, Inge's original Academy-Award-winning screenplay of 1961, applies to the plays as well: "The film was a typical Bill Inge work, a soap opera until suddenly it appears there is a little more depth and humanity there, as well as a balanced view of life."[4]

A further hallmark of Inge's stagecraft resides in his expert use of parallel plots and subplots involving sharply distinctive minor characters. As the playwright himself comments in the foreword to *Four Plays*, his interest has never been in "creat[ing] new forms, but always in "keep[ing] the stage bubbling with a restless kind of action" and "keep[ing] several stories going at once. . . . I use one piece of action to comment on another, not to distract from it." And so in *Come Back, Little Sheba*, Lola and Doc, as they look back in regret, are played off against the sexually alive young couple Marie, their boarder, and Turk, her satyrlike, javelin-throwing lover. Lola, as voyeur and accessory to their affair, gazes at the muscle-bound Turk as he poses in his track suit for Marie and sees a past that never was, or at best only fleetingly was, in her relationship with Doc; her concentrated stare makes the otherwise ordinarily unembarrassed Turk "self-conscious" about his seminude physique. Doc, as he gazes at the negligee-clad Marie, sees his lost dream: she is what Lola was and is no more, and to him what every girl should be. Torn between jealousy of Turk and disgust that such ideal beauty—he associates Marie with his mother, and both women with the ethereal "Ave Maria" playing on the radio—suffers defilement under his roof with Lola's acquiescence,

Doc goes on a drunken binge. He returns to the house in a hatchet-wielding rage, trying to attack Lola and threatening to castrate Turk. Forcibly restrained by Alcoholics Anonymous members whom Lola has called in her justifiable panic, he is taken away to dry out. When a chastened Doc arrives back home, now completely sober, Marie has deserted Turk to marry the more dependable if less passionately exciting Bruce. Lola has completely reformed herself; initially spurred on by her impulse to impress Bruce, now with revitalized energy, "contentment," and "angelic demeanor," she goes about her housekeeping chores ready to satisfy a repentant Doc's need for her to sustain him during his recovery.

The dream Lola recounts at the end of the play helps chart the extent of her change and indicate the nature of her renewed life. In its first segment, Lola and Marie watch Turk at the Olympic competition ready to throw the javelin, which to Lola's utter fascination he had earlier described in orgasmic imagery, "stick[ing] in the ground, quivering like an arrow," when it landed. But the referee, in the person of Lola's father, disqualifies Turk, and he is replaced in Lola's dream by Doc, who "picked the javelin up real careful, like it was awful heavy. But you threw it, Daddy, clear, *clear* up into the sky. And it never came down again." Although Inge has often been criticized for the obviousness of Lola's phallic dream, that has not prevented its inspiring two quite opposite interpretations: the first, since the javelin fails to land and penetrate the earth, sees the imagery confirming Doc as totally emasculated; the other, however, takes the same imagery as signifying his return to full potency, "physically active and very powerful."[5]

One of the few critiques of a modern American dramatist that might legitimately be termed "notorious" is Robert Brustein's lengthy review of *The Dark at the Top of the Stairs*, which appeared in *Harper's*. Largely on the basis of the subplot in that play, Brustein generalizes about Inge's entire body of work during the 1950s, designating the playwright as "the first spokesman for a matriarchal America," penning "she-dramas" in which the "hero gives up his one distinguishing characteristic [of] sexual dynamism" since "marriage demands a sacrifice of the hero's image (which is the American folk image) of maleness. He must give up his aggressiveness, his promiscuity, his bravado, his contempt for soft virtues, and his narcissistic pride in his body and attainments."[6]

For 30 years, Brustein's reading of Inge's women as triumphant castrators tended to dominate the critical commentary. Yet, as Inge's biographer Ralph Voss suggests, "such a view distorts the poignant situations that Inge's women find themselves in."[7] Janet Juhnke, shifting the focus from domesticated men to severely circumscribed women, perceptively claims that Inge's "female characters are more tamed than taming," finding Lola's "infantilization, boredom, passivity, dependence, emptiness" as evidence for "Case Study 1 . . . of the effects of the feminine mystique" (104–5). In 1963, Betty Friedan first published her book arguing that at the very "core of contemporary American culture" rests a myth that relegates women to finding "fulfillment in sexual passivity, male domination, and nurturing maternal love."[8] She writes in a summative passage: "It is my thesis that the core of the problem for women today is not sexual but a problem of identity—a stunting or invasion of growth that is perpetuated by the feminine mystique. It is my thesis that as the Victorian culture did not permit women to accept or gratify their basic sexual needs, our culture does not permit women to accept or satisfy their basic need to grow and fulfill their potentialities as human beings. . . . And there is increasing evidence that women's failure to grow to complete identity has hampered rather than enriched her sexual fulfillment, virtually doomed her to be castrative to her husband and sons, and caused neuroses, or problems as yet unnamed as neuroses, equal to those caused by sexual repression" (77). The terms of Friedan's description, as Juhnke has noticed, apply almost perfectly to Lola as daughter in her father's house and wife in her husband's: the idealized beauty, once defiled, is either ostracized or ignored; without children, denied purposeful activity outside the home, and with her femininity fading with time, she is left identity-less.

The second section of Lola's dream concerns her dog, Little Sheba. The play has been punctuated by plaintive cries for the dog, whose disappearance has been equated with youth "vanish[ing] into thin air," to "come back." Now, in her dream, Lola sees Little Sheba lying dead, and Doc refuses to let Lola take care of her, saying "we gotta go on." Lola's decision to "not call [Sheba] any more" and thus admit she is never "coming back" indicates an acceptance of present reality over past illusion and future daydreams. In the face of diminishment, Lola, shorn of her youth, and Doc, denied his drink, must go on in mutual need and support. Like Beckett's Didi and Gogo, they can be certain only of one another's presence.

Picnic (1953), for which Inge received the Pulitzer Prize for drama, bears the subtitle "A Summer Romance" and occurs on Labor Day, which traditionally signals the end of summer and the beginning of fall; yet the promised harvest may sometimes be bitter. Once again, Inge writes of the fleetingness of youth and beauty, of seemingly unlimited possibility being superseded by restriction and disillusionment. He continues to explore as well how women either succeed or fail in their attempts to break free from their thwarted condition. What most consistently delimits these women is their almost total subjugation to what might be called the curse of the romantic imagination, to which Lola in *Come Back, Little Sheba* also fell prey. Here, Flo Owens, the mother of two teenage daughters and herself disappointed in love, tries to control the parameters of their existence by encouraging them to pursue an it-only-happens-in-the-movies life of "comfort . . . with charge accounts . . . automobiles and trips," reminding them that a "pretty girl doesn't have long—just a few years. Then she's the equal of kings and she can walk out of a shanty like this and live in a palace with a doting husband who'll spend his life making her happy."

This image of domestic bliss, very much tied to the feminine mystique, is countered in *Picnic* by the pull toward freedom and self-definition, symbolized by the frequent whistle of trains heard in the distance. That too, however, holds an equally unreal and therefore destructive promise of happiness somewhere over the rainbow, à la Hollywood, where the older daughter, Madge, dreams of being discovered. The beautiful Madge, envious of her sister Millie's brains, never considers that her incompleteness might actually reside in a kind of spiritual vacuity, a perception beyond a girl who resorts to narcissistically "looking in the mirror [as] the only way I can prove to myself I'm alive." Flo, who believes that loving a man can be humiliating because it makes the already weaker woman "feel—almost helpless" and "seem so dependent," still wants Madge to pursue the well-to-do college boy, Alan. She acts taken aback and even disappointed that he has *not* been more sexually demanding with her daughter and finally utters "a cry of loss" when Alan gives up on Madge, for it signals that Flo will be unable to recapture vicariously a past she herself never experienced.

Competing with Alan for Madge's affections is Hal, the muscle-bound swaggering jock, barechested or T-shirted in the manner of Williams's Stanley Kowalski. A good-hearted drifter with a dark past (alcoholic father dead in jail, reform school for stealing), Hal, as the cock in the henhouse, sets the women in a tizzy. He may dream of becoming a star in Hollywood, but his immediate future is as a bellboy in Tulsa; Madge, much to Flo's dismay, sacrifices any chance for security with Alan to follow Hal and the whistle that beckons. (In *Summer Brave*, a version of *Picnic* written earlier but not produced until 1962, Inge in his eyes made the play's ending "more humorously true" by having Madge remain behind, to be ogled and pursued by the local boys.) Women, Flo seems to believe, might temporarily escape their appointed condition in life through media-fostered daydreams, but in reality domestic servitude remains the order of the day. Moreover, what makes a woman like Madge so ill-prepared for marriage is precisely the prettifying of domesticity that Flo has fostered, for life with Hal can never be what Madge expects. Flo's neighbor, Helen Potts, whose mother had Helen's marriage annulled, condemning her to a life as daughter/martyr and never wife/mother and therefore a reminder to audiences of the effects of a selfish control of daughter by mother, has, however, a more realistic grip on human relationships; reminded by Hal's presence of her thwarted womanhood, she advises Flo, "You don't love someone 'cause he's perfect."

In *Picnic*, Inge intends to show that women cannot do without men, as much as they might like to fool themselves into believing otherwise; as he has commented, "The women seemed to have created a world of their own, a world in which they seemed to be pretending men did not exist."[9] In the double plot, the spinster schoolteacher, Rosemary, aware of time's fleet foot, sacrifices her independence to marriage. With representatives of both youth and middle age on stage, *Picnic* becomes partly a seasonal ritual of youth blossoming into its prime, threatening to supplant age. It is mating ritual as well, as seen in the dance at the play's center, through which Inge masterfully dramatizes the dynamics of the characters' relationships. The dance, with traditional sexual definitions temporarily thrown askew (as they often are in journeys into "the green world" in Shakespeare's romantic comedies, which share Inge's emphasis on generational conflicts and gender roles), becomes a contest of the sexes, eventuating in a reconfirmation of the woman as subservient to the man who offers salvation from repression and loneliness. The woman even pleads to be allowed an unchallenging identity.

At the start of the dance in act 2, which dramatizes visually woman's need for sexual fulfillment, the independent Rosemary pairs off with Millie, though the younger girl insists "I gotta lead!"; when Howard, Rosemary's beau, and Hal, acting the "coy female," embark on their own single-sex parody of the dance, Rosemary demands that they stop. Millie then dances with Hal, succumbing to his demand that he lead ("you gotta remember *I'm* the *man*") and actually coming to "feel like Rita Hayworth!" as "she is whirled around." After Howard has danced with the ravishing Madge, she moves into Hal's arms; then a jealous Rosemary, in a pathetic attempt to assert her youth, pulls Hal away from Madge and dances sensuously with him, "clutching at him" and eventually "tearing off a strip of his shirt." She has realized the impossibility of ever setting back the clock and possessing him. Meanwhile, Alan, by appearing in an apron, has visually displaced the macho image that would confirm him as an appropriate husband for Madge.

In her shame, and after she and Howard, a boozer and mama's boy and a far cry from Hal, have spent the night together, Rosemary begs him to take her as his wife and thus save her, now sexually awakened, from a life of profligacy. Earlier, Rosemary had worn a mask of excessive propriety by chiseling the sexual organs off the school's statue of a gladiator and objecting strenuously to books by D. H. Lawrence; furthermore, out of a long-standing fear of sex instilled by her "strict, God-fearing" father, she had denied her own needs by preventing Howard from getting fresh with her. Howard hesitates to marry and be "stuck," and so must rationalize that it is past time to "settle down" and that it will be good for his business. Rosemary, however, needs him more desperately than he needs her. When she tells him he must relinquish his bachelor habits to marry, Howard bristles, "I'm not gonna marry anyone that says, 'You gotta marry me, Howard.' . . . If a woman wants me to marry her—she can at least say 'please.' " Rosemary not only begs "please," but "sinks to her knees," aware that this may be her last chance. Howard's show of strength, however feeble, and Rosemary's decision to submit to the stronger, may do little more than satisfy a stereotypical image of the male as the source of female identity and fulfillment that Inge's women in *Picnic* foster and perpetuate. Yet this myth of maleness, differently understood by both sexes, may ultimately be destructive for both.

Inge's Vulnerable Males

Although Inge asserts that *Bus Stop* (1955) was "meant . . . only as a composite picture of varying kinds of love, ranging from the innocent to the depraved," it becomes an examination of the necessity for breaking down destructive stereotypes, particularly about what constitutes manliness, before love can be (re)defined and recognized. Although Inge tells at least four contrapuntally interrelated stories in this play about a group of travelers snowbound overnight in a "dingy" small-town Kansas cafe, the central one concerns Bo Decker, a small-time rodeo cowboy, and Cherie, an "absurdly" outfitted and heavily made-up night club "*chanteuse*," or as she pronounces it, "chantoosie"—engagingly brought to the screen by Marilyn Monroe—whom he has practically kidnapped for marriage on a ranch in Montana.

On the surface, Bo plays the irresistible, highly experienced ladies' man, equating one night of sex with him to the promise of a lifetime's love. Underneath, he is a pussycat, too tenderhearted even to go deer hunting; if "a fella" risks showing that side, however, "then someone comes along and makes a sap outa him." To verbalize his feelings and admit to being lonesome makes him "sound like some pitiable weaklin' of a man." When Will, the sheriff who protects Cherie from being forced into marriage, subdues Bo in a fistfight, Bo concludes Cherie could never respect him now that "she saw [him] beat." Yet Cherie no longer wants, if she ever did, the type of macho man society demands that Bo try to be. Tired of being used by men as a sex object, Cherie emerges as an early proponent of a "softer" male: a man should be respectful yet not domineering, thoughtful yet not so solicitous as to make the woman dependent. At the same time, the woman must not make the man feel inadequate for failing to conform to society's expectations. When Bo confesses to Cherie that his swagger is just that, and that she has been his "first gal," she sensitively responds, "I never woulda guessed it." Only then can he begin to peel off some of the outer layers and admit that he "couldn't be *familiar* . . . with a gal I din love," apologize for the peremptory way he treated her, and kiss her gently.

In the maturing of his love, Bo has a number of tutors. Will convinces him that a man must first prove he "deserves" the things he loves, and that to display a little humility "ain't the same thing as bein' *wretched*," while the guitar-strumming older cowboy, Virgil Blessing, Bo's surrogate father/guardian, counsels him to "take a chance" and show tenderness. As Virgil's surname indicates, he resembles the priest who prepares the young couple and then officiates at their union; that mission fulfilled, his duties as Bo's surrogate father are complete. Virgil, who refuses to remain ranch foreman and sends Bo and Cherie off alone, knowing that Bo's former dependency must give way to mutuality with Cherie, now admits there was something immature, even shameful, about his own decision to "live his whole life dependin' on buddies" and not commit himself to another person in love. Such commitments, though, do not necessarily ensure a surcease of loneliness, as seen through Grace, the restaurant proprietor. Sick of being on her own in an empty apartment that was lonesome even when her husband was there, she invites the bus driver, Carl, to join her upstairs; if not on the highest level, these 20 minutes snatched now and then help ease the restlessness of this vital woman whose existence under small-town eyes is severely constrained.

Another character in *Bus Stop* who, like Virgil, freely chooses aloneness, redefines the concept of manliness in passages that are thematically central to the dramatist's canon as a whole. Dr. Lyman, thrice divorced and dismissed from his college teaching position when his second wife, a student of his, sued him on grounds of incontinence and drunkenness, tries to arrange an assignation with Elma, the teenage waitress enamored by his veneer of learning and oblivious to his true intentions. Despite his own shortcomings, he possesses considerable abstract wisdom about matters of the heart. Implicitly alluding to the atomic cataclysm, Lyman reasons that contemporary "man's anxiety about his mere survival" may be one source of a "miserly" clinging to self rather than "giv[ing] of himself in any true relation" with another; yet "men are afraid" of such unselfish giving, counting it a reduction or emptying out. Rather than constituting a lessening of self, Lyman claims it reveals "people strong enough inside themselves to love . . . without humiliation" and to be loved without "fear[ing] it as a burden." His answer to what Alva Myrdal has called "the problem of two-someness," that is, of becoming one with another and yet maintaining one's own identity as an individual, is akin to the biblical notion of losing oneself to the other, so that both find themselves more fully in and through the other.

Ironically, Inge's characters who reach the deepest intuition about this process are often, like the playwright himself, the ones left most physically alone. Lyman makes the moral choice to call off his spree with Elma; always resentful before of "having anyone *over* [him and] tak[ing] *orders* . . . from anyone," he will seek help by committing himself to a clinic. If Lyman, for his moral failings, seems justifiably excluded from the generative community at the play's end, Virgil hardly deserves to be, and so his permanent outsidedness proves more painful for the audience. Witnessing this winter's night's pairings has been educational for Elma, an initiation into understanding love and sex. Her knowledge reaches a higher level of maturity than Millie's in *Picnic*, who mistakenly thinks that the observations of the artist—she is a budding writer—can always be an adequate substitute for full participation in a lived life, shared with another in love.

Though overly obvious at times in its characterization and themes, *The Dark at the Top of the Stairs* (1957)—a rewrite of Inge's first play, *Farther Off from Heaven*, which had been produced by Margo Jones in Dallas in 1947—is on several counts the playwright's richest drama, not least in its depiction of the social milieu and its handling of stage space. Once again focusing on the insecurities and vulnerabilities that cause separations and alienation and that prevent individuals from forming intense bonds of communion with one another, Inge weaves an intricate tissue of connections among half a dozen important characters. Set in an Oklahoma town during the "oil boom" of the early 1920s, against the background of the transition from a cowboy/agrarian to a mercantile/industrialized economy, *The Dark at the Top of the Stairs* treats in part the impact of change on cultural stability and traditional institutions. The Flood family, because of Rubin's precarious livelihood as a traveling salesman of harnesses, a soon to be outmoded commodity, find themselves pushed farther to the fringes of the newly monied local society where, as Cora comments, "people distrust you" if you are outside the group. Because of prejudicial attitudes, however, not even money can guarantee admission to places like the country club for some people, such as the Jewish businessmen.

As do virtually all Inge's works, *The Dark at the Top of the Stairs* focuses centrally on the relationship of a man and woman within marriage. Cora's past history much resembles Lola's in *Come Back, Little Sheba*. Swept off her feet at 17, she was pregnant and married within six weeks, wife to a man her parents never fully accepted. Unlike Lola, Cora became a mother of two, though she "live[s] like a widow" because Rubin is away so much, using his absence as an excuse to pamper little Sonny, to whom she turns as "top man" of the house. Perhaps her attentions to Sonny have contributed to Rubin's resuming his drinking and womanizing, but because of his unfaithfulness Cora now rejects sex as simply an "animal" act, throwing him out of the house after he strikes her. She eventually recognizes that she has kept Sonny too "close" by protecting him from the taunts of the other boys and taking him into her bed when he is afraid and when she needs "to have *someone* close to [her]."

For Rubin, marriage, entered into reluctantly, has from the beginning always restricted doing what he pleases. Nor has fathering been expansive for him. Like a teenager chafing at the bit, when faced with attempts to curb his unruly conduct, Rubin's "just gotta go out and raise more hell, just to prove to [himself he's] a free man"; he needs his space and his sense of his own worth, but (as is true for almost all of Inge's men) to openly admit this would belie an unmanly cast of character. Absent during the whole middle section of the play, he returns somewhat chastened and more considerate from having lost his job in midcareer and having recognized the challenge in re-educating himself for another.

Finally, Rubin can share with Cora his "doubts" and "fears" about his ability to face the changes that events outside his control are forcing upon him: feelings of inadequacy and alienation in a world where economic and social progress have left him behind, where the future and his place in it are unknown.

Partly, Rubin did not share his doubts about himself as a provider to protect Cora from worry; partly also, he could not reveal these insecurities because to do so would admit his inadequacy and lack of control, putting him in a situation similar to that of Cora's brother-in-law, Morris, who indeed seems to fit Brustein's categorization of the domesticated male, though this unhappy man who escapes through long, solitary walks may be in the throes of a clinical depression. Inge again skillfully employs the relationship in his subplot to foil his main plot. Cora's sister, Lottie, has become "bossy," but only because she thinks Morris wants it that way. She may say she never wanted a family, actually blaming Morris for their childless state. The real source of her domineering behavior resides, however, in her awareness of having "missed out on" life. Sexually unfulfilled—she attributes never enjoying sex to a repressive upbringing—she has turned to voracious eating to satisfy her emotional emptiness. Intolerant of religious differences and unschooled in the social graces, she still remains sensitive enough to others' hurt to advise that Cora "beg" Rubin to come back to her bed, which Rubin will do only on his terms, saying that he refuses ever to be "rearrange[d]" by anyone else and commanding gently but firmly that Cora "come on" up the stairs where he waits with "growing impatien[ce]."

Inge handles the theatrical space at the top of the stairs almost expressionistically. In the opening set description, he specifies that "[d]uring the daytime scenes, this small area is in semidarkness, and at night it is black. . . . We are conscious of this area throughout the play, as though it holds some possible threat to the characters." Twice during act 2, Inge calls particular attention to that stage place: when the obsessively shy and withdrawn daughter, Reenie, at first lacks "courage" to come down and meet her blind date for the country club dance, the audience sees her "feet go scurrying back to safety"; at the act curtain, when Sonny fears the dark because "you can't see what's in front of you. And it might be something awful," Cora must hold his hand and go up with him "to face the darkness hovering there like an omen." Symbolically, then, the dark suggests fear of the unknown, of the forbidden. Yet from another perspective it might also be the entrance to a place of safety, a sheltering womb where artificial defenses against an open acceptance of human weakness and need can be abandoned.

Theater poster for the original Broadway production of William Inge's *The Dark at the Top of the Stairs*. By courtesy of the William Inge Collection, Independence Community College Library, Independence, Kansas.

When Rubin beckons to Cora from the top of the stairs, the audience "see[s his] naked feet standing in the warm light at the top" as it hears Cora's final curtain line, "I'm coming, Rubin. I'm coming," with both its note of willing acquiescence to his control and its sexual connotation. Rubin's nakedness at this point symbolizes his full acceptance of his vulnerability. (Significantly, when Lola in *Come Back, Little Sheba* wondered why males like Turk did not model in the nude as women did, Doc replied, "A man, after all . . . well, has to protect himself.") Like Spencer with the body of Joker in the private place at the end of "Boy in the Basement," Rubin for once stands totally uncloseted before others, unafraid to reveal his weakness as well as his strength to Cora, knowing that in his need she will provide not just the reassurance of physical love but "a feeling of decency . . . and order . . . and respect." Like Bo in *Bus Stop*, Rubin finds his salvation as a man by acting counter to the prevailing stereotypes of acceptable gender behavior.

Rubin's open admission of vulnerability and insecurity provides an important clue to understanding how another of the play's subplots, often maligned for its seeming excrescence, links up carefully with the rest of the drama. This subplot, moreover, constitutes one of the central expressions of Inge's continuing concern with the fate of the outsider in society. Reenie's date for the dance is Sammy Goldenbaum, who might as well be an orphan, since he was shunted from one military school to another by his mother, a minor Hollywood star fearful that knowledge of his existence would hurt her career. Inge risks sentimentalizing difference in his portrayal of Sammy, mature beyond his years, "darkly beautiful" and "something about him seem[ing] a little foreign" in an exotic sort of way. Sammy possesses a natural ability to put the socially untutored Reenie at ease; can calm Sonny's temper tantrums with loving firmness; and resolutely refuses to hold his mother accountable for her lack of attention, recalling only a weekend when, more like a lover, he escorted her in the big city. He also claims: "It doesn't bother me that I'm Jewish. Not any more." Yet when the anti-Semitic Mrs. Ralston insults Sammy for dancing with her daughter and tells him that Jews are not "allowed" at the club, Sammy commits suicide by jumping from a hotel window. In a final indictment of the vacuity of Hollywood—the sought-after utopia in the dreams of several Inge characters from Lola in *Come Back, Little Sheba* through the autobiographical Sonny with his picturebook of the stars in *The Dark at the Top of the Stairs*—Sammy's mother absents herself from his funeral, fearful of adverse publicity.

Through the gentle questioning of Cora, Reenie comes to understand her involvement in Sammy's death. Because no other boys cut in while they were dancing, she hid in the bathroom out of embarrassment; so she was not there when Sammy, hurt by Mrs. Ralston's attack, sought her out for help. If her father's insecurities prevented his opening up honestly with Cora, Reenie's own insecurities, her "being so shy and sensitive and afraid of people" were "nothing but selfishness" that caused her to fail Sammy in his moment of need. Inge's motif here of the necessity to respond compassionately to others, sometimes at great personal cost, recurs again and again in Tennessee Williams as well. Reenie's emergence from her shell of self-involvement is revealed, as R. Baird Shuman suggests,[10] in her decision to play the piano for her father; whereas before she had always used her art as an excuse for and a means of withdrawal, now she shares it communally with another.

Art, too, becomes Inge's means of breaking out of the shell of self; yet, ironically, it also makes him vulnerable. For much of the 1950s, with a string of four Broadway successes from *Come Back, Little Sheba* in 1950 through *The Dark at the Top of the Stairs* in 1957, it looked as if Inge might join the triumvirate of the later O'Neill, Miller, and Williams as an American dramatist of the first rank. As was true for Williams, too, though for different reasons, Inge found success difficult to bear; in his case, the discrepancy between what he reached for in his plays and what he actually achieved left him dissatisfied. When critical rejection hit, especially with Brustein's attack and the negative reviews of *A Loss of Roses* (1959), Inge felt personally rejected, unable to effect any separation between the work and the person who created it: "If [the play] is rejected, he can only feel that he is rejected, too. Some part of him has been turned down, cast aside, even laughed at or scorned."[11] Like so many of America's playwrights who achieve early acclaim only to face later rejection, Inge came to see too well the dark underside of the bitch-goddess of success, stating: "We're vicious to failure in this country."[12]

Oedipus in the Midwest

In *A Loss of Roses,* Inge divides his attention, some would say fatally for the play's success, between a young man's delayed resolution of his Oedipus complex through making love with a mother substitute, and a down-on-her-luck actress's attempt to discover physical and emotional stability and a renewed sense of self-worth. Inge in his prefatory remarks makes explicit his intention that it be "really Lila's play,'' and the title, with its heavily mythic overtones, supports his contention that the work concerns the diminishment of beauty and innocence with the passage of time. Lila's past is even more traumatic than Lola's: the victim of sexual abuse by her stepbrother, and later of attempted sexual molestation by her father-in-law when she escaped the confines of a small Oklahoma town by marrying into a vaudeville troupe, she attempted suicide. The only man who had ever been different and who became the ideal by which she measured all others was big Kenneth, on whom she had a crush when she roomed as a teenager in his and Helen's house and helped care for little Kenny. Lately, she has been on the road with a group of itinerant actors, forced out of work because of economic hard times.

Now in Kansas City at Helen and Kenny's home (Kenneth had given his life to save Kenny from drowning), Lila experiences a vague sense of being somehow responsible for her own victimization. Though she does not believe people are "really sinful," she does blame herself for being "weak and soft," whereas "You have to be hard to be good." Displaying any need for closeness with others reveals evidence of human frailty, leaving one easy prey to being used and abused. Experiencing guilt over being exploited, she must "atone," choosing Helen as her mother confessor. Although Lila, through going to bed with him, provides Kenny the necessary reassurance "that *someone* can love [him]," he goes back on his commitment to marry her, and Lila again attempts suicide. All that remains is a humiliating life with the jealous and manipulative Ricky, performing in blue movies and live sex acts that she knows will destroy "any feelings about anything" and "make [her] ashamed."

At the play's close, Lila, whose surname "Green" hints at the verdant and paradisal, "surveys the morning scene as though it were her last day of grace upon the earth" as Inge introduces a new walk-on character, an innocent little girl dressed in ribbons and lace, clinging to her mother's hand and carrying a bouquet of roses for the teacher on her first day at school. As with Doc looking at Marie and remembering what Lola had been, Lila sees in the girl exactly what she once was, but remembers her own teacher slapping her "hard" for talking in class; when Lila asked for *her* roses back, the teacher had refused, which should have taught Lila the deterministic lesson that some things—for instance, innocence—once wrenched away can never be regained. Like Margaret in Gerard Manley Hopkins's poem "Spring and Fall," Lila is perpetually "grieving / over goldengrove / unleaving," mourning her lost self.

Robbed of the illusion that she could find love as a saying grace and protection, Lila submits to the final degradation in a cycle begun with the death of her mother and arrival of an abusive stepbrother. She takes with her the wristwatch, bought by Kenny for his mother, Helen, to commemorate her wedding anniversary but given to Lila after they have slept together, as a symbolic reminder of time's passing and, with it, the loss of innocence and failure to find lasting love. Like Lola, Lila is another in Inge's gallery of women whose lives are circumscribed and unfulfilled; being a party to society's male-fashioned mystique of beauty and youth becomes a catch-22, restricting rather than freeing them, in Lila's case even condemning her to a life of exploitation.

Oedipal attachments appear recurrently in Inge's canon, beginning with Doc and his mother in *Come Back, Little Sheba*, and form the central tension in *A Loss of Roses* and the play that follows it, *Natural Affection*. In *A Loss of Roses*, the mother Helen has for some time fought the temptation to "be dependent" on Kenny or to let him "still be making love to [her] like [he] did when [he was] a baby," already knowing what Cora in *Dark at the Top of the Stairs* must learn: that "if [she'd] loved [him] any more, [she'd] have destroyed [him]." Aware now that she was wrong to allow Kenny's hatred for other men and her guilt over deserting her son to keep her from remarrying, Helen encourages him to take a job out of town, rejects his attempts to kiss her, and refuses his gift of a watch to replace the one his father had given her. But Kenny needs to prove to her "that *someone* can love [him]." Sleeping with Lila, the mother substitute, although Helen claims it was done simply to demonstrate his "manliness" and to "spite" her, finally allows him to break free and leave home after Kenny "dreamed that [Mom] died." Yet Kenny's affair with Lila still does not evidence a mature ability to form a responsible relationship with woman.

In *Natural Affection* (1963), the least resonant of Inge's full-length stage works because of its blandness and predictability, Donny can only sever his Oedipal attachment and strike back at what he perceives as his mother Sue's rejection by brutally killing a surrogate, in the person of an unkown woman who makes sexual advances toward him. Inge justified what many critics consider the ending's gratuitous violence by arguing that the play was actually "written as a release from the tension [he] felt living in the late fifties and early sixties, when the newspapers were so full of violence." In his reading, violence not only springs from and reflects the social atmosphere that spawns it—Inge is writing, of course, at the beginning of a decade of political assassinations and racial upheaval—but is just the most virulent evidence of the terror of personal "rejection that continues to make man feel less and less important." If one accepts Inge's analysis, violence embodies the ultimate response to being pushed to the outside and marginalized, for whatever reason.

Staging Sexual Difference

Pinky in Inge's last full-length play, Where's Daddy? (1966), the only openly homosexual character in any of the dramatist's works for Broadway, is analogous to Virgil and Lyman from Bus Stop in dramatic function. (The possible latent homosexuality of several others, including Virgil in Bus Stop and Vince in Natural Affection, has frequently been remarked upon.) Like Bus Stop, Where's Daddy? celebrates married love as the culmination of a young hero's maturation into responsibility. It considers as well the bafflement of the older generation confronted by rapid social change, even upheaval, and forced to re-examine its system of values, probing the degree to which traditional mores can coexist with a liberated approach to making concrete moral choices. Looked at as the story of the young couple, Tom and Teena, Where's Daddy?, subtitled "A Comedy," is a forgettable failure; considered, however, as an exploration of Pinky, and secondarily of Teena's mother, Mrs. Bigelow, it deserves more than passing attention.

Living in a Manhattan coldwater flat with pop art posters covering the walls, Tom and Teena play at being a thoroughly contemporary couple, unencumbered by any traditional notion of the nuclear family. Having married only so that their soon-to-be-born child will not be illegitimate, as Tom was, Teena refuses to stand in the way of Tom's freedom to desert her and the baby for his career as an actor. They do, however, disagree over whether the baby should be given up for adoption—he for, she against—since all she has ever desired is motherhood, maybe to prove she can provide a child with love whereas her own parents offered only indifference, or perhaps to discover some purpose in an otherwise empty existence that already includes one suicide attempt. That Tom sees Teena as defying his wishes only shows that ingrained habits of thought die hard.

Pinky must do for his surrogate son, Tom, what Virgil (and the others) do for Bo: convince him that men should not fear being loved as a sign of weakness; and that claiming to lack the emotional maturity for a relationship is just an excuse for being "scared shitless" over fatherhood. Accepting parenthood need not mean that Tom will sacrifice his "integrity" by becoming a part of the world he rebels against for its complacency and ineffectuality. Tom's new understanding that all of existence is both "so frightening . . . at times [and yet] very beautiful at times" runs counter to his earlier touting of absurdist theater as a valid representation of humanity's universal predicament in a world "full of fear and violence, and hatred, and prejudice, and corruption and hypocrisy." Pinky, who has felt society's prejudice and rejection in a way few others have, deplores the Beckett-like plays "with people coming out of ashcans and urinating on the floor," disagreeing about the necessity "to be sordid [just] to be real." For someone like Pinky, marginalized by sexual orientation and possessed of a sad understanding that he has grown into an "old boy" with his knitting and TV shows, the modernist notion of inescapable alienation must seem a clichéd and bitter message. While Tom may kid himself into thinking it is easy to throw off the old rules, Pinky, always conscious of the taboos he is breaking, lacks that luxury, and so he has remained "an old-fashioned man" who embraces those comforting mores that are today considered "terribly reactionary."

Pinky decries, in fact (as Inge himself might well have, coming from a home with a largely absent traveling salesman father), the disappearance of Daddy "from civilization," not intended as a heterosexist or hegemonic remark but rather as a comment on the absence of those, like himself, willing to assume responsibility for others. But his basic conservatism does not prevent his being socially liberal and unconventional in his response to concrete situations, in a way that Mrs. Bigelow, who "stopped changing her thinking" years ago and so is unusually dogmatic and even inadvertently racist, never could be. Society has said to Pinky, fated by biology to be different, as it did to the playwright himself, that a fully open, long-term relationship is not available to him. That one of Inge's most prescient and admirable characters should suffer denial and marginalization in this way is simply added reason for rejecting society's stereotyping and victimizing of the "other."

Several explanations have been advanced for the abruptness with which Inge's string of successes turned into failures. Some commentators, like Bigsby, feel he was simply unable to adapt to the changing climate of the New York theatre in the late 1950s, when the avant-garde became the order of the day, "when art was more self-consciously experimental, more single-mindedly concerned with social and political issues."[13] And yet, that movement was almost exclusively an off-Broadway rather than a Broadway phenomenon during the 1960s, rarely touching in any measurable way the commercial theater for which Inge wrote. A contributing factor may certainly have been his shift from midwestern, small-town settings in his first five plays to urban Chicago and then Manhattan in *Natural Affection* and *Where's Daddy?*, respectively. The insularity of the small community, like that of Inge's own hometown of Independence, Kansas, perhaps provided an essential ambiance and caged atmosphere for him to work out characters' conflicts that tend more often to the darkly personal rather than the social in nature.

Neither can one discount as a decisive factor Inge's lack of freedom to explore certain subjects such as homosexuality; even had "The Boy in the Basement" been written as a full-length work in the early 1950s, it remains doubtful that a play so explicit about the physical love of one man for another could have received a commercial production at that time (in 1955, Williams would still find it necessary to be circumspect about the subject in *Cat on a Hot Tin Roof*). Inge, though, despite these limitations, managed to broach topics whose currency would not become widespread in the American theater until almost three decades later, providing compelling portraits of those who were marginalized as outsiders for their difference, be it racial or sexual, and of women who found their channels of fulfillment severely circumscribed by stereotypical notions of what should be allowed the feminine. In many of his insights, Inge wrote ahead of his time; his works are indeed a barometer of currents that lay hidden beneath the artificially placid surface of the 1950s, ready to burst forth in the decades that followed.

Retaining a focus on midwestern life, Inge laid bare the prejudices of the small town, while centering his attention on what would come to be called family and sexual politics: Within the marriage relationship, who will be dominant, and on what terms? What does the partner who submits to the other sacrifice? How can one remain free to develop an individual identity within constraints of gender and race and sexual preference imposed from without? But his peculiar gift, closely allied to his own troubled identity as a homosexual, was to limn those characters who, made vulnerable and insecure by an awareness of their own difference from the supposed norm, had somehow to find the courage to admit their difference, without in the process becoming diminished by self-pity, as well as to understand that although society might name that difference—and the vulnerabilities shown in proclaiming it—a weakness or worse, it could instead be a source of individual moral strength. As Inge admitted, to accomplish that requires making a separate peace, perhaps the hardest of all to achieve.

6

Other Voices of the 1950s:
Marching to Different Drummers

In various essays, Arthur Miller comments on what he considers the limitations of American playwriting during the late 1940s and early 1950s: "The plays of the forties, which began as an attempt to analyze the self in the world, are ending as a device to exclude the world. Thus self-pity and sentimentality rush in, and sexual sensationalism. It is an anti-dramatic drama. . . . the line of development has been toward more and more intimacy of statement by playwrights and less attention to the older ideas of craft, of stage logic. . . . [by the mid-1950s] the theater was retreating into an area of psycho-sexual romanticism, and this at the very moment when great events both at home and abroad cried out for recognition and analytic inspection. In a word, I was tired of mere sympathy in the theater" (*Theater Essays*, 209, 229, 231). Miller's assessment is borne out by a number of critics, especially Gerald Weales and Robert Brustein. The latter, decrying the "aspirin fantasies" rather than "radical surgery" doled out by many post–World War II stage realists, rebukes "the newer American playwrights [who] often confuse themselves with psychological counselors, for deeply imbedded in their plays you will generally find an object lesson about the diagnosis and treatment of romantic, emotional, family, or social disorders."[1] Many of these writers worked in several media; along with his stage plays, Robert Anderson, for instance, wrote radio and television scripts, novels, and film scripts, two of which, *Tea and Sympathy* and *The Nun's Story*, garnered Academy Award nominations. Most of this group solidified their lasting reputation through one play: Anderson with *Tea and Sympathy*, Arthur Laurents through *The Time of the Cuckoo*, Jerome Lawrence and Robert E. Lee with *Inherit the Wind*, William Gibson through *The Miracle Worker*, and Paddy Chayefsky with *The Tenth Man*.

Robert Anderson

To some degree or other, these dramatists, perhaps reflecting the suspicions and paranoia of the McCarthy era, write about the notion of freedom in one of its many guises: the individual versus the constraints of a patriarchal society; the development of a moral relativism as an antidote to a too restrictive religious authority; and even, when focusing on the marriage relationship, the potential sacrifice of individuality and the objectification and victimization that one partner might experience at the hands of the other. Anderson's works in particular display a more than usual thematic unity and consistency. He focuses typically on middle-aged males, disillusioned that their lives have not turned out as planned, annoyed that time's passage severely restricts future options, embarrassed by openly expressing feelings that those around them regard as unmanly, and yet sublimating their fears in sexuality, though oftentimes leaving their wives emotionally starved in the process. And Anderson reiterates over and again certain motifs: the necessity for setting aside traditional moral codes that prevent responding openly to the emotional wounds of others; the idealization of physical sexuality that, while countering mortality and a terror of the void, hampers communion; the fathers' tendency to confuse strength with manliness and thus not foster sensitivity in their sons; the women's propensity to sublimate their own identity and fulfillment in another.

Although *All Summer Long*, Anderson's adaptation of a Donald Wetzel novel, would not finally reach Broadway until after *Tea and Sympathy*, it premiered at Washington's Arena Stage early in 1953. Each of these Anderson works shows the influence of one of the dominant strands of modern drama: the first a Chekhovian mood play about a young boy's rite of passage into adolescence; the second an Ibsenite well-made drama about a young man's coming into adulthood. The family in Wetzel's novel shares similarities with Anderson's own: an authoritarian, emotionally distant father; a caring, nurturing mother; and brothers who are closest of friends rather than sibling rivals. In *All Summer Long*, young, vulnerable Willie undergoes the end of innocence and the beginning of knowledge. He sees his brother, Don, paralyzed in an accident for which the father is partially culpable. He earns his father's disparagement for dabbling in the sissified hobbies of art, poetry writing, and afghan knitting rather than athletics. He hears sex and birth named "filthy" and "disgusting" by his narcissistic sister, Ruth, who attempts to abort her baby on a fence wired to electrocute stray chickens. In the face of this family's petty bickering and moral paralysis, Willie attempts the herculean task of constructing a stone wall to save the family home (unsuccessfully) from the encroaching flood waters. At virtually every point, the symbolism underpins Anderson's central theme of creation and destruction, both nature's and humankind's, in what proves philosophically the darkest of his plays.

In the words of one reviewer, if *All Summer Long* was "a tone poem," then *Tea and Sympathy* (1953)—starring Deborah Kerr and John Kerr for 712 performances on Broadway, and Ingrid Bergman in its Paris version—was "a symphony." Just prior to its opening, Anderson was admitted to membership in the Playwrights Producing Company, founded back in 1938 by five of America's then leading dramatists— Robert Sherwood, Maxwell Anderson, S. N. Behrman, Sidney Howard, and Elmer Rice—as an alternative to the domination of theater by producers who exercised complete artistic control. As he wrote *Tea and Sympathy*, Anderson had Thoreau's notion of marching to the music of "a different drummer" in mind, and he was not unaware, in focusing on how any deviation from perceived norms of behavior may prompt "judgment by prejudice" and persecution, of the possible application of his play to the prevailing atmosphere of the witch hunt unleashed by the HUAC/McCarthy hearings. In the play, the "very lonely," "very sensitive," and sexually naive 18-year-old Tom Lee finds himself branded as "an off-horse" by his father as well as his housemaster at boarding school, both presented in an irredeemably negative light more appropriate to melodrama, because he hurts their pride by refusing to be pigeonholed into the stereotypical pattern of the manly man. He walks "light," wears his hair long, takes female leads in plays at the all-boys school, wants to be a folksinger, and, though champion, "doesn't even play tennis like a regular fellow. No hard drives and cannon-ball serves." Being discovered sunbathing nude on the dunes with one of the "sexually suspect" teachers only exacerbates the suspicion of others that Tom is homosexual, increasing his sense of being ostracized. To regain his self-confidence and prove his masculinity, he allows himself to be goaded into visiting the town prostitute. Unable to perform sexually when there is no "tenderness, gentleness, consideration," he attempts suicide. Before hearing the full story, Tom's father, Herb, actually feels proud to be able to call his son a "regular fellow," while the housemaster, Bill Reynolds, taunts him: "You couldn't be with her. Do you understand what I mean?"

Bill's deep aversion to Tom belies his own latent homosexuality; as his wife, Laura, openly charges, he persecutes Tom for "the thing [he] fear[s] in [him]self." Long a bachelor, "in some vague way [he] cried out" for "help" and married Laura to quiet his doubts, though he would still rather be off with the boys backpacking, leaving Laura lonely and starved for affection and with no outlet for her need to pity others. Like many Anderson women, she loves her man not so much for what she believes at the time she can give to him and do for him as for the sense of responsibility and feeling of being indispensable that he provides for her. Laura realizes that she can no longer "save" Bill, and also sees that she was wrong when she clung to moral qualms and refused to hazard helping Tom "in his misery," instead sending him away. To expiate her guilt for having earlier rejected him, Laura now gives herself to Tom sexually and, by so doing, restores his belief in his own manhood. In an electrifying curtain line as indelibly imprinted on rapt audiences as Blanche's exit line in A Streetcar Named Desire, she beseeches Tom: "Years from now . . . when you talk about this . . . and you will . . . be kind." The restoration of Tom through confirmation of his heterosexuality, which Anderson seems to have taken for granted, begs the issue for several recent critics of the play, who find Anderson even less able than Williams would be in Cat on a Hot Tin Roof to admit the possibility of his protagonist's homosexuality.

Anderson's last play of the 1950s, Silent Night, Lonely Night (1959), makes more explicit his emphasis on physical sexuality as redemptive and on the ethical imperative of setting aside traditional moral codes to respond compassionately to another. The story of this virtually static play, in which exposition largely substitutes for drama, is simple. Katherine Johnson and John Sparrow, both married but temporarily alone and lonely—her husband off in Europe on business, his wife in a nearby asylum—meet in a New England inn on Christmas Eve, come together in a long night's confession of their domestic problems culminating in a one-time sexual encounter, and then part, each returning to his or her spouse. Although Anderson skillfully handles a young couple on honeymoon who serve as foils, the play remains essentially a two-character drama centering on a moral dilemma symbolized by a strange "eye of God" pendant that Katherine's puritanical father had given her; she must choose whether to be bound by an inhibiting set of absolute "shalt nots" that fosters guilt or live by a situational ethic that recognizes a higher, affective morality. Anderson's secularization of the Christmas holiday helps underscore the human-centered nature of Katherine and John's religion of love.

Anderson's playwriting career extended through the 1960s and into the 1970s, beginning with *The Days Between* (1965), originally conceived for the arena theater being constructed at Lincoln Center, where the thrust stage preordained, he thought, a structure that moved melodramatically "from climax to climax." *The Days Between* became, instead, the initial offering of the American Playwrights Theater, produced in college and community theaters nationwide. The brainchild of Jerome Lawrence and Robert E. Lee, the APT was to provide an alternative theater for works "of ideas" and "relevance" incompatible with the "hit-or-miss syndrome" of Broadway. David Ives, the failed writer-teacher in *The Days Between*, has arrived at middle age cynical and angst filled, obsessed with "nothing[ness]," "death," and "liv[ing] in crud." Still plagued by an adolescent romanticization of marriage as "eternal passion" and suffering from writer's block, alcoholism, and sexual impotence, David is ripe to experience jealousy over an author of "successful, sentimental trash" who offers himself to David's sexually unsatisfied wife, Barbara. Anderson's technical novelty resides in consciously considering David's midlife crisis from the viewpoint of the woman. Barbara constitutes a textbook example of the woman who freely submerges her own identity in the roles of wife and mother, becoming nothing more than an appendage of her husband. "Terrified" of the freedom that would come with divorce, in order to free David to pursue his "dream" of "days of glory" as a famous novelist she even aborted a child, ironically enslaving herself to guilt. Following upon so much blunt honesty, their "remarriage" out of the ashes after David destroys his notes when he learns of his complicity in the death of the child strains credulity, as do other forced "happy" endings in Anderson.

David comments to a fledgling author that every writer starting out must essay his "God damn the father book." Though not written until Anderson was in his early 50s, *I Never Sang for My Father* (1968) might be seen as his "damn the father" play. As a "memory" play and examination of a survivor's guilt over having failed to love adequately, it seems derivative of Williams's *Glass Menagerie* and Miller's *Death of a Salesman* in structure and conflict (interestingly, it boasted the same set designer, Jo Mielziner). The father of the title is Tom Garrison, a cranky authoritarian, difficult to love. As a young boy who hated his father for deserting, and as a man dismissive of his wife's emotional needs and overly demanding of his children, Tom excuses his actions in the name of pursuing self-reliance and the American dream of success. A failed son and husband, he seems intent on wanting his widower son, Gene, to fail also, trying to prevent his remarrying. Although his sister charges Gene with indulging the "seductive . . . image of the eternally bereaved husband [and] dutiful son," Gene finds it impossible to relinquish his moral code and makes "the most loving gesture" of inviting his father into his home to live. When Tom rejects him because the arrangement will not be on his own terms, Gene understands that his father wants "to possess him . . . entirely and completely!" If the son has failed to love his father, it is not through any lack of trying; yet he cannot forgive himself. Gene, by masochistically lacerating himself for not being perfect, not only cannot sing for his father but ends in self-pity and self-recrimination.

  With *You Know I Can't Hear You When the Water's Running* (1967), Anderson joined that select group of playwrights, Noel Coward and Neil Simon among them, able to turn evenings of one-act plays into Broadway bonanzas (760 performances). The title is taken from its opening one-acter, "The Shock of Recognition," in which a none-too-attractive actor tries to convince a writer and producer of his rightness for a part that requires he come naked from bathroom to bedroom—which he never does in Anderson's play. Continuing Anderson's attack on the myth of masculinity as aggressiveness devoid of sensitivity, his playwright protagonist wants to reveal not everyman's virility but instead his "mortality and ridiculousness." In "The Footsteps of Doves," buying twin beds to replace a double signifies a couple's separation over the question of continued physicality in a middle-aged marriage. He fears that infrequent sex squeezed together in a coffin-sized twin bed will send him into the arms of someone younger, while she mistakenly believes that the physical changes of menopause necessitate a dulling of her affectionate side. In the farcical and fuguelike "I'm Herbert," Anderson pens a Pirandellian and Pinteresque sketch about how the subjective truths of memory, confused by the process of aging, can offer a sense of communion to blunt the vicissitudes of time. The most substantial of these short plays, "I'll Be Home for Christmas," remains unique among the playwright's canon for being his only "blue-collar" play. Its protagonist, the "brawny," beer-drinking Chuck Berringer, is, however, one of Anderson's typical males, "at war with the inevitable"—that is to say, up against mortality, disillusionment, loneliness, and a wife who holds a hedonistically utilitarian notion of sexuality as opposed to Chuck's idealistic one. Despite his insight and sensitivity, masculine restraint makes him unable to communicate his deep love to his children, and so the "Can't Hear" of the play's title comes to connote all those artificial constraints that separate human beings from one another.

Anderson's last work produced on Broadway, *Solitaire/Double Solitaire* (1971), is another evening of long one-acters, this time only two. The curtain raiser, "Solitaire," features a dystopian technocracy in which the only relief from total loss of human identity comes via Call Families for temporary hire in state-sanctioned houses of illusion, reminiscent of Genet's *The Balcony* (1965). The more consequential "Double Solitaire," Anderson's finest achievement since *Tea and Sympathy*, uncompromisingly maps the fissures in a marriage on which the dramatist refuses to impose a happy ending. Nowhere is Anderson's tendency toward archetype more apparent. For elements of his structure he returns to the medieval morality play, artfully blended with the modern multimedia effects of a home video and photographic slides. Barbara and Charley each listen to two tempters: she to a mother-in-law who argues that sexuality ends at menopause, when the drift toward death begins, and to a divorced friend who advises a succession of men to assuage the loneliness within (or after) marriage; he to his father, who puts great stock in abiding by vows, and to a friend who flaunts the sexual freedom of an open marriage. The family's third generation, Charley and Barbara's son, Peter, and his lover, Melinda, put no faith whatsoever in external forms and old rituals; with both his father and grandfather, Peter shares an incurably romantic image of the bliss that sexuality would confer. Anderson's married men remain romantics long after their wives have come down from the clouds, always to the detriment of the marriage.

Charley's adolescent fixation on sex harms his relationship with Barbara, so that she feels exploited and victimized, reduced to an object in a marriage she has come to "hate." Because of their opposing attitudes toward sexuality, Charley seeing it as a means of confounding the existential void, Barbara as a source of increased loneliness, marriage becomes like the game of double solitaire, in a play Anderson felt contained a "synthesis" of all he had ever attempted thematically and technically in the theater. Anderson linked himself thematically with Inge for the way in which they each focus on "normal" sexual relationships within marriage; an even more telling connection arises, however, with Tennessee Williams: in the sympathy they both offer to the lonely in need of solace and in their compassion for those willing, if need be, to violate long-standing moral codes to answer unselfishly the human cry for help.

Arthur Laurents

If Arthur Laurents belongs to any group of post–World War II American dramatists, his closest affinity lies with those who might be called psychological realists, especially William Inge and Robert Anderson. Like them, he focuses primarily on emotionally distraught characters, oftentimes portraying women caught up in the age of anxiety, beset by self-doubt or even self-loathing. Yet unlike either Inge or Anderson, Laurents reveals a solid measure of Thornton Wilder's influence in his generally optimistic outlook as well as in the nonrealistic stylistic techniques of some later plays.

In the preface to *A Clearing in the Woods* (1957), Laurents formulates the clearest statement of his central insight: If men and women are lonely, they are so because they cannot accept themselves as flawed, imperfect creatures; until they arrive at such self-acceptance, they will be unable to feel sufficiently, or to give of themselves adequately, to experience a sense of completion and fulfillment. When Laurents's characters hurt within themselves, they lash out and, attempting to deflect their own misery, hurt others. The diminished sense of self-worth exemplified by so many of Laurents's characters rests on an individual psychological basis, but it can also be greatly exacerbated by social forces, such as prejudicial attitudes and the drive to conform. The prejudice may be racial, as in *Home of the Brave* (1945) (see chapter 1), while the conformity may reside either in perpetuating the success syndrome by seeking a comfortable economic status—as in *Clearing in the Woods* and *Invitation to a March* (1960)—or in an inability to break free of repressive sexual mores and conventions, as in *The Time of the Cuckoo* (1952) and, again, *Invitation to a March*.

Perhaps because of the perennially popular 1955 Katharine Hepburn movie *Summertime* adapted from it, *The Time of the Cuckoo* will likely remain the best remembered of Laurents's plays. This bittersweet romance involves a clash of cultures when Leona Samish, a thirtyish American presented as a spinster, has a brief affair in Venice with the older Renato Di Rossi. As Leona remarks, Americans abroad carry with them "more than a suitcase"; they bring a whole trunk load of attitudes and values, manners and mores. New World brashness confronts Old World charm, money meets culture, and puritan guilt and repression come up against an instinctive lust for life. Di Rossi, regarding himself as a spokesman for Mediterranean culture, believes that abstract notions of right and wrong have no validity; to live fully and to make contact with others is the only good, and so he bemoans the tendency of Americans to always "feel bad" and wallow in sexual guilt. The owner of the pensione, Signora Fioria, who had an affair while her husband was alive and is having another now, also deems as "impractical" any morality except discretion, urging others to leave life a little "sweeter" than they found it by entering upon a giving relationship. The values of these two Italians gain added weight when Laurents shows the shortcomings of the traditional notions of sexual morality espoused by an American couple, the beautiful, blond Yaegers. Eddie Yaeger, an artist experiencing painter's block, after straying sexually returns to the unquestioned belief that love requires absolute fidelity; his wife, June, suffers from the less tangible but equally destructive romantic ideal that a wife must be her husband's complete life.

What finally prevents Leona and Di Rossi from achieving a permanent relationship turns out not to be their differing attitudes toward sexual morality but a failure within Leona herself. A woman who prides herself on independence but increasingly hides her insecurities behind drink, she underestimates her attractiveness to Di Rossi. His gift of a garnet necklace, a gesture so overwhelming that she—together with the audience—literally hears a waltz, temporarily melts her. When it appears, however, that he has made money off her by exchanging her dollars for counterfeit on the black market, she rejects him. Her souvenirs of Venice, two wine-red eighteenth-century goblets and the garnet necklace, suggest by their color her long-repressed passion. That she insists on keeping the necklace as something tangible to take home with her indicates her insecurity and need for things as a proof of feelings. Although it remains unclear whether she will return to America any the wiser, she at least stays in Venice to complete her vacation instead of fleeing further experiences that would test her conventional moral code.

A Clearing in the Woods concerns a woman who must confront the past to move into the future, thus continuing Laurents's exploration of the need for psychological wholeness. The most theatrically intricate and, according to the playwright, most difficult yet satisfying of his plays to write, A Clearing in the Woods does not lend itself to simple categorization. Laurents himself discounts all the formulas—flashback, dream, nightmare, hallucination, psychoanalysis, psychodrama—that might readily describe this work in which not only the woman Virginia but also her three former selves all appear onstage. Even stream of consciousness does not seem an accurate enough classification; perhaps nonrealistic fantasy, with a dose of expressionism, comes closest. Each of Virginia's three younger selves reveals herself mainly in the way she interacts with a man—father, teenage lover, husband—in acted-out fragments of past experience. Jigee, Virginia as a little girl of 9 or 10, rebels against both the restraints and lack of attention of her father, Barney; in a plea that he pay attention to her, she cuts off his necktie, wishing it were the tongue that had lashed out. Virginia's initiation into sexuality is seen through Nora, her 17-year-old self, who goes off with a woodchopper, while her lack of success in marriage is probed through 26-year-old Ginna's relationship with Pete, who had married her thinking she was pregnant.

Like Virginia now, neither Nora nor Ginna wanted to be ordinary; each coveted a life set apart from others. This same desire has stood in the way of Virginia's marrying Andy, whom she thought would always be simply a competent researcher rather than a brilliant discoverer. Virginia now invites him to cross over the magic circle and enter a fantasy world. She demands, however, that Andy live up to her goals for him and will be angry if he fails, while he is happier accepting and living within his limitations. Never satisfied with herself, Virginia places destructive expectations on others. Andy acts as a kind of therapist for Virginia, helping her recognize that she has never really loved anyone, even herself, and that she has consequently destroyed the men in her life. Yet as each of the men returns in the present, she discovers that her impact on them has not been wholly negative. By becoming content with herself rather than pursuing a false image that could never be, Virginia can finally accommodate rather than deny her former selves. Having achieved integration, she moves with hope into the future.

Invitation to a March is a charming romantic fairy tale about people's need to keep time with no drummer at all, even to break out and dance. DeeDee and Tucker Grogan have come East to see their son, Schuyler, married to Norma Brown. DeeDee and Norma's mother, Lily, are conventional, status-happy women. DeeDee has wealth, Lily, social position, and both are morally proper; yet their limited lives remain dull, dreary, without adventure. The bride-to-be's one peculiarity is her propensity to fall asleep for no apparent reason. This odd habit constitutes her quiet revolt against the conformity and complacency that surround her. She sleeps because life is not worth staying awake for, that is, until Aaron Jablonski, envisioned as riding on a horse in the rose-colored light, arrives to fix the plumbing and wakes her with a kiss.

Although several of the characters at times face front and ingratiatingly address the audience, Aaron's mother, Camilla, functions as chief of these narrators and the playwright's mouthpiece. She displays more than a little of the down-to-earth philosophizing of Wilder's Stage Manager from *Our Town* about her, and the play more than a bit of Wilder's point of view. A wacky individualist and free spirit who treasures the adventures life offers, Camilla knows that one can deaden life by not living it the way one desires; since time passes and one does not have many chances, one must take the opportunities that present themselves, as she did 20 years earlier when she found her magic during a summer romance with Aaron's father, who turns out to be Tucker Grogan, and thus will be the father of the groom no matter what.

Norma's similarity to Camilla reveals itself in her penchant for tearing up calendar pages, an act symbolizing her desire to break free from the restrictions of a confined, regimented life. In the play's title passage, Camilla warns about all the marchers in the world who try to thwart one's individuality, who want one to toe the line and move in lockstep. It may be easier and safer to submit than to assert one's difference, but to do so is finally deadly dull. Norma feels no guilt after her first night with Aaron; nevertheless, it takes some time before she can break free and dance by giving up the prospects of a secure and success-oriented life in suburbia with a lawyer-husband and replace that goal with her love for Aaron. Although Schuyler, so much the prisoner of conventionality that he cannot respond to feelings, finds the shoe Norma kicks off before she dances away, he is no Prince Charming; in fact, he confesses to not believing in princes anymore and so he symbolically falls asleep, a victim of the march, while his fully awakened and alive beauty waltzes off with another. With its reversals of motifs from the popular fairy tales Cinderella and Sleeping Beauty, and its deft handling of tone and comfortable assimilation of Wilder's philosophical outlook and stage techniques, *Invitation to a March* may come to be seen as Laurents's most significant play.

Because Laurents's major efforts vary so in form and structure, he remains difficult to categorize. He resembles both Hellman and Miller in his hatred of prejudice and his compassion for those who must hide a facet of themselves, whether racial or sexual, to avoid rejection. In Laurents, however, it is not only, or even primarily, the other person or society that seeks to limit his characters' world; rather, the protagonists themselves, through their psychological inhibitions and moral or sexual repression, circumscribe their own existence. Like several other playwrights from the decade immediately following World War II, Laurents has not always escaped criticism for his "group therapy session" or "pop psychologizing" plays, which, admittedly, sometimes end with victories too contrived or too easily won. Laurents's accurate reading of the injured modern psyche, awash in the anxiety and self-doubt that inevitably accompany any search for an ethical system that would replace traditional social and sexual mores, remains in somewhat uneasy balance with his innately positive view that the individual can win through to a sense of personal wholeness. Laurents dramatizes this tension, however, with understated honesty. Like his spokeswoman Camilla in *Invitation to a March*, Laurents at his best can be an adroit stage manager, gently pulling the strings that continue to move audiences in the theater.

Lawrence and Lee

As the epigraph for their 1970 play, *The Night Thoreau Spent in Jail*, Jerome Lawrence and Robert E. Lee chose the same famous passage from Thoreau's "On Civil Disobedience" that Anderson had in mind when he wrote *Tea and Sympathy*: "If a man does not keep pace with his companions, perhaps it is because he hears a different drummer. Let him step to the music which he hears, however measured, or far away." This encapsulates the overriding emphasis in the theater works that these two Ohio-born playwrights produced during a collaboration of more than 40 years: a person is obligated to listen to the voice of conscience within and follow it wherever it leads, asserting his or her freedom, though that might entail violating societal mores or authoritarian decrees. Even such a work as their perennially diverting high comedy, *Auntie Mame* (1956), skillfully adapted from Patrick Dennis's novel, comes down squarely on the side of individualism against conformity. The eccentric and occasionally wacky Mame, suddenly finding herself guardian of her nephew, son of a stuffed-shirt businessman, decides to release all the stops to ensure that he will experience life's bounty. With her motto, "Life is a banquet, and most poor sons-of-bitches are *starving* to death," Mame preaches

"cultural enlargement" and expansiveness. Despite reveling in "the adventure of molding a new little life" by opening amazing doors and windows for him, she comes to accept that Patrick is not hers and must finally be his own person, although that does not prevent her undertaking a similarly progressive educational program for his son.

Lawrence and Lee base their two most lasting plays, *Inherit the Wind* (1955) and *The Night Thoreau Spent in Jail*, on historical incidents wherein a law is broken for some higher moral claim; in each instance, they dramatize events so as to imply parallels between past history and current political affairs. Lawrence, writing under his given name of Jerome Swartz, had explicitly utilized the interplay between past and present to ironic effect in his first short work, "Laugh, God!" published in *Six Anti-Nazi One Act Plays* (1939). In it, the death in 1855 of the German romantic poet Heinrich Heine in exile in Paris is framed by a prologue and epilogue set in 1933 Germany, both showing the "vulgar, cheap mob" throwing books into a bonfire and shouting "Burn, JEW BOOK!" Heine's nationalistic fervor remained so intense that he refused to renounce citizenship in his homeland even for election to the Academie Francaise. Though he repudiated his Jewish religion as "a misfortune," a century later his Jewishness would ironically be taken as the sole measure, and a condemnatory one, of his acceptability by the masses.

Lawrence and Lee's most justly famous work continues to be *Inherit the Wind*, first produced to acclaim in 1955 at Margo Jones's Dallas Theatre and later that year on Broadway. Although based on the 1925 Scopes "monkey" trial in Tennessee that pitted Clarence Darrow for the defense against William Jennings Bryan for the prosecution, the play, the authors claim, should be regarded as neither journalism nor history but as theater intended to transcend the specific historical moment: " 'Not too long ago.' It might have been yesterday. It could be tomorrow." Bert Cates's decision to read to his high school science class a passage from Darwin's *Origin of the Species* precipitates a conflict between science and religion, doubt and faith, pluralism and unity, the progressive North and the more conservative South, and individual rights and the laws of society. Through their presentational handling of stage space, so that the small town is always present by suggestion, the playwrights implicate the social organism as one of the central players in this dispute, indicating that the community is "on trial," too.

Torn between devotion to Bert and obedience to the community's mores is Rachel Brown, daughter of the town's minister. Wanting him to take the path of least resistance, she urges that Bert admit to breaking

the law. Speaking in free-verse dialogue, one of the three outsiders, the Baltimore newsman E. K. Hornbeck, looks with bemused cynicism at this ignorant town of Hillsboro that has adopted a carnival atmosphere for the occasion, complete with a prophet of Armageddon come down from the hills, banners ordering "READ YOUR BIBLE," and an organ grinder's monkey that Hornbeck gaily hails as "Grandpa!" Dominating stage productions of *Inherit the Wind*, however, will always be the attorneys, Matthew Harrison Brady for the prosecution and Henry Drummond for the defense.

Welcomed as a savior by this insular society that fears new ideas, Brady upholds the revealed Truth of Scripture against what he terms "the blasphemies of Science." Believing that law should be the servant of religion and so a handmaiden, in this instance, to fundamentalist theology, he upbraids Drummond as "a creature of the Devil," labels all scientists agnostics, and judges Darwin's scientific theories false without even having read them. Drummond, on the other hand, an agile legal mind with a flamboyant manner, asserts the power, even sanctity, of the human mind as it reasons for itself. There exists a plurality of truths; there can be no comforting abstract grid to arbitrarily plot the rightness and wrongness of every act, and every individual must always retain "the right to be wrong."

Although the jury, selected for the conformity of their opinions, finds Bert guilty, the judge can uphold the law's letter as well as ferret out its underlying spirit and proclaim a moral victory for Drummond and Bert by fining Bert only $100 to be appealed. Bert announces that he will continue to "oppose" such an unjust law, as there must always be those pariahs willing to take a stand and push change a few inches farther; even Rachel accedes that thinking must be evolutionary, "like a child inside our body. It has to be born." The play's final image of Drummond, with Darwin in one hand and the Bible in the other, symbolizes the coexistence of a multiplicity of truths of different kinds, old knowledge always ready to be expanded by new without necessarily being discarded. Hornbeck, in fact, sees no paradox in saluting Drummond as "an atheist / Who believes in God." Coming, as does Miller's *Crucible*, after the HUAC hearings, *Inherit the Wind* forcefully dramatizes the necessity for a unitary society to forsake narrow prejudices in order to valorize the autonomy of human conscience.

Lawrence and Lee continue to focus on the "right to be wrong" and on doubt as a heuristic for approaching the truth in *The First Monday in October*, a play centering on the appointment of the first woman

Associate Justice of the Supreme Court (historically, that did not occur until 1981, with the confirmation of Sandra Day O'Connor). Written in 1975 to celebrate the sixtieth anniversary of the Cleveland Playhouse—one of the nation's oldest regional theaters—it is, like *Inherit the Wind*, a drama whose chief tension comes from the collision of two value systems, each conscientiously formed; furthermore, it posits, as did the earlier play, this dialectic as necessary to the health of a free society. Again, Lawrence and Lee write an issue-oriented drama, considering four timely and even prescient topics: censorship versus free artistic expression, unbridled capitalism, judicial impropriety, and women entering careers once closed to them.

The playwrights' chief spokesman on the first three issues is the most junior of the currently sitting justices, Daniel Shaw. An absolutist in the areas of freedom of speech and expression and the right to privacy, he argues that even though it personally turns his stomach to defend a pornographic film under review, the filmmaker's "right to speak" and "be wrong" is inalienable. To censor and put limitations on artistic expression because a work might potentially offend standards of morality or taste also risks "wip[ing] out . . . unforgettable music and powerful plays!" Any "moral dry cleaning" courts danger because it renders the least common denominator the supreme arbiter. Yet in the case of a large corporation deliberately neglecting to develop an alternative energy bank that would render internal combustion obsolete, Shaw argues for regulations on big business, which has begun to "cripple itself by its own self-interest."

When the newly confirmed justice, Ruth Loomis, believes she must resign because her late husband was party to the business conspiracy in a case before them, Shaw convinces her that since she had no knowledge, no conflict of interest exists and she did nothing improper. And Ruth herself, tired of journalists distinguishing between her and the eight men on the court, retorts tartly: "A woman *can* ovulate and think at the same time." Precisely because of their intellectual differences on the issues, Shaw, at first skeptical, comes to welcome Ruth's presence on the Court. The coexistence of adversarial positions that can be openly avowed and debated remains essential to a democracy.

Lawrence and Lee's last play of the 1950s was the forgettable *The Gang's All Here* (1959), about cronyism running, and potentially ruining, the presidency. Set in an indefinite past time of "quite a while ago," the play is, the authors remark, "about the Presidency itself: the father image, the godhead we send to Washington." Like several other political dramas of the period (see chapter 1), it assigns the blame for electing incompetent leaders squarely to the voters themselves; again, as in *Inherit the Wind*, the community shares collective responsibility for its myopia.

Lawrence and Lee's strongest contribution to American theater outside of *Inherit the Wind* came in 1970 with *The Night Thoreau Spent in Jail*. Written for the American Playwrights Theatre, it might be seen as a dramatization of Thoreau's manifesto, "On Civil Disobedience." In its nonrepresentational technique, its handling of time and space, and its form as an examination of conscience, it recalls *Death of a Salesman*; specific visual and aural echoes of Miller's play twice occur in "the flute melody . . . and leafy-green projection[s]." With "Time and space . . . awash here," the protagonist ranges freely between present and past starting with the day in 1846 when he is jailed for refusing to pay a poll tax to support what he believes to be an immoral war effort, its horror made palpable both to him and to the audience through two extended, expressionistic segments of almost "Goya-esque nightmare." The jail itself serves as a symbolic representation of all those social, political, and narrow religious systems that imprison one's thoughts and actions.

As a "majority of one," Henry values the right to be different. Irreverent of authority, he rebels against conformity, ownership, and work for money that only enslaves. He chooses celibacy, despite loneliness; he preaches ecological awareness instead of "poisoning paradise"; finally, he embraces transcendentalism and favors imagination and creativity over life's infernal chain of getting and keeping. Though the authors could be accused of simplifying and sentimentalizing Thoreau to remake him as a "NOW THOREAU" related to the "angry young men" of today, still there exists genuine power in his insistence that man must be willing to declare an unjust law wrong, that to do otherwise he would be "a criminal. To [his] Conscience. To [his] God. To Society" and his fellow human beings. Thoreau ultimately attains sufficient wisdom to see that the gadfly or conscience of society cannot fulfill his role by withdrawal; he must disavow returning to Walden as a place of safe retreat. Yet, now he can internalize Walden and the values it embodies, being there without being physically so. As an evocation of the individual who holds true to the light of individual conscience above subservience to an unjust law imposed from without, Thoreau becomes the quintessential Lawrence and Lee character. While highly critical of the oftentimes complacent masses, they implicitly affirm the American experiment that reaches its apotheosis in the actions of people like Thoreau, or Bert Cates in *Inherit the Wind*.

William Gibson

From the earliest days of his writing career, as the author of a play about young Shakespeare in Stratford-upon-Avon and an award-winning teleplay about Helen Keller and her teacher, William Gibson has specialized in writing imaginative reconstructions of historical personages. These "biodramas" differ both from traditional history plays—with their usual aim of discovering lessons applicable to current societal conflicts through the prism of the past—and from docudramas—which, like the documentary films of which they are an extension, employ only actual dialogue in their presentation of characters and events. Gibson uses the biographical drama to explore the toll that commitment to a vocation exacts on one's personal life, especially for the woman whose work defies a stereotypical model. Whether public (such as that of a politician) or more private (artist or teacher), the vocation conflicts with imperatives of the heart, the need of the self and others for affection and love.

These characteristic concerns were not, however, central to Gibson's first hit, *Two for the Seesaw* (1958), a bittersweet comedy about two maimed loners attempting to connect in the big city. In *The Seesaw Log* (1959), a "travelogue" or "physiognomy of theater," Gibson reflects on the frequently demoralizing process of bringing to Broadway a play destined for commercial success. Recognizing that drama must always be "a popular art or it is nothing," Gibson expresses a growing uneasiness over art's subservience to commerce, fostering a "commodity" type of writing "likeable" rather than "serious." Although Gibson acknowledges that "ultimately our audiences write our plays" by determining what they will pay to see and the values they insist be confirmed, he nonetheless finds disheartening the hit-or-miss syndrome that controls Broadway. Gibson "entered the theater thinking of it as a church, and emerged thinking of it as a brothel" that potentially destroys the writer's "soul."[2]

Gibson managed in his two-character (and a telephone) *Two for the Seesaw* to pull off two un-Broadwaylike feats: present an unappealing "hero" and an unhappy, or at least non-Hollywood, ending. Jerry, a lawyer from Nevada undergoing a divorce, comes across as a heel. Feeling himself "drowning" and "in limbo," he seeks someone "weaker" whom he can help and protect as a compensation for having been so long and so willingly on the receiving end of a father-in-law's "charity" and a wife's "smothering." Once he re-acquires self-confidence from "be[ing] needed," he can re-embrace his vows to one wife for life and go back to support her. So the wimpy Jerry in his own way actually uses and abuses the however willing Gittel, a spunky and outspoken Bronx Jewish dance teacher. While counseling her against being "a born victim" and treating herself "like a hand-me-down snotrag any bum can blow his nose in," he continues to demean her by projecting his own past victimization onto his definition of her. If she learns anything from their on-again-off-again relationship, it is her right to make a "claim" on a man that she not "share" him with someone else; even though she is "scared" of being lonelier than before, she refuses to trap an unwilling Jerry into staying. Having taught him something he needed to know about himself, and thus inadvertently getting the once-married couple back together, Gittel finds strength, actually a reassertion of a quality she possesses all along, in a painful decision to stay apart, thereby guaranteeing independence.

Gibson's other stageplays all employ some variation of nonrepresentational scenic design, à la the "bare platform and a passion or two" of the Elizabethan theater, beginning appropriately enough with A *Cry of Players* (1948, revised for New York 1968). This "portrait of the artist as a young man" dramatizes Will Shakespeare, randy and in rebellion against all authoritarian institutions, chomping at the bit to escape Stratford for London. Will, believing the best part of himself goes "unused" and "thwarted" in his marriage to Anne who "throttl[es]" him, can discover no easy accommodation between the "contraries in him." Like Tom in Williams's *Glass Menagerie*, either he remains "fettered and locked" in obeying his responsibility to others, or leaves home to embrace and develop his art.

Gibson continues his cinematically fluid handling of time and space in his most famous play, *The Miracle Worker* (1959). Based on his television drama of two seasons earlier, it featured memorable performances by Anne Bancroft and Patty Duke. With a text drawn "almost exclusively" from the letters of Annie Sullivan appended to the autobiography of her renowned pupil, Helen Keller, the play, much more than an uplifting look at how physical handicaps and impairments can be overcome, dramatizes two forces: the power of love, which oftentimes must be disciplined and even critical of the loved one, and the power of words, as a link between the mind and experience, the self and the world outside.

Two parallel movements structure the play. The lesser, though by no means unimportant one, traces Annie's release from the haunting memories of her "desertion" of her younger brother, Jimmie, after they were orphaned. The second, and for audiences undoubtedly the unforgettable one, dramatizes Helen's release from the prison of being blind, deaf, and mute following a babyhood illness. Since the beginning of knowledge and self-sufficiency resides in the word, to name things assumes biblical power; as Annie says, for Helen language can be her sight now that, like the eyeless rag doll her aunt sews for her, she can no longer see and thus master experience or, shut into herself, speak in other than the "inarticulate" noises of a trapped animal. Helen must be retaught the connection between the word and the object or emotion, the signifier and the thing signified.

To accomplish that, her teacher Annie must "discipline her without breaking her spirit," which demands a love freed from destructive pity and predicated on Helen's potential and desire to learn, which are the instructor's best aids. The breakthrough is finally achieved when Helen spells "wah wah" (water) in Annie's hand, the water symbolizing all that is internal and hidden bursting forth. Then Annie, first received with skepticism by the family because of her young age and lower immigrant social class, can openly confess "love" for her pupil. In Gibson's terms, *The Miracle Worker* demonstrates "the artist's struggle with [her] raw material" and the reciprocal salvation achieved by the selfless teacher and receptive student. The vocation of teaching becomes the medium through which the human form is shaped and perfected.

Gibson, by drawing on "major happenings" that are "factual enough," carries forward the story of Annie and Helen in his *Monday after the Miracle* (1982), which picks them up 20 years later. John Macy, a young writer who, appropriately enough, admires the "struggles of the underprivileged for speech" in literary works by the American naturalists, arrives to upset the closed relationship, turning it into a triangle even before he marries Annie. More centrally, *Monday* focuses on Annie's awareness of how her vocation has deprived her of a life; having suppressed her needs and found her sole definition in her commitment to "the other," she now doubts whether this is "enough." Unable to dispute John's assessment that spinsterhood is "leaving [her] arid. . . . an empty vessel," Annie "want[s]—a life, as a woman." To achieve that with John would require deserting and even betraying Helen, for whom the word "Teacher" is a "poem." Indeed, Helen thinks of Annie as the sculptress who "hewed" her and who will be Helen's "answer, in the dark, when death calls." Annie has, in fact, released in Helen feelings that cause a fleeting moment of passion between John and Helen herself; and John, unsure of Annie's love and too insecure to live in the shadow of celebrity, becomes like a child in a tantrum: "John and Helen and Teacher are one huge love turd." Alone again after John leaves, Helen and Annie can only "accept" the "pain" as "useable" and find solace in their "work . . . as seed sown," though Annie can probably never be as philosophical as Helen about the terms of her diminished life.

Monday is a much better drama than the critics allowed, as is the play that immediately preceded it about a similar conflict, *Golda* (1978), which Gibson terms "a documentary fantasia on a moral theme." One of the beauties of the multimedia *Golda*, which may finally be Gibson's most impressive achievement, lies in the complexity of its structure, fitting because of Golda's own decision to leave the private domain and enter history, finally serving as Israel's Prime Minister from 1969 to 1974. It proceeds, as Gibson explains, on three levels: that of "suspense," the hinge of the 1973 Yom Kippur War; that of the "witnesses," a half dozen narrative passages recounting episodes from 1921 on; and that of "memory," another half dozen sequences from 1904 on in the mind of Golda.

Reared in a paternalistic and sexist household, and in a religion that marginalized women by forbidding them even to talk in the synagogue, Golda rebelled by making her own decision about whom to marry. But Morris, the man she chooses, holds to the traditional notion that a wife should "make a nice home, read a book, be happy," which leaves a woman who desires to "make a new world" feeling small and circumscribed. When Golda answers the call to public responsibility and separates from her family for political office, Morris, ironically, becomes a housemother.

In victory, however, Golda regrets both that she "didn't do very well by [her] children" and the "price" Morris had to pay. Most poignantly, she understands the pain suffered by those who died for the dream of a homeland and the sacrifices inevitably demanded by such idealism. Like Will, who found power in using language, and Annie, who found it in giving language, Golda understands that true power resides not in abstract ideology but in washing a dish, in being free, in protecting the children, in taking in homeless brothers. But using that power for others or imparting it to them inevitably entails for Gibson's protagonists some sacrifice of self, as true of Golda as it is of Annie and Gittel. Jerry might offer Gittel the consolation that "After the verb to love, to help is—the sweetest in the tongue." Consistently, however, Gibson remains unafraid to showcase his perception that the two responsibilities are often at odds: to aid the stranger may mean to sacrifice those one loves closer to home.

Paddy Chayefsky

Like Gibson, Paddy Chayefsky first attained national prominence writing for television, a medium he called "the scorned stepchild of drama" even while musing that it "may well be the basic theater of our century."[3] In *Marty* (1954), he created the era's most famous small-screen drama; adapted to the movies in 1955, it won an Academy Award for best screenplay, an honor Chayefsky would repeat twice more with *The Hospital* (1971) and *Network* (1976). Distinctive among the writers in this chapter for his urban settings, Chayefsky focuses on the anomaly of loneliness in the big city that can grind little people down. Even when treating fairly mundane subject matter, he creates an aura of metaphysical angst as his predominantly Jewish characters question whether life has any purpose and, if it does, how it can be found. Because of Chayefsky's ethnic background, critics have tended to use as a frame of reference Clifford Odet's urban ghetto plays of the 1930s, yet Chayefsky's works are less concerned with the nuclear family—and strong mother figures, à la Sean O'Casey's *Dublin Trilogy*—or with political and socioeconomic issues than with a more generalized search for meaning in a world edging toward absurdity. Chayefsky was, in fact, together with Archibald MacLeish, the chief popular expositor of the absurd in the commercial Broadway theater before the movement entered into common parlance off-Broadway at the end of the 1950s. The stage plays that frame Chayefsky's career offer two possible responses to the perception of absurdity: discovering meaning through human love, or effecting a wider awareness of humankind's constricted condition.

The first, *Middle of the Night* (1956), which began as a television drama and was later filmed, is an introspective if rather turgid story of a May/December, Gentile/Jewish love between two wounded people, interesting for its sensitivity in handling such issues as aging and sexuality. Jerry Kingsley, a 53-year-old widower already rebuffed once in his attempts to remarry, experiences middle-age doubts and mild depression over fear of impotence, a fear that temporarily becomes fact. Aware of "something dying inside" when not being loved physically, he falls for the younger and "emotionally very immature" Betty Preiss, herself on the rebound from a failed marriage. The other women close to Kingsley, a sister who lives with him and fears being displaced by "that tramp," and a daughter who sees Betty as usurping her rightful relationship, act from unconscious sexual motivations and uneasiness over Kingsley's sexual desires. Falling into jealousy over Betty's returned husband, Kingsley momentarily thinks himself a silly "old fool" in an exploitative "tabloid story."

Chayefsky's characterization of the neurotic Betty becomes a too pat psychological study: rejected by her mother and reared by a neighbor lady, she eventually married to compensate for what was lacking in her life and now discovers in Jerry the father she never had, with her mother objecting to both his Jewishness and his age. Despite these obstacles, the on-again-off-again relationship eventuates in marriage. Only through love can two human beings counter emptiness and discover their "meaning." Set, like Gibson's *Two for the Seesaw*, in two Manhattan apartments that delineate their inhabitants' class differences, the play only once compels much visual interest. At its final curtain, an apparently submissive Kingsley, ready to abide by society's stricture against the impropriety of age finding sexual fulfillment, sits stooped under a shawl, "huddled and tired and cold." But Betty's return satisfies his need to be needed and, rejuvenated, he throws off the shawl to embark on a renewed life.

The May/December union in Chayefsky's last stage play, *The Latent Heterosexual* (1967), is grounded not on mutual need but on selfish gain. Termed a "Kafka-esque fantasy" by John Clum,[4] the play mixes Elmer Rice's expressionism with Eugene Ionesco's absurdism to castigate corporate America's ethics and values and offer a satiric look at a materialistic society that forces man to violate his integrity in order to prosper. The broadly comic/pathetic protagonist, a modern-day Volpone who deifies money and can assert an identity only through a series of poses, seems intended as a type of existential Everyman. John Morley, the fortyish vulgarian and homosexual author who finds his first success in a quarter century with a tawdry book, is slapped with a bill for a half million dollars in back taxes and penalties. On a lawyer's advice, he marries, and later divorces, to set up phony corporations and other tax dodges. His abstract corporate identity is such that to liquidate the corporation is to liquidate the self, which he does when, acting again at his attorney's prompting, he kills himself. But not before Chayefsky generalizes Morley's "insufferable" situation into a definition of angst-ridden existence: "a lost, frightened soul in terrified flight across the great yawning terror of doubt—a human being, in short!"

Chayefsky's *The Tenth Man*, loosely based on S. Ansky's famous Yiddish drama *The Dybbuk* (1925) and produced on Broadway in 1959, remains the most assured and substantial of his stageplays. Focusing on the conflict between faith and reason, belief and uncertainty, religion and psychiatry, it comments on the importance of rootedness in a community held together by a common culture and a shared ritual as a way of staving off the dislocation inevitable in the modern world. It proposes as well the union of two individuals as the one clear evidence of God's presence today. The Jewish community in the play evidences signs of breakdown and decline: a converted shop houses their synagogue; they are increasingly unable to muster the requisite 10 men for daily prayers; the Rabbi, himself in need of renewed belief in the spiritual order, has resorted to sponsoring a baseball team as a ploy to fill up Sunday school.

The characters, most elderly, constitute a microcosm of Jews in the modern world: the devout cabalist, Hirshman, is a near-mystical seer who has been doing penance for years after giving up the rabbinate; the high school biology teacher, Foreman, is an empiricist who "report[s] . . . only what [he] see[s]"; the journalist, Alper, though a reformed Jew, maintains an interest in the occult, while Schlissel has become an atheist and rationalist. Into this group come two young people: Foreman's granddaughter, Evelyn, given to bouts of catatonic schizophrenia and occasional violence, who is possessed by the dybbuk of Hannah Luchinsky, dishonored in her youth by Foreman himself and now "a migratory soul" attempting to "return to heaven"; and Arthur Landau, a lawyer on a bender who has found that psychiatry does not hold the antidote for his sense of worthlessness and alienation.

Arthur, who facetiously "think[s] of God as the Director of Internal Revenue," claims to believe only in disbelief; Hirshman calls him "a man possessed by the Tangible." Arthur's worst heresy, however, is to disbelieve in the fact of "love anymore." While Arthur understands his mission as spreading an awareness of meaninglessness, Evelyn quirkily regards him as searching for meaning, and thus a kind of "mystic." Her wild dance to the Chassidic chant in act 2, like Nora's tarantella in Ibsen's *A Doll House*, allows free reign to her repressed "lasciviousness" and "abandon and wantonness." And the ritual exorcism in act 3, while it successfully releases the dybbuk of Hannah, more importantly and unexpectedly liberates Arthur from his own unacknowledged dybbuk: his terror of the "idea of love." Arthur now re-embraces life, praying for the ability to love, which will help him both cure Evelyn and redeem himself. As Alper makes explicit, believing in God and "wanting to love" are synonymous. The power of human love becomes contemporary man's religion, the crutch he can lean on instead of God in his search for purpose and definition.

The seeming incompatibility between God's existence and man's significance pervades Chayefsky's next play, *Gideon* (1961), based on the biblical narrative of the defeat of the Midianites. Tired of "grim gods," the Israelites have "defaulted" on the Covenant and turned away from the "jealous God" Yahweh, who in the form of an Angel appears to Gideon. Despite finite man's need to concretize the object of worship so that it does not remain "too vast a concept"—a subject Edward Albee will later pursue in *Tiny Alice* (1964)—the Angel resents being defined in human terms, claiming only "I am what is" and demanding absolute love. For God to be great, his creatures must be kept little and will-less. Gideon nevertheless boldly questions: "If the Lord is with us, sir, then why are we as we are?" Following the miraculous victory over the Midianites, Gideon, who began as a reluctant warrior/redeemer of his tribe, becomes an overreacher and braggart warrior, akin to the *miles gloriosus* of old. Although in word he attributes all credit for success in battle to God, in deed he is vainglorious and a "pompous ass." Yet by defying the deity's capricious command to smite the elders of Succoth, he earns sympathy; for to pity those at the point of death means that human life, despite what Yahweh says, holds value.

Gideon's example challenges God to learn from his creatures and reconceptualize himself as merciful. Rejecting a God who condemns men to being "suspensions of matter, flailing about for footholds in the void, all the while slipping back screaming into endless suffocation" as just "too hideous, an intolerable state of affairs," Gideon, another in the line of Chayefsky's timeless Everymen, concludes: "I cannot love you, God, for it makes me a meaningless thing." Believing that he "must aspire," Gideon chooses the burden of finding meaning within oneself. In opposition to the Angel's command that he not make a cult of man, Gideon assumes the golden ephod, a garment intended only for God. With no longer any illusion of something outside the self to provide meaning, it proves a heavy yoke.

Gideon is oftentimes linked with another "biblical" play of a few seasons earlier, Archibald MacLeish's Pulitzer-Prize-winning *J. B.* (1957), perhaps the most impressive drama on a religious subject yet produced by an American and, along with Robert Lowell's *The Old Glory* (1964), the best of the post–World War II verse plays. To retell the Book of Job in modern dress, MacLeish returns to the medieval mystery play for his form and to the morality tradition, with its conflict between God and Satan over the soul of Everyman, in this instance a successful businessman seen celebrating Thanksgiving Day, the American feast that expresses most forcibly the connection between spiritual election and material prosperity. Living, however, not in the medieval age of faith, but in the postbomb nuclear age of anxiety, J. B.'s wife, Sarah, remarks in the last lines about the church candles and stars having been extinguished in a God-is-dead, indifferent universe; moreover, the recurrent imagery of dungheaps and cesspools decidedly pictures a modern wasteland. One of the characters, in Beckettian lines, echoes the dark vision of the absurdists: "We never asked to be born / We never chose the lives we die of / They beat our rumps to make us breathe." To be human is to *be* a Job, for to be is to suffer.

J. B. plays itself out concurrently on four levels: first, an acting contest between two out-of-work performers, Mr. Zuss, who believes that God's inscrutable ways remain providential, and the cynical Mr. Nickles, who holds that consciousness of suffering denies any possibility of happiness; second, a battle between God and Satan for the allegiance of J. B.; third, a conflict between a capricious God who indiscriminately orders suffering and a modern Everyman who demands purpose and logic as opposed to whim and irrationality; and finally, and perhaps centrally, a dispute that expresses the radically different religious beliefs of husband and wife. As loss after horrendous loss befalls them, Sarah edges toward despair, admonishing J. B. to "curse God and die." Unless J. B. denies the existence of a just God, his only avenue to restoring meaning is, apparently, to demean himself by pleading guilty to a sin he did not commit: "God is unthinkable if we are innocent." If MacLeish is here asking whether any rational grounds for faith exist, the answer would seem to be no. Sarah, however, journeying from unquestioning piety through despair to a dynamic new faith in humanity—a humanism arising from a romantic response to nature—offers an alternative basis for belief. In an epiphanic moment, she finds a forsythia twig growing in the ashes, a promise of life springing from death, and it teaches her not to demand justice. The ultimate value resides in affective feelings and emotions that are here deified: if the churches are dark, then "blow on the coal of the heart" and there shall be light. The final, some might argue sentimental, image is of a paradise regained, peopled by a modern Adam and Eve setting to work with a restored confidence in the American ideal of self-reliance, a faith in human love as salvation not unlike that which concludes *Tenth Man*. Meaninglessness has been averted.

When Chayefsky's Gideon rejects miraculous explanations for the victory over his enemies, he concludes that sociopolitical forces alone explain historical events. In one final play, *The Passion of Josef D.* (1964), Chayefsky further questions if historical processes can provide humankind with enough of a grounding, or whether they must resort to embracing some illusion or false god to give purpose and significance. Chayefsky adopts a quasi-Brechtian form, structuring *Josef D.* in 11 scenes, complete with songs that provide commentary and several narrative passages in which he achieves considerable novelty, since the speakers step out of character and jump-cut the narration. Like Brecht, Chayefsky seems more intent on presenting a problem to be studied than in the historical events of the Russian Revolution and its aftermath

Stalin, whose young wife died in inexplicable agony, desperately searches for a justification: "A man can endure life if there is a reason for it, even an incomprehensible one. But to suffer for no reason at all is too hideous. . . . I could not endure to live without a God." Lenin, on the other hand, advises that he accept meaninglessness as a given and then move ahead from there. Meaning can never come from accepting a God who exalts suffering, but only from acting so as to become the "historical forces" of one's time. But Stalin cannot live without a god, so he "commends [his] soul" to Lenin as his new god, who will render him meaningful and significant, and then, after Lenin's death, sets himself up as the latest in a line of false gods. Even historical processes prove inadequate. Faced with nothingness, humankind must reinscribe itself through its illusions. Chayefsky's presentation of modern man's dilemma thus looks backward to O'Neill, who charted humankind's search for a God "to comfort his fears of death with," as well as forward to Albee, who characterizes the contemporary man and woman as adopting a succession of illusions in order to face the void.

Tennessee Williams
in the 1940s and 1950s:
Artist of the Fugitive Kind

Tennessee (born Thomas Lanier) Williams, indisputably the major figure writing for the American theater in the period from 1940 to 1960, and the most important southern dramatist yet to emerge, spent the formative years from his birth on 26 March 1911, until after World War I in Mississippi, when the family moved to St. Louis. The tension between these two cultures, an agrarian South that looked back nostalgically to a partly mythical past of gentility and refinement and an industrialized North that rewarded business acumen and practicality, would haunt Williams throughout his life. By 1940, when he was readying *Battle of Angels* for his first New York production of a full-length work, he had, according to the catalogue of his longtime agent, Audrey Wood, already completed dozens of plays of various lengths, hundreds of poems, and numerous stories while on the road from St. Louis, to Iowa, to New Orleans, and on out to California and Mexico. *Battle of Angels* never reached Broadway, closing in Boston, where it sent audiences, some of them already outraged by the subject matter, fleeing up the aisles to escape a malfunctioning smoke machine.

Battle of Angels, to which Williams attributes an "epic quality" and "sweep,"[1] may be gothic and overwrought, yet is not lacking in raw power. Furthermore, the play introduces virtually all of the motifs that become central in the Williams canon: a romantic valorization of the poetic misfit or dispossessed outsider; an almost Manichean duality in the patterning of imagery and symbology, particularly of "shadow and light"; a consideration of the artist's vocation and near-sacred function in the community; the place of illusion and dreams in otherwise thwarted lives; the relationship between madness and vision; an emphasis on repressed sexuality or neuroticism, and on the redemptive power of sexual love; the necessity for breaking free from the shell of self and responding compassionately to others; the need to accept human frailty without despair and to move from guilt to expiation; a discussion of how societal mores and economic dependency constrict individual freedom; and a desire that civilization be feminized and humanized as a counter to masculine power and aggression.

The Myth of the South

Throughout his career, Williams was an inveterate reviser of his own works. *Battle of Angels* finally opened on Broadway as *Orpheus Descending* in 1957, but ran for only 60 performances. The pervasive critical emphasis on myth and symbolism and sexuality in the play's various permutations has tended to obscure the fact that, with the possible exceptions of *Sweet Bird of Youth* (and there mainly act 2) and the much later *Red Devil Battery Sign*, Williams here makes his most explicit foray into sociopolitical drama. He castigates several social wrongs: the racial superiority and bigotry against ethnic groups that create a climate for ostracization and violence; the distrust and defamation of liberal political views; and the class insularity and stratification evident both in the prejudice of the old propertied southern aristocracy against the new mercantile class and in the middle-class condescension toward and exploitation of poor whites. Although Williams denies any "acquaintance with political and social dialectics" and claims "Humanitarian" as his only party affiliation, he still believes that no "writer has much purpose back of him unless he feels bitterly the inequities of the society he lives in."[2] For Williams, that society was initially the South, where he felt most urgently the contest between civilization and materialism: "the South once had a way of life that I am just old enough to remember—a culture that had grace, elegance . . . an inbred culture . . . not a society based on money, as in the North. I write out of regret for that [and] of the forces that have destroyed it. . . . I write about the South because I think the war between romanticism and the hostility to it is very sharp there" (*Conversations, Williams,* 43, 45).

As Carol Cutrere says to the audience near the end of *Orpheus Descending,* "This country used to be wild, the men and women were wild and there was a wild sort of sweetness in their hearts, for each other, but now it's sick with neon, it's broken out sick with neon, like most other places." Society, in trying to tame the elemental and primitive in human beings in order to bring it under control, may actually succeed in routing it out and destroying it. Carol describes herself as having once been a "Christ-bitten reformer." She protested the massacre of the African-American majority in their county, set up free clinics for the poor, and objected to the imprisonment of a black who had relations with a white whore, for all of which she was arrested on a hopped-up charge of lewd vagrancy. So the South in Williams, as in Faulkner, is home to the venal despoilers of the land, its people, and its heritage. It continues to house a deep-seated, unresolved sense of guilt over the region's original sin of slavery; and, if it no longer reels under the economic dislocation of Reconstruction, it has not yet totally escaped its impress. It continues, as well, to promulgate a (mis)definition of women according to the Cavalier myth, which perpetuates a double standard and an idealization of womanhood that leads to victimization and dependency.

Orpheus Descending occurs in the rural South; prominent in the stage set is the sign "Mercantile Store," the establishment that Lady (Myra) Torrance runs now that her husband Jabe lies dying of cancer and that establishes the play's overriding metaphor of commodification. As an Italian and daughter of an immigrant, Lady is an outsider; her class dislocation resulted, in fact, in her aborting her child by the prominent David Cutrere when he threw her over for a socially acceptable wife, causing her heart to be "cut . . . out with it." Associated with her youth and innocence is the wine garden that her father opened out on the lake, but that the Klan-like Mystic Crew burned to the ground, with her father in it, when he sold liquor to blacks. Afterward, she allowed herself to be "bought" as wife by Jabe, "sold [her]self" as "whore" in a loveless and, significantly, sterile union.

Val Xavier (close to Savior), a 30-year-old dispossessed wanderer of "wild beauty" turned store clerk who wears a snakeskin jacket and plays gospel songs like "Heavenly Grass" on his guitar, restores Lady to life and fertility. If the destruction of the wine garden was for Lady like an expulsion from paradise, then the alcove where she and Val make love, curtained by a cloth with "a gold tree with scarlet fruit," is like an Eden regained. Val feels disgust over people being bought and sold, and he admits to living in corruption, since he has sold himself for money; yet he denies being "corrupt," because he always reserves a part of himself that is never branded. He exhibits an almost absurdist awareness, wanting things to "make sense" but realizing that the universe refuses to provide any answer to the "why" of existence; until he comes to truly love Lady, his code proclaims that even physical contact is suspect and might simply increase a person's sense of estrangement from the other. His perception that "we're all of us sentenced to solitary confinement inside our own skins, for life" echoes what the dramatist has called "perhaps the major theme of my writings, the affliction of loneliness."[3]

Williams terms *Orpheus Descending* and its progenitor "the emotional record of [his] youth" and refers to *Battle of Angels* specifically as "a lyrical play about memories and the loneliness of them" (*Where I Live*, 81). Certain autobiographical references do arise in one or both versions of the play: Val composes on shoebox lids; the artist Vee Talbot, whose sight, like Williams's, was blurred by a caul or cataract, "paint[s] a thing how [she] feel[s] it instead of always the way it actually is," that is, impressionistically, an apt commentary on how the playwright often imagines and adorns his theatrical environment. In a more basic sense, *Orpheus* becomes a lyrical remembrance insofar as the past to which Lady Torrance desires to return materializes for the audience on stage as the play progresses.

In drama, the attempt to objectify memory, because it depends on and is even tied not only to a more imagistically evocative language but also to certain poetic and nonrealistic theatrical devices, might be seen as a female mode of discourse, in contrast to the more patriarchally embedded male texts that comprise ongoing narrative. Williams visualizes Lady's subjective memories in "the confectionery, shadowy and poetic as some inner dimension of the play," through which she hopes to resurrect the taverna of her father. The store's back room has been transformed physically into the garden Lady associates with life and love, in contrast to the space connected to buying and selling, formerly a male province. "The ghostly radiance of her make-believe orchard" delineates a female space, linked with her womb that is "alive once more" and "won't wither in the dark"; like the no-longer-barren fig tree, she decorates herself with tinsel and ornaments in a kind of fertility ritual. The confectionery at the rear of the set that recaptures the past functions as well as a theater on the stage, a house of potentially salvific illusions/art; to enter and live in it becomes analogous to recovering the lost or repressed feminine from the grip of a masculine mindset that resists creation for destruction and unleashes a kind of nihilism.

For in *Orpheus* masculine hate and aggression ultimately destroy feminine softness and reverie. Lady's husband Jabe, who in the original *Battle of Angels* might be seen as a not-too-veiled allusion to the forces of darkness unleashed by World War II, disrupts quiet moments of possible communion between Lady and Val by incessantly knocking on the ceiling. Finally, he rises from his bed to stalk onto the stage as "death's self, and malignancy," gleefully confessing that it was he who led the raid on her father's wine garden. Now his shots kill Lady and Val's love child, thus ending generativity, except on the level of myth, to which Williams, straining somewhat, tries to raise his protagonists.

In Williams's version of the American story, the pursuit of, and faith in, Edenic innocence has been undercut and routed by a rejection of difference and an exploitation of the weaker that are somehow endemic to the American search for material and cultural domination. Violence has invaded the garden; Jabe sets fire to this realm of art and the spirit, and will have Val hunted down and killed by blowtorch. What will be passed on as a token "so that the fugitive can always follow their kind" will be Val's snakeskin jacket, a regenerative talisman. For the audience the other powerful talisman is the work of art itself.

Repeating Val's words, Williams specifically links the voice of the isolated and the alienated fugitive to the technique of "personal lyricism," so termed to designate the style and emphasis of his particular type of theater: "Personal lyricism is the outcry of prisoner to prisoner from the cell in solitary where each is confined for the duration of his life" (*Where I Live*, 76). Vee, the main artist-figure in the play and wife to the bigoted Sheriff Talbott, who abuses his power, encapsulates Williams's belief that nothing human, no matter how shocking a part of the "dark world," can be outside the proper realm of the transformative power of the artist. Yet the artist tends to become marginalized as society's archetypal fugitive the more he or she insists on "a very healthy extension of the frontiers of acceptable theme and subject matter" (*Where I Live*, 117), as Williams consistently does. Vee, whose lack of physical outlet and emotional fulfillment has resulted in a confusion of erotic fantasies and mystical experience—she conflates Christ's eyes with Val's and senses that the hand of the crucified and risen Savior "touched" her breast—propounds the visionary inspiration essential to her creativity. Val privileges the revelatory power of her art, claiming that she "paint[s] as if God touched [her] fingers" and that her art helps "make sense" out of otherwise random and meaningless "Existence!" which is filled with "Awful! Things!" such as "Beatings!," Lynchings!," "convicts torn to pieces by hounds." In bearing "witness," the artist gives voice to "the fugitive kind," to all those whom Williams in his 1941 "Poem for Paul" hails as earth's "crooked child[ren]"—"the strange, the crazed, the queer. . . . the lonely and misfit . . . the brilliant and deformed."[4]

Williams's "Personal Lyricism"

In virtually all of Williams's works during the 1940s and 1950s, delineating and probing character psychology takes precedence over all else. The dramatist's own claim that the "chief aim of playwriting is the creation of characters. . . . My characters make my play. . . . I always start with them" (*Where I Live*, 116, 72) is borne out by the extensive descriptions and stage directions that impart to the printed texts a novelistic quality. His goal of verisimilitude reflects an attitude toward and a conception of character enshrined in method acting, as practiced by trainees from the Actors Studio—many of whom, including Marlon Brando and Geraldine Page, would star in Williams scripts—under the direction of people like Elia Kazan—who would likewise have a long collaborative partnership with Williams—to achieve what has been called "heightened emotionalism."

And yet, in a daring strategy for a work that would finally introduce Williams to Broadway, he begins *The Glass Menagerie* (1944) with lines unique in the annals of classic American drama in that they are explicitly theoretical in nature, demanding that their audience process information about dramaturgical concepts before they become the least caught up in the characters or action. Williams's authorial character, the narrator Tom Wingfield, opens the play by addressing the audience: "Yes, I have tricks in my pocket, I have things up my sleeve. But I am the opposite of a stage magician. He gives you illusion that has the appearance of truth. I give you truth in the pleasant disguise of illusion." These lines not only prepare viewers to expect an unconventional theatrical experience, as they had, for instance, with Thornton's Wilder's *Our Town* (1938) or *The Skin of Our Teeth* (1941). More essentially, they define the difference between, on the one hand, the realistic theater that asks its audience to make believe they are not making believe by accepting the illusion for the real thing, and, on the other, the nonrealistic, which tells its audience to acknowledge themselves as playgoers and have fun with the make-believe by recognizing the theatrical experience for what it is, just an illusion.

In his "Production Notes" preceding the text of *Glass Menagerie*, Williams penned a significant manifesto, raising a clarion call for "a new, plastic theater which must take the place of the exhausted theater of realistic conventions if the theater is to resume vitality as a part of our culture." Questioning the continued ability of the "straight realistic play" to any longer probe beneath the surface, Williams underlines "the unimportance of the photographic in art: that truth, life, or reality is an organic thing which the poetic imagination can represent or suggest . . . only through transformation." He goes on to describe several elements of this theatrical plasticity, including legends and images on a screen, evocative lighting, and atmospheric music, that combine to create his style of "personal lyricism," as realized in the original productions of his plays by such influential masters of American scenic design as Jo Mielziner and Boris Aronson. Like Miller's later *Death of a Salesman*, which Mielziner would also design, *The Glass Menagerie* is an elegiac memory play, in this instance evoking Williams's years with his mother, Edwina, and sister, Rose, in the late 1930s in St. Louis, where they had moved from Mississippi in 1918. Its form as memory controls its episodic structure—isolated scenes from the remembered past introduced and linked by narrative passages in the present—as well as its visual concept, complete with a gauze scrim whose rising indicates the viewer's entrance into the mind of Tom as he does the remembering, creating something analogous to the first-person point of view in fiction. As Mielziner commented, "My use of translucent and transparent scenic interior walls was not just another trick. It was a true reflection of the contemporary playwright's interest in—and at times obsession with—the exploration of the inner man."[5]

Tom undergoes the process of remembering in order to justify his decision to leave a constricting job at the warehouse, where he wrote poems on shoebox lids, and join the merchant marines and inhabit the larger world now "lit by lightning" of the coming conflagration of world war; to do this, however, involved deserting his mother, Amanda, and his unmarried, minimally disabled sister, Laura.

Amanda has already been left once before by her husband, "a telephone man who fell in love with long distance" and whose grinning portrait adorns the living room wall as a model to Tom of successfully escaping a coffinlike existence. Overbearing if well-meaning, Amanda rules the family by incessant loquacity, a refusal to face reality, and a retreat into illusion. She torments Tom for the uncouth way he eats, the "dirty" novels he reads by the likes of D. H. Lawrence, and the nightly movies he escapes to; she denies that Laura is "crippled" and so makes her already shy daughter even more self-conscious and withdrawn. She compensates for her own diminished life by regarding her children as a second chance at success, nostalgically reliving, in her lyrical jonquil speech that poetically embroiders the facts, her youth as the belle of Blue Mountain with her flurry of gentlemen callers, and receiving Laura's potential beau in old clothes retrieved from a trunk. Yet to live in the past is, however unintentionally, to circumscribe the present and the future. As played by the legendary, terminally ill Laurette Taylor, whom Williams compared with Sarah Bernhardt and Elenora Duse, Amanda both charmed and exasperated audiences for 563 performances after an opening night with 25 curtain calls. (Such formidable actresses as Helen Hayes, Maureen Stapleton, Katharine Hepburn, and Joanne Woodward would later essay the part on stage and screen.) Taylor's portrayal was so strong, in fact, that the director, Eddie Dowling, who also acted the role of Tom, eliminated from the production the images and legends Williams had wanted flashed on a screen to guide the audience through the plot discontinuities.

Most of those images and legends, which might also function to replicate how memory works by association as well as to diminish any excessively sentimental response in the manner of a Brechtian distantiation device, are linked with Laura, who is as physically, emotionally, and psychologically fragile as the collection of miniature glass animals that serves as her central symbol. The collection, like the phonograph records left by the absent father, is her means of escape from reality into fantasy, equivalent to her mother's serialized romances and her brother's nightly adventure films. Her world of imagination is peopled as well by memories of Jim O'Connor, the gentleman caller/emissary from the world of reality; she has taken his mild attentions from high school days when, misunderstanding her ailment of pleurosis the high school hero nicknamed her "Blue Roses," and enlarged them into a romantic attachment. The reality, however, not only fails to fulfill the dream but actually ruins it.

Jim arrives on a Friday, the day of Christ's sacrificial death on the cross, heralded by the word "Annunciation," imparting a Dale Carnegie gospel of self-confidence designed to release her from her shell, making her more normal and "less freakish." But the promised salvation he brings, as foretold by the interrupted supper that should have served as a kind of secular communion, is short-lived, since, figuratively, he refuses to die for her. They exchange "Souvenirs" (another of the play's legends): "with a flourish" he autographs her treasured program from *The Pirates of Penzance* in which he starred; she gives him what remains of her favorite glass animal, the unicorn now lacking its horn that he broke off, suggestive of lost sexuality, while they danced together. Most important of all is the kiss that Jim shares with Laura which "lights her face inwardly with altar candles" in hope and expectation. But when he reveals his engagement to someone else, "the altar candles are snuffed out," replaced by "a look of almost infinite desolation." Having tasted physical sexuality in a moment that has been the climax of her emotional life thus far, Laura, the play suggests through its system of visual signs, is never likely to experience it again. Her condition seems destined to be one of perpetual loneliness and loss; nothing of the dream remains to retreat into. As a character in Maxine Kumin's novel, *The Designated Heir*, laments: "I wish it had never happened. . . . It's because a taste of happiness is hard to bear."

Tom faces the tension, which can never be resolved satisfactorily, between self and selfishness, between responsibility to developing his own potential and the obligation to help others, particularly his sister. In choosing to escape the limiting confines of the family in a boxed-in urban apartment, he incurs guilt, which he then tries to work out through the process of remembering. The text of *Glass Menagerie*, at least on one level, suggests that the process proves therapeutic. He has been haunted by the shadow of Laura in his restless wandering, seeing her over his shoulder as he peered into shop windows at bottles of colored glass; the thought of her has pursued him into movie theaters and bars where he met friends, one of the few forthright hints in the intensely autobiographical *Menagerie* of Williams's own homosexuality.

Now, however, he begs her "blow out your candles, Laura." That she accedes indicates not only her release of him but perhaps also her acceptance of her final condition of aloneness, since the lighted candles had been associated with hope of a loving relationship with a man. Her world closes in upon her, emotionally, psychologically, sexually. In life, Williams felt guilty over an inability to do anything to prevent the prefrontal lobotomy performed on his schizophrenic sister, Rose, that left her calmed but permanently limited, a guilt he would atone for the rest of his life by paying for her care in a number of sanitariums. Yet there remains a darker undercurrent to Laura's final gesture: her being permanently untouched by another human being leaves her pure and undefiled to become the imaginative source of many of Williams's most famous creations, from Laura in *Glass Menagerie*, through Blanche in *Streetcar Named Desire*, to Catherine Holly in *Suddenly Last Summer*, herself threatened with a lobotomy. Without Rose Williams, there might never have been a Tennessee. Yet if his art is a way of possessing her, it involves as well a violating of her by objectifying her as his subject. Paradoxically, it also becomes a means of atonement by memorializing her forever.

Williams's Southern Heroines

In *A Streetcar Named Desire* Williams gave audiences not only what he considered his "best play" but what may arguably be the finest work ever written for the American stage, possessing as it does, along with technical brilliance, what relatively few other American dramas attain, the psychological and thematic complexity most often attributable only to the novel. The play opened on Broadway on 3 December 1947 to a half-hour's standing ovation and critical acclaim—one reviewer wrote, "Williams is certainly the Eugene O'Neill of the present period"[6]—and went on to run for 855 performances. It has provided a stellar role on stage and screen for a succession of fine actresses: Jessica Tandy, Uta Hagen, Vivien Leigh, Tallulah Bankhead, Claire Bloom, Ann-Margret, Blythe Danner, Jessica Lange. Setting his play in the ethnically and racially mixed French Quarter of New Orleans, Williams dramatizes what results when a southern woman's dream of beauty and refinement is challenged by the vulgarity and brutality of the mechanistic world, a brutality with which she, at one point at least and however unintentionally, cooperates.

Williams structures his drama using a vast network of dichotomies in characterization, imagery, and ideas as a means of expressing how fragmentation of experience and dissociation of sensibility lead inevitably to a tragic imbalance. Desire (Eros) is set over against Death (Thanatos); bright silks, colored lights, and jazz music against delicate pastels, a shaded lightbulb, and cathedral bells; the crudeness and violence perpetrated by the virile executioner against the gentility and kindness espoused by the fragile victim; fact against fantasy and body against spirit; the strength of the industrial North against the decadence of the agrarian South. Williams uses this system of binaries not to suggest that any one facet of existence should be privileged over or preferable to another, but rather to insist on life's organicism and to posit an androgynous ideal; to see experience as unresolvable antinomies ("either/or" instead of "both/ and") rather than integrative and whole constitutes one of humankind's most debilitating illnesses.

Blanche DuBois, herself both tigress and moth, unable to integrate sexual longings with an ideal of gentility—she wears a red satin robe as well as light pastels—is the illusionist who confronts Stanley Kowalski, the literalist who regards the unempirical realms of morality and the heart as totally expendable. Panicky over physical beauty that fades with time and drink, she must avoid the unremitting glare of the naked light bulb, and so covers it with a Chinese paper lantern. Yet the lantern can easily be torn off, as both Stanley and Mitch do, and crushed as if violated, and so becomes symbolic of Blanche herself. Williams's dramas regularly depend on visual symbolism, which he refers to as "nothing but the natural speech of drama": "symbols, when used respectfully, are the purest language of plays. Sometimes it would take page after tedious page of exposition to put across an idea that can be said with an object or a gesture on the lighted stage. . . . Art is made out of symbols the way your body is made out of vital tissue" (*Where I Live*, 45, 66).

Blanche, who constantly reinvents herself by creating the text in which she plays and artfully sets the stage for her many fluctuating roles, insists on the place of illusion in life, proclaiming, "I don't want realism. I want magic! Yes, yes, magic! I try to give that to people. I misrepresent things to them. I don't tell the truth. I tell what ought to be truth." As the critic and director Harold Clurman notes, she is "the potential artist in all of us. . . . Her lies are part of her will to beauty; her wretched romanticism is a futile reaching toward a fullness of life."[7] Just before her violation, in an attempt to recapture life as it was, or as she "remembers" its having been at the family plantation Belle Reve ("beautiful dream"), Blanche attires herself in long white evening gown, silver slippers, rhinestone tiara; but in a symbolic act, she breaks the hand mirror, for art cannot camouflage life or stop time, and reality will always betray the dream.

Belle Reve was lost through the "epic fornications" of her ancestors, and all of the old generation have fallen victim to "the Grim Reaper." Blanche herself has also endured the loss of her poetic young husband, Allan Gray, who shot himself after she discovered him in the arms of his homosexual lover and impulsively condemned him, "You disgust me." Her failure to respond compassionately and nonjudgmentally to another in time of need, even though she denies having acted premeditatedly from "deliberate cruelty," has led to a disrespect of self and a sense of guilt; she is haunted by "hearing" the strains of the Varsouviana polka that was playing when Allan pulled the trigger. Her guilt recalls that of Tom over his desertion of Laura in *Glass Menagerie*.

Blanche tries to assuage her sense of failure by running from "death" to "desire" through a compensatory series of liaisons with young soldiers that eventually result in her being fired from her high school teaching position. Yet Blanche deludes herself by attempting to deny that this sensual side, which runs counter to her dream of purity, is a part of her nature. Her repressed side demands expression in excess; her seductiveness, her exhibitionism, her hyperemotionality and developed fantasy life are all symptoms of her neurosis. Blanche, as Williams himself says, "is an hysteric" who distorts by exaggeration normal feminine characteristics and seeks sexual gratification to compensate for her powerlessness, under a system of male domination forged by the Cavalier myth of southern womanhood as an object put on a pedestal and kept economically dependent.

If Blanche turns to fantasy and the imagination as sources of strength in her vulnerability, Stanley overcompensates for his incompleteness, insecurity, and suspicion of tenderness as a sign of weakness through violence. He is a smasher of things and people, tearing up treasured letters, throwing food and dishes off the table and a radio out the window, verbally and physically abusing his wife, Stella, and finally raping the intruder Blanche on the night his son is born. Aggressive and apelike, Stanley wears "gaudy shirts" that are the "richly feathered plumage" of the male bird; the first image the audience sees of him is of "the gaudy seedbearer" bringing fresh meat home from the hunt and tossing the bloodied package to Stella. Although there may initially be something appealing about the down-to-earth humor of this returned soldier—indelibly played by a T-shirted Marlon Brando, who became an iconic image for later "angry young men" actors—as an agent of democratization who undercuts or erases class distinctions, nothing justifies his rape of Blanche. A creature of facticity and of the isolated moment of experience, Stanley does not think in moral terms at all, claiming to be without "a guilty bone" in his body. At times almost a parody of machismo, ordinarily he relates to others only through brute physicality.

Stanley does display a softer, even dependent, side, though, in his neo-Lawrentian love for his wife, a kind of pagan naturalism that "narcotizes" yet nevertheless invigorates her and guarantees new life for the family line. If sex can be a brutalization, it can also be a salvation. Stanley, however, desecrates that love at the very moment it reaches its highest fulfillment in the birth of the child. And Stella, in her guilt over choosing to believe Stanley's lie rather than the truth of Blanche's rape, might now turn from Stanley emotionally and center herself on the child. The play's final image is hardly that of a holy family, with Stanley reaching inside Stella's blouse to fondle her breast while she holds the swaddled babe, relating on the only level that Stanley can, the purely physical.

Blanche's last chance to make real the "magic" in her life comes in her relationship with Mitch, the "gentleman caller" who seems ready to marry and restore the self-respect she lost through failing Allan. Outwardly a sensitive mama's boy, Mitch seems inwardly to hate the woman who has controlled and limited his options for so long. When Blanche feels certain of their mutual love as a saving grace and affirmation of existence, she exclaims, "Sometimes—there's God—so quickly." Appropriately throughout the play, while indulging in calming and cleansing hot baths, she sings in the well-known lyric from "Paper Moon," "It wouldn't be make-believe / If you believed in me!" Yet Blanche's belief in Mitch's saving power is short-lived, for when he discovers her past indiscretions, he fails her as she had failed Allan; ironically, he treats her like the refined lady she claims to be by acting the perfect gentlemen who could never marry and bring home to mother the fallen woman.

As Blanche approaches her ultimate abasement, Williams dramatizes expressionistically her extreme vulnerability and the mental disintegration she undergoes through the screeching of alley cats, the glare of the locomotive headlights, the jungle cries, the grotesque and "lurid" reflections, the piano out of tune. She leaves the stage a violated madonna, dressed in the Della Robbia blue of the Renaissance religious painters. Her famous exit line, the poetic "I have always depended on the kindness of strangers," is, nevertheless, countered by the play's harsh and prosaic curtain line, "This game is seven-card stud," as the men, including a stunned and ineffectual Mitch, resume their poker game. For Blanche's retreat to the sanatorium may ultimately prove not all that "kind": the doctor on whose arm she exits actually entered to the strains of the dreaded Varsouviana; the stern and cruel nurse seems almost a reincarnation of the earlier woman in black selling "flowers for the dead"; and Blanche is not so far gone in madness that she does not realize that this doctor is not Shep Huntleigh, the mythical man of her romantic dreams come to rescue her. The kindness may be only temporary—

and the image of Rose Williams looms once more over the end of the play.

Whatever trace of vanity, selfishness, and deceit mars Blanche's character, Williams makes it perfectly clear that the Blanches of this world will always be infinitely preferable to the Stanleys who increasingly threaten their existence. Destruction is preferable to barbarism. In a passage central thematically to the play, Blanche utters Williams's twentieth-century reformulation of Shakespeare's Renaissance humanism as expressed in the "What a piece of work is man" soliloquy from *Hamlet*: "Maybe we are a long way from being made in God's image, but . . . there has been some progress. . . . Such things as art—as poetry and music—such kinds of new light have come into the world. . . . In some kinds of people tenderer feelings have had some little beginning! That we have got to make grow! . . . In this dark march toward whatever it is we're approaching. . . . Don't—don't hang back with the brutes!" These lines express the artist's premonition of entropy, of disorder and return to primal chaos.

This apocalyptic jeremiad to modern civilization on the brink of moral and aesthetic backsliding comes not from the mouth of the literalist but from the heart of the fabulist, and it intimates Williams's own statement of the play's meaning as "the ravishment of the tender, the sensitive, the delicate, by the savage and brutal forces of modern society." In the insistence of *A Streetcar Named Desire* on the need for mutuality among human beings; on the need for moral categories that are compassionate and flexible enough to admit differences, especially in the area of human sexuality; on the need to accept one's nature as fallen yet not become so mired in guilt as to despair of forgiveness; on the need for courage and gallantry in the face of hostility and rejection; on the need to accept time's passage and one's mutability without allowing one's spirit to be broken; and on the need to recognize art as a kind of secular sacrament that can sanctify by reaching beyond empirical data into the realm of ethics and the heart, Williams felt that the play really expressed "everything" he ever wanted to say.

Although the label "morality play" has been used to describe other Williams works, such as *The Milk Train Doesn't Stop Here Anymore*, it designates most accurately the nature of *Summer and Smoke*, first produced by Margo Jones at her regional theater in Dallas and then in New York in 1948. The play did not come into its own as a major work until José Quintero triumphantly directed it with Geraldine Page in her first starring role at the Circle in the Square in 1953, which might almost be said to mark the beginning of the off-Broadway movement. Elements in the stage setting represent the flesh or body, the spirit or soul, and eternity or the otherworldly, carrying on the pattern of oppositions noticed in the characters, imagery, and symbolism of A *Streetcar Named Desire.*

Set in Glorious Hill, Mississippi, during the first 15 years of this century, the play employs a split set. One side of the stage features the tracery of a Victorian Gothic house, with a romantic landscape on the wall, that is the Episcopal rectory; on the other side is a similar house, with an anatomy chart on the wall, that is the office of the Doctors Buchanan, father and later son. In between sits the town park, with a fountain in the shape of a stone angel named "Eternity"; overarching all by day is a sky of the Renaissance blue of religious art, abode of some universal force or power, and by night revealing the constellations and the Milky Way. Yet unlike the medieval morality play in its most widely known iteration in *Everyman,* which concerns how properly to prepare for and face death, *Summer and Smoke* focuses on how to live so as to prevent a death-in-life.

Partly because Williams himself spent his early days in the Episcopal rectory of his maternal grandfather, in "the shadow" of the church, he felt a particular kinship with his creation Alma Winemiller, a minister's daughter whom he believes "may very well be the best female portrait [he has] drawn in a play. She simply seemed to exist somewhere in [his] being and it was no effort to put her on paper" (*Memoirs,* 109). When first seen in the prologue as a child of 10, Alma, whose name in Spanish means "soul," assumes the attitude of the angel, hands cupped "in a way similar to that of receiving the wafer at Holy Communion." By the time of the play proper, which begins on one Fourth of July just before the war, the hardly independent Alma has become an excessively proper premature spinster given to palpitations and "nervous breathless laughter" that suggest her hysteria, symptom of the restraints and unreal expectations that social mores have placed on her.

Young Dr. John Buchanan diagnoses her problem as "a doppelgänger"; she has repressed her true nature, a hidden self, rather than grant it free expression. Sowing his wild oats through drinking, gambling, and whoring, John hardly fulfills Alma's elevated, idealized notion of what humankind in general, let alone someone with a doctor's vocation, should be: "more religious" than even a priest, he should "serve humanity" by relieving "the fearful suffering—and fear" endemic to the human condition. So his life, she judges, is a "desecration." Even Buchanan himself grants that his research for a cure to a fever should bring him closer to the Creator; though a microscope cannot show you God, it can reveal "a mysterious . . . universe . . . Part anarchy—and part order!" that might be seen as "[t]he footprints of God!"

In a speech reminiscent of Blanche's Hamlet-like encomium to humankind's potential for becoming more, so long as it does not "hang back with the apes," Alma employs the image of the Gothic cathedrals with their arches and vaults and spires all reaching heavenward to express her restraining of the flesh ("All of us are in the gutter") in order to reach the stars: "that is the secret, the principle back of existence—the everlasting struggle and aspiration for more than our human limits have placed in our reach." Although Williams never denies that there exists something more than the purely physical, the body cannot, as Alma seems to desire, be completely bypassed to reach it, as the eyes of the poet know; there is, in fact, something oddly similar in the images of the cathedral spire and the exploding roman candles to which John had earlier given a decidedly sexual thrust. To be stone, like the angel, is to be less rather than more human; men and women must live first in time and not for eternity, since that would mean denying full participation in life.

The lesson Buchanan draws for Alma from the anatomy chart in the doctor's office parallels hers on the Gothic cathedrals. Saying that the brain hungers for truth, the belly for food, and "the sex . . . for love because it is sometimes lonesome," he claims: "I've fed all three, as much of all three as I could or as much as I wanted." For him, as Shakespeare would say, the "soul is sense." He goes on to accuse Alma of having "fed none," since she is roped in by "hand-me-down notions!—attitudes!—poses." Because he has read the anatomy chart only with the eyes of someone who admits nothing beyond empirical data, he has misread Alma. For it is not that she denies human sexuality; rather, she refuses to accept that love is not a matter of the heart as well as of the genitalia.

After Papa Gonzales, to whom John is indebted over gambling and whose daughter, Rosa, he has taken as a lover, shoots and kills the elder Dr. Buchanan, the young doctor undergoes a reformation that he attributes in part to the influence of Alma, but who can never be more to him than a substitute for the mother he lost as a child or an inviolate older sister, "a lady." Lionized for his medical discoveries, he gives over the fiery and exotic Rosa for an engagement to the innocent Nellie. More important, he comes to believe that there is, indeed, "an immaterial something" not visible on the anatomy chart. Some critics have suggested that Williams's play follows the hourglass structure: John begins in the flesh and ascends to the spirit, while Alma begins in the spirit and descends to the flesh, replaying Blanche and Mitch, who come close to a consummation but who pass in the night without achieving it. Yet *Summer and Smoke* deflates any notion that life can be seen in simplistic binaries. The play suggests strongly that sex and love will be more easily fused and balanced in the marriage between John and Nellie because John had never bifurcated his identity by denying the flesh. Alma, who admits a fragmentation or division within herself, comes to recognize that a spiritualized angel is a creature of an unearthly existence, not of the here and now, for "her body is stone and her blood is mineral water."

The final scene of the play, in which Alma gives herself physically to the lonely traveling salesman, should not to be seen as a descent into a life of profligacy, but as the beginning of Alma's initiation into integrated personhood. The pills that calm her and that she shares with the man are one of life's "little mercies" so that "we are able to keep on going": "The prescription number is 96814. I think of it as the telephone number of God!" she says. Williams, whom Nancy Tischler, one of his first important critics, calls a "rebellious puritan," sees sexuality as part of that grace, too. Alma had always possessed spirituality. But now she begins to experience humanity.

A Dionysiac Interlude

The Rose Tattoo (1950) brims over with color and vibrancy, earthiness and sensuality. Williams's most forthright expression of sexuality as sacrament, it celebrates the victory of life over death, of generativity over sterility, opposites symbolized onstage by the dressmaker's mannequins of an appropriately appareled "widow and a bride who face each other in violent attitudes, as though having a shrill argument." In his *Memoirs*, Williams calls *Rose Tattoo* his "love play to the world" (162), and it does show him somewhat uncharacteristically exuberant, partly over his relationship with Frank Merlo, who introduced him to Sicily and the spirited people who would be his play's prototypes. Yet it also finds him carried away with an excess of symbolism, what Tom Wingfield in *The Glass Menagerie* acknowledged as the "poet's weakness." Just as Amanda's home in Blue Mountain was overrun with daffodils from admirers, here everything's coming up roses, the flower of sexual passion and love after which his sister was named: people wear clothes made of rose-colored silk and roses in their hair, sometimes doused with rose oil; there is rose-patterned wallpaper and rose-colored carpet, and a bowl of roses adorns a table while a design of roses decorates a paper fan. (Arthur Kopit will later satirize William's obsessive symbolism in this work and elsewhere in his parodic farce, *Oh Dad, Poor Dad, Mama's Hung You in the Closet and I'm Feeling So Sad* [1961].) As Bigsby notes, Williams's symbols when "most effective . . . share with poetry an ability to condense experience and also, by implication, to evade the deceptive nature of language. At their worst . . . they are an alternative to action, a radical simplification of complex issues."[8]

The "exclamatory . . . brightness" of the setting in *Rose Tattoo* is intended as a visual "projection" of the voluptuous Serafina delle Rose, whose "heart [is] passionately in love" with her husband, Rosario; feeling a sharp pain and seeing the rose tattoo miraculously transferred from his chest to her breast after their love making, she knows that she has conceived a child. Their love, she deceptively believes, can stop time; it is not subject to change and loss. Rosario, nevertheless, is shot and killed and his truck burned while smuggling contraband goods for the Brothers Romano along the Gulf Coast, and Serafina miscarries. In an action the parish priest regards as self-indulgent and idolatrous, she reserves Rosario's ashes in an urn before a shrine to the Virgin so they will "stay clean" and "don't decay"; in her despondency, for three years she barely dresses and never leaves the house, believing she would be "cheap and degraded" to ever love another. Serafina's religion is more pagan superstition than Catholic; she holds with signs and miracles and wonders, and fears the neighborhood Strega, or witch. Indeed, the local doctor has greater wisdom than the priest, understanding that people "find God in each other. And when they lose each other, they lose God and they're lost." For as long as she can, Serafina resists and declares as a lie what the community knows: that Rosario had been having an affair with the blonde Estelle Hohengarten. Her contention that "known facts" do not tell the whole story, that matters of the heart reign superior to empirical data and can sustain one while facts only diminish, echoes William's own insistence that "[i]t is the dissatisfaction with empiric evidence that makes the poet and the mystic" (*Where I Live*, 55).

Alvaro Mangiacavallo, a swarthy Mediterranean type who also drives a banana rig and claims to be grandson to the village idiot, arrives to turn back time and restore Serafina to life and love in a "world gone cold." Mocked by a local novelty salesman as a "Wop," "Dago," and "greaseball," Alvaro, feeling himself unmanly, breaks into tears, which releases Serafina's grief. He accuses her of having denied life by putting her "heart in the marble urn with the ashes" and counsels it is time to allow her daughter, Rosa, to move from innocence to experience in the arms of the sailor Jack; as she finally sends them off with her blessing, she neglects to give Rosa the watch she bought for a graduation present, signifying that love does conquer time, if only temporarily. When Serafina accepts the truth about Rosario and Estelle, she rejects the Blessed Mother and smashes the urn; the ashes blowing free symbolize her heart now released for renewal. As she and Alvaro make love, the sky takes on the color of the Madonna's robes; physical nature and the instinctual are not only sanctioned but sanctified. The pain in her breast and the transference of Alvaro's rose tattoo recur, as the women pass the rose silk shirt of the "seed bearer," sewn for Rosario but worn only by Alvaro, amongst them in a Dionysian ritual, to conclude a play that Williams saw as "being a true celebration of the inebriate god" (*Where I Live*, 57), complete with a live goat running free across stage. For once in his drama he had broken unabashedly and unashamedly free of the Puritan within.

Dramatizing the Closet

The action of *Cat on a Hot Tin Roof* (1955) really begins, like that of *A Streetcar Named Desire*, long before the curtain goes up, in one character's ill-measured response to a revelation of homosexuality; the awareness of failure is followed, in each case, by self-disgust and guilt. Williams underlines the similar pattern through aural imagery: Blanche, in the more expressionistic *Streetcar Named Desire*, literally hears the strains of the Varsouviana polka until the sound of the gunshot obliterates them; Brick Pollitt, in *Cat on a Hot Tin Roof*, drinks until he hears "the click" of a telephone disconnection, quieting his pangs of conscience and fear of facing his sexual identity.

Brick exists in a state of physical disability and spiritual disrepair. A former football player turned sports announcer, he tried to turn back time the night before and recreate his former glory days of athletic prowess by jumping the hurdles on the high school track; he fell, and now hobbles around with the aid of a crutch. The injured leg is clearly meant to symbolize a loss of power; without the crutch he is dependent on others, whereas with it in hand he is armed with a kind of weapon. The deeper malaise from which he suffers depends on a different kind of crutch,

Barbara Bel Geddes as Maggie and Ben Gazzara as Brick in the original Broadway production of *Cat on a Hot Tin Roof*. *Bob Golby Collection, Harry Ransom Humanities Research Center, The University of Texas at Austin.*

drink, to see him through. One of the two most prominent items on stage, in fact, is "a monumental monstrosity peculiar to our times, a huge console combination of radio-phonograph . . . TV set and liquor cabinet. . . . a very complete and compact little shrine to virtually all the comforts and illusions behind which we hide from such things as the characters in the play are faced with."

Despite his disgust with "mendacity" in all its myriad forms, what the sullen and seemingly indifferent Brick hides from is his moral culpability in the death of his friend Skipper. Although Brick claims that on his part the relationship was a perfectly "pure" and noble one completely devoid of anything "dirty," the only physical manifestation being clasped hands across the space between the twin beds when they were roommates, clearly on Skipper's part it was homoerotic in desire if not in act. Williams leaves the exact contents of Skipper's phone call to Brick unstated, but Skipper apparently confessed his homosexual desires. Unable to bear the truth that sullied and shattered his ideal, and/or thrown into turmoil over a recognition that he shared in those feelings, Brick hangs up on Skipper. Afterward, Skipper, like Allan in *Streetcar Named Desire*, commits suicide.

Williams's protestations that "Brick is definitely not a homosexual" (*Conversations, Williams,* 35) notwithstanding, several critics have found the playwright evasive or even dishonest in his characterization of Brick, rather than simply imbuing him with the ambiguity that he claims desirable in any drama: "Some mystery should be left in the revelation of a character in a play, just as a great deal of mystery is always left in the revelations of character in life, even in one's own character to himself." The pained subtext in *Cat on a Hot Tin Roof* might very well be, then, that of the latent homosexual forced by societal pressures and family expectations to "cure" his sexual orientation through a heterosexual union; in David Savran's terms, what happens in the bed after the final curtain will be a "perpetuation of a homosexual economy and [witness] to the force of Maggie's fetishistic appropriation of Skipper's sexuality."[9] Bigsby chooses to explain the ambiguity of Brick's character from a slightly different perspective: "In some fundamental sense it is less a potential homosexuality which is the heart of Brick's dilemma than his fear of life, his desire to resist a process which pulls him into the world of sexual and emotional maturity with its tensions, its profound ambivalences and its causal implications. This is, in a sense, the fundamental dilemma of the Williams protagonist" (Bigsby 1984, 93).

In the early 1950s when *Cat on a Hot Tin Roof* was written— and long thereafter—the American atmosphere was as militantly antigay as it was anti-Communist; indeed, the House Un-American Activities Committee impugned both groups almost equally as security risks. What Williams could write of openly in several of his short stories, including "One Arm" and "Desire and the Black Masseur," had to remain unspoken on stage, or at least hidden from largely homophobic audiences and critics. As Savran notes, Williams negotiated this forbidden territory by writing " 'under a number of screens and covers' which would allow him to represent his homosexuality in other guises: as a valorization of eroticism generally and extra-marital desire, in particular; as an endorsement of transgressive liaisons that cut across lines of social class, ethnicity and race, and violate mid-century social prescriptions; and as a deep sympathy for the outside [*sic*] and the disenfranchised, for 'the fugitive kind' " (58–59).

Even if one accepts the dramatist's extratextual designation of Brick's sexuality, and so finds the homosexual character still absent from the stage (present only through discussion of Skipper), in *Cat on a Hot Tin Roof* Williams does stage the homosexual closet. The bed-sitting room of the plantation house, dominated by an ornate double bed, had once been occupied by the two bachelors, Jack Straw and Peter Ochello.

This room, shared by the two lovers for 30 years, "is gently and poetically haunted by a relationship that must have involved a tenderness which was uncommon." Brick's father, Big Daddy, was taken in by them, and inherited the land from them, so their patrimony, the power they pass on, is financial as well as sexual. As even John Clum, who unlike Savran ordinarily criticizes Williams as decidedly heterosexist, comments: "The bed of Jack Straw and Peter Ochello represents an unstated ideal relationship that seems unattainable for the heterosexual marriages in Williams [sic] play. In positing this ideal, the play is subversive for its time. . . . The paradox in Williams' presentation of his homosexual characters is that the feared homosexuality, for which there is not positive language [except silent hints in the stage directions], also has the potential for creativity, sensitivity, and, as we see in Jack Straw and Peter Ochello, abiding love."[10]

Williams, along with leaving a deliberate vagueness in Brick's character, further decenters him by not referencing him in *Cat on a Hot Tin Roof*'s title. Instead, the title character (who has proved a marvelous role over the years for such actresses as Barbara Bel Geddes, Elizabeth Taylor, Elizabeth Ashley, and Kathleen Turner) is his tough-skinned and sensual wife, Maggie, who clings tenaciously to her husband and her marriage, and to her goal of having a child by Brick who will inherit the land. Although not entirely free from greed and a desire to secure her position in the family after a girlhood of deprivation, her actions are other than merely selfish. Granted, she is determined not to let her marriage fail partly because she is eaten up with sexual longing. Her motive, nonetheless, also involves taking hold of Brick and restoring to him some measure of self-respect: "Oh, you weak . . . beautiful people!—who give up.—What you need is someone to—take hold of you—Gently, gently, with love! And—I do love you." She never claims to be "good," only "honest"; she admits to having gone to bed with Skipper as a way for the two of them to get closer to Brick, but also to prove Skipper's homosexuality, which she now realizes "destroyed" him.

Maggie hopes to find her definition and sense of completion as a woman in her ability to restore Brick to wholeness, although it is unlikely that any woman could accomplish this, just as it appears that Blanche could never save Allan. Williams, however, at the urging of the play's director, Elia Kazan, rewrote the third act before its Broadway opening to clarify and confirm in the audience's mind Maggie's success in accomplishing Brick's regeneration. When she avers in the revised third act that there is "life" in her, she is not yet pregnant and so appears to be lying, but the lie is potentially true. Her love and determination to hand Brick's life back to him "like something gold [he] let go of" is the life that she exudes and that Big Daddy, who "hates" all lies and liars, affirms when he proclaims, "this girl has life in her body, that's no lie." The potential for giving life physically will become actual when, having thrown out Brick's liquor bottles and crutch, she leads him off to bed.

In an extended and astute commentary, Williams's fellow playwright Arthur Miller analyzes Brick's capitulation as symptomatic of his failure to "question absolutely everything." Whereas earlier Brick clung to his image of friendship "as to a banner of purity to flaunt against the world, and more precisely, against the decree of nature to reproduce himself, to become in turn the father, the master of the earth, the administrator of the tainted and impure world" of "money-lust, power-lust," Brick now does not see through to or force "the ultimate question of the right of society to renew itself when it is, in fact, unworthy"; he shirks from "weigh[ing] . . . the question of [the race's] own right to biological survival—and one thing more, the question of the fate of the sensitive and the just in an impure world of power" (*Theater Essays,* 190–91). Brick himself, however, in the version the firstnighters saw—but that Williams would later reject—admires Maggie and assents to the creativity within her, admitting "truth is something desperate, an' she's got it." Literally occurring on his father Big Daddy's sixty-fifth birthday, the play marks a kind of birth day for Brick as well.

Yet it is also tantamount to a death day for Big Daddy, since he finds out that he is dying of bowel cancer. Like the crutch and the liquor cabinet, the cancer becomes heavily symbolic, in this instance of the avariciousness tearing the family apart as Brick's brother, Gooper, and his wife, Mae, a virtual baby factory producing little "no necked monsters," vie with Brick and Maggie for control of the plantation. The family patriarch possesses a bounding lust for life, tenaciously clinging to it because "There's nothing else to hold onto." When he must die, he wants his chance at immortality through leaving the land he loves ("twenty-eight thousand acres of the richest land this side of the Valley Nile") to a son who will see that the inheritance is nurtured as Big Daddy would want it to be.

In William's original draft, Big Daddy disappeared after act 2, but Kazan felt instinctively, and probably correctly, that he was too potent a force not to be brought back on stage, if only to tell a ribald elephant joke, "bless" the (re)union of Maggie and Brick, and prepare to "give up" his land, before the audience would hear his cries for morphine and be reminded of the finiteness facing even the strong. In the brilliantly handled confrontation between father and son in act 2, Brick and Big Daddy thrust and parry verbally, and at points physically, either deliberately or inadvertently moving closer to the truths about the cancer that is consuming the father and the guilt that is festering and eating away at the son. At a climactic moment, Big Daddy knocks the crutch out from under Brick, and the human gesture of a hand clutching another hand makes a powerful visual statement. Williams gives voice to one of the central literary themes of the postwar period: the difficulty, and yet the inescapable need for, communication between individuals. This need was even underscored in the original production by having the central characters speak directly to the audience across the footlights in what Brenda Murphy calls "recitatives" that "foreground[ed the] production's theatricality,"[11] as suggested in William's vision of walls that dissolved in the open sky above.

In *Suddenly Last Summer* (1958), the longer of two one-act plays presented together under the collective title *Garden District* because of their common setting in the upper-crust area of New Orleans away from the raffish French Quarter, the homosexual character is still absent and unseen, though his darkness is made visible through the extended narrative of his cousin, Catherine Holly. One of this taut play's brilliances, in fact, resides in William's ability to maintain suspense about an "action" already completed in the past and only reported, rather than shown as it would be in the highly successful screen version starring Katharine Hepburn, Elizabeth Taylor, and Montgomery Clift. The tension in the play, however, finally has more to do with how the other characters onstage, and the theater audience, "read" and judge Catherine's text.

Suddenly Last Summer moves simultaneously on three levels. On one level, it dramatizes the struggle between the poet Sebastian Venable's mother, Violet, and Catherine, threatened with a lobotomy if she spreads her horrific tale of cannibalism, to possess him by controlling his memory and reputation. On another, it limns the failure of a poet with a unique if obsessional vision who is completely inverted and turned in on himself, rejecting any public role for his art. On yet a third, it serves as a parable or allegory "of our time and the world we live in," though the play's detractors might judge its depiction of a cannibalistic world as merely "hideous" and deny its claim to universality.

The work's overarching image of cannibalization, established through "a tropical jungle" garden setting, complete with Venus flytrap, where the "massive tree-flowers . . . suggest organs of a body, torn out, still glistening with undried blood" and where "there are harsh cries and sibilant hissings . . . of savage nature," stems at least in part from Williams's own horror over the lobotomizing of his beloved sister, Rose. Indeed, one of the central characters, Dr. Cukrowicz, performs just such "radical" and "risky" operations at his hospital; though the surgery succeeds in pacifying his patients, Cukrowicz remains haunted over whether there will be "any possibility, afterward, of reconstructing a— totally sound person, [for] it may be that the person will always be limited afterwards, relieved of acute disturbances but—limited."

The garden here is partially internalized, representing a psychological state of mind. Everyone in the play preys on or uses others, thus reducing them to objects: Sebastian employed first his mother and then, when her attractiveness had faded, his cousin as procurers of his young lovers; his mother had used Sebastian as an escort to ensure the illusion of youth; Sebastian had come to consider his lovers as if they were just so many "new items" on some "menu"; Mrs. Venable, along with threatening to have Catherine's story "cut out" of her, tries to bribe the doctor with the promise of research funding if he helps destroy Catherine; Catherine's insufferably materialistic mother and brother think almost wholly in terms of securing the inheritance from Sebastian; and the flock of naked boys finally strip and attack and devour Sebastian under the Georgia O'Keefe-like image of a sun that looked as if some "huge white bone had caught on fire in the sky." Nor are nature and nature's God exempt from the charge, for just as the birds in the Encantades attack the newly hatched sea turtles, a capricious God seems to use his creatures, both animal and human, for "his sport."

The jealously demanding Violet Venable lives for and through her son, protecting him so that he could write and privately print for a tiny coterie one perfect poem each summer of his life, as if he were bringing forth a child; with an "exalted" look, she raises the volume "as if elevating the Host before the altar." Yet Sebastian's life that last summer becomes a perverse ritual, almost a Black Mass in which he, "look[ing] like a big white-paper-wrapped bunch of red roses had been torn," becomes the sacrificial victim. As in Melville, the power of darkness can come clothed in white. Admitting no disjunction between his life and his poetry, Sebastian's final work of art, his death as substitute for his last poem that is never written, seems subconsciously chosen and embraced so that it will conform with and affirm his dark version of existence. Watching the devouring of the sea turtles by the birds in the Encantadas, Sebastian claims to have seen God in the savagery and ferocity; Cukrowicz, who believes that scientists must "look harder for [God] than priests," admits that "such a spectacle could be equated with a good deal of— experience, existence!" but denies it could be equated "with God!".

At the same time that the artist must see the truth, no matter how horrifying, still he or she must not distort it. Catherine's tale, accepted by all the listeners except Violet as honest and containing "the possibility" of truth—even her brother George backs off from his mercenary concerns—is valorized by Cukrowicz as a "vision," moving her narrative into the realm of art. Once again, Williams holds that nature "tooth and claw" and the evil in humankind must never be negated by the artist; neither, of course, must they be exaggerated to the exclusion of all else as the sum total of life's meaning. As Williams claims in an essay of a few years later, "I dare to suggest, from my POV [point of view], that the theater has made in our time its greatest artistic advance through the unlocking and lighting up and ventilation of the closets, attics, and basements of human behavior and experience" (*Where I Live*, 116–17). In *Suddenly Last Summer*, while still keeping the homosexual offstage, Williams unmasks as in almost no other of his plays.

Acts of Interconnectedness

Williams's long-held conviction that "time is the enemy" of physical beauty, of the giving heart, and of the creative artist coalesces in his last important play of the 1950s, *Sweet Bird of Youth* (1959). Academic critics might point to several deficiencies in the work: structural diffuseness— even Williams felt that act 2, written to expand the play to full length, was almost a play in itself; stylistic incoherence—the nonrealistic devices appear to lack integration with the rest of the text; a mix of too-insistent symbolism—Williams blends extensive classical, Christian, and archetypal imagery; and questionable universality—the hero, who undergoes castration, hardly seems morally representative. But audiences responded favorably, and with good justification, for 375 performances to the original production starring Geraldine Page and Paul Newman, who went on to repeat their roles in the 1962 film version.

If cannibalism, the fate and sacrificial punishment of Sebastian, became the overriding symbol in *Suddenly Last Summer*, here physical castration, the fate and atonement of Chance Wayne, becomes centrally symbolic: in the "flesh-hungry," "blood thirsty ogre country" along the

Mississippi Gulf coast that these characters either inhabit or pass through, time castrates; fame castrates; fear and hate castrate; racial bigotry castrates. And all of these things, because they cause one to be obsessed with self, prevent the loss of self necessary for going out to and embracing the other, as is seen through Williams's dual protagonists.

Alexandra Del Lago, the Princess Kosmonopolis, an aging movie queen, finds refuge from what she thought was a disastrous film comeback by taking drugs and going to bed with a handsome young stud who has Hollywood aspirations beyond his talent. The movie screen can foster illusions and even, in rare instances, raise experience to the level of art, yet it also magnifies flaws; when Alexandra saw her fading physical beauty enlarged and made permanent on the screen, she misread the viewers' reaction as mockery and ran from the theater. A former sex object herself, she now uses Chance for pleasure and reassurance; people treat each other as commodities, asking only what they can get out of them.

Sometimes, however, the gulf of incommunication can be bridged and the other becomes a person rather than an object. When Chance performs a little act of grace by responding to the Princess's desperate need for oxygen, it reawakens within her a feeling of self-dignity and concern for another that she thought gone forever; not totally a hardened "monster," her heart can go out to him. Yet as soon as she learns from the gossip columnist that her comeback has been an extraordinary success, she pulls back into absorption with the self. Grasping at what she knows can be at best a temporary reprieve until the next rejection, she grows harsh and cold, justifying self-sufficiency in the guise of a Beckettian endurance of going on alone. Williams dramatizes this destructive egoism and solipsism through Alexandra's frequent gazing at herself narcissistically in the mirror that is to be imagined as in "the fourth wall," as well as through the monologues that the characters fall into when they seem to have retreated into interiority, cut off from others.

Williams's other protagonist, Chance Wayne, an Adonis beginning to show his age, is a former chorus boy turned masseuse who exacts from the Princess the promise of a Hollywood screen test. He stops in St. Cloud on the way to the promised Eden to renew his relationship with Heavenly Finley. In their teens, Chance and Heavenly were regarded as a golden couple; their love ended in a pregnancy Heavenly was forced to abort by her politician father, making her sterile. This leaves Chance troubled by guilt, in much the same way that Tom in *Glass Menagerie* is tormented over Laura's aloneness and perpetual virginity as the love object of the writer/brother's imagination. Chance learns that love can eventuate in hurt and that it cannot necessarily turn back time, or renew creativity or generativity, or restore lost innocence. Given the choice to leave or stay, he chooses to remain and face castration at the hands of Finley's henchmen. What secures him the right to such an atonement is not only his remorse but, more important, his positive response to Alexandra's earlier cry for help. The fugitive chooses to rest in active suffering.

In a challenging and often misunderstood speech that ends the play, Chance addresses the audience from the forestage: "I don't ask for your pity, but just for your understanding—not even that, no. Just for your recognition of me in you, and the enemy, time, in us all." The recognition that he desires is a moral insight by the audience so that they might respect him as the Princess did at his best moment, when, despite his later retreat back into putting self before others, she saw that his inherent instinct toward good still exists. The religious imagery that adumbrates the play is both classical (the waxing and waning of the god Adonis; the sacred palm groves associated with the fertility kings) and Christian (church bells, lilies, palms, the "Alleluia Chorus" of Passiontide and Easter), and it speaks to pain and death leading to resurrection and rebirth. But although the play occurs on Easter Sunday, it ends not on the morning of the Resurrection but on the Easter evening of doubt and challenge to the disciples' faith and belief.

Williams expresses this doubt and anxiety through the Heckler at the political rally in act 2, who challenges Boss Finley's portrayal of himself as an anointed prophet of the Old Testament God of vengeance and jealousy, protecting the racial purity of southern womanhood, even though to do so means fetishizing his daughter, Heavenly, to manipulate the crowd's reaction. Though only a minor character, the Heckler holds a privileged status as the audience's onstage representative, and so his central utterance, "that the silence of God, the absolute speechlessness of Him is a long and awful thing that the whole world is lost because of," assumes added weight. The theatergoers share in his moral indignation and—like Chance, who becomes an onstage audience as well—experience outrage over his beating. Like Chance, the Heckler, too, undergoes a kind of castration by being silenced and denied a voice.

Williams has conceived the stage setting for act 2 so that at one point Chance looks at the imaginary fourth wall as if it were a TV screen showing the crowd at the rally; but because those whom Chance "sees" and the audience are one and the same, the theater audience is translated into the mob at Finley's gathering and thereby faced with the political and moral challenge to reject all he stands for. In almost Brechtian fashion, they are called upon to respond intellectually, to distrust the steamroller tactics of media magnification, and to read the text correctly as the Heckler does. The metatheatrical moments in *Sweet Bird* constitute some of the most subtle and astute uses of the physical stage as a potential purveyor of meaning in all of Williams's dramatic output.

Williams's least characteristic long work from the 1940s and 1950s—it could almost be argued from his entire playwriting career—is *Camino Real* (1953). It was never given an entirely satisfactory New York production, either in its original staging by Elia Kazan, starring Eli Wallach and Jo Van Fleet, or in its full-scale revival at Lincoln Center in 1970, with Al Pacino and Jessica Tandy, the original Blanche DuBois. Conceptually more a dramatic poem than a traditional play, what Williams himself calls a "fairy tale or masque" (*Conversations, Williams,* 31), it has always proven difficult for audiences, perhaps because its very lyrical theatricality and diffuseness have distracted them from following its line of action, so that the subtle climactic moment passes unnoticed. Evidently forgetting some of Thornton Wilder's experimental techniques in *Skin of Our Teeth,* Williams overemphasized the innovativeness of the staging in *Camino Real,* claiming to be the first dramatist to send characters up the center aisle of the auditorium and into the boxes and balcony. Such free use of the playing space contributes to a carnivalesque fantasy not intended to appeal to the logical mind; deliberately "meant most for the vulgarity of performance," the text is a mere "blueprint" that demands to be choreographed as much as staged—indeed, Kazan was assisted by the dancer, Anna Sokolow.

What Kazan sees as Williams's most personal work, one "as private as a nightmare that penetrates the soul of the artist" (494), has, predictably, always been dear to its author's heart and has provoked extraordinarily explicit comments about what he was attempting to convey: Williams is telling the "romantic nonconformist in modern society" about the absolute necessity to "cling to romanticism, not out of weak sentimentality, but in the sense of adhering to gallantry as far as you can go" (*Conversations, Williams,* 67). He continues by saying that he feels he is propounding "a religious attitude in an august, mystical sense" in this play that holds forth the poets and the artists and the creatures of their imagination as the ultimate fugitives and outsiders in an increasingly materialistic society.

If *Glass Menagerie* is expressionistic insofar as it attempts to objectify the inner reality of Tom Wingfield, *Camino Real* is expressionistic in that it stages the subjectivity of Tennessee Williams himself, through casting it as a dream vision in the mind of a literary figure, Miguel Cervantes's knight errant, Don Quixote. In the prologue, Quixote arrives in the town square of Tierra Caliente, where the "royal highway" has diminished into simply the "real road." On opposite sides of the square, Williams juxtaposes the Siete Mares Hotel—a watering hole for the well-to-do run by the somewhat sinister Gutman, who also serves as Stage Manager, calling out each of the 16 "Blocks" (or scenes) on the Camino Real—and the Ritz Men Only, a low-life flophouse whose overseer bears the unsavory name of A. Ratt. This setting throws the haves into sharp contrast with the have-nots. Periodically traversing the desolate plaza, which at one point resembles a city devastated by bombardment, are the street cleaners, actually collectors of the dead. Given the country's social conditions, and because an unseen Generalissimo rules this banana re-public by force of military police, *Camino Real* has been considered by Donald Spoto to be Williams's only "frankly political play to open in New York" (185); and, indeed, Williams himself claimed he was reflecting a "reduction in human liberties" whereby the "wild of heart [are] kept in cages" (*Conversations, Williams,* 31–32).

The text contains explicit references to a kind of thought patrol ("the exchange of serious questions and ideas is regarded unfavorably") to an intolerance of rebelliousness, and to a squelching of the "spirit of anarchy." In fact, although Williams proved always to be more interested in "humanitarian impulses" rather than "partisan prejudices," the origi-nal production was even "attacked" by columnists Walter Winchell and Ed Sullivan "as anti-American" (Spoto, 187, 189). Yet it seems finally more richly metaphysical than blatantly political in its import, as is suggested by a further element of the stage set. Beyond "the ominous arch" between the city and the distant mountains sits the Terra Incognita, a fearful "wasteland" or "void" that faces any of life's permanent transients who would dare venture forth. The human condition is one of suspension between birth and death, wherein all creatures tend to be "maimed, . . . deformed and mutilated" and whose luck runs out the day they are born; they are "a work in progress. . . . guinea pigs in the laboratory of [a] God" who has been lulled to sleep by all "the Mumbo Jumbo" hu-mankind subjects Him to. The only means of possible escape comes via a plane aptly named the Fugitivo that people clamor to board, though it is destined to crash.

In the play's prologue, Don Quixote, the ultimate romantic ideal-ist, arrives at this place where "the spring of humanity has gone dry."

Deserted by Sancho Panza, and believing it "inexcusably selfish to be lonely alone," he determines to choose a new sidekick. Then he falls asleep, and the play becomes his dream vision wherein other legendary figures, both real and imaginary, appear to him, including Proust's Baron Charlus; Lord Byron; Jacques Casanova and Marguerite Gauthier/Camille; and Kilroy, the archetypal wanderer who ultimately ventures into the Terra Incognita with Quixote to enter the world of myth. For his part, Lord Byron decries the way he has allowed the seeking of pleasure to interfere with fulfilling his vocation, though he blames this on the need to find "agreeable distractions" from "the frightening solitude of a poet." Yet he still understands, and this could just as well be Williams speaking, that the role of a poet is a transformative one, "to influence the heart . . . to purify it and lift it above its ordinary level," so that the heart can translate *"noise* into *music,* chaos into . . . *a mysterious order!"*

The vagrant, ailing Kilroy enters wearing the golden gloves and CHAMP belt buckle that point to his former glory; his "golden-heart" as big as a baby's head has meant that he can no longer risk satisfying his wife sexually, and so he sacrificed the rarely found warmth of love and unselfishly left her rather than turn her life of "light into night." Gutman sees the former hero as a patsy, and so during the fiesta makes him don the embarrassing clown outfit, just as he has Casanova crowned king of the cuckolds, but Kilroy and Casanova, both believers in the importance of romance, help each other remove these degrading outfits. Infinite "patience" and "courage" are the requisite virtues.

When the gypsy girl, Esmeralda, to the surprise of everyone designates the unheroic and maimed Kilroy as king of the festival, he, unlike all others, recognizes something sensitive in her, refuses to violate her physically, and urges her to respect herself and change her life. His climactic choice constitutes a little act of grace that parallels that of Jacques Casanova to Marguerite Gauthier. Even though the fading, tubercular Camille, an escapee from a sanatorium whose heart has become cold, twice betrays Casanova, first by stealing his papers and trying to fly away on the Fugitivo and then by cruelly deserting him for the bed of a younger man, he unquestioningly takes her back into his comforting embrace that transcends physical sexuality; for she had once taught him "the part of love that's tender." Such little acts of grace are paradigmatic in Williams, making *Camino Real* a key to understanding the subtle moral choices of such later plays as *Sweet Bird of Youth* and *Night of the Iguana* (1961).

Because of these human responses of one person to another that refuse to settle for using the other, the world outside the self is affected, even transformed and saved as Quixote, awakened from his dream, proclaims in the play's curtain line: *"The violets in the mountains have broken the rocks!"* A few moments earlier, Quixote had pronounced the "Amen" to Esmeralda's valedictory prayer for all the earth's fugitives: "all cats without pads," "all con men and hustlers," "all two-time losers," "the courtesan and the cuckold, the poet," "the last cavaliers," "those fading legends that come and go." In the vision of a romantic poet such as Williams declares himself to be in *Camino Real*, these fugitives alone have it in their power to restore "honor" by refraining from self-pity and "going *on* from—*here!*" supported only by each other, and by art.

Tennessee Williams in the 1960s and 1970s: Death and the Artist

The works of the second half of Tennessee Williams's career generally differ from those of the first by their tendency to allegorize rather than psychologize character, oftentimes presenting two characters as fragmented sides of one, and by their obsessive handling of a more personal and limited range of themes, sometimes ponderously overstated and frequently concerning the artist as victim of time and death. They also experiment with dialogue, employing expository or reflective monologues delivered in spots of light as well as truncated lines that one character seems helpless to complete alone and that can only be finished by another.

A Diversion into Comedy

Williams began the 1960s, however, with an atypical and uncharacteristic foray into what he called a "serious" romantic comedy about marriage in southern suburbia that might have been written by Robert Anderson.

Period of Adjustment (1960), subtitled "High Point over a Cavern" after the name of the subdivision of "cute" Spanish-style bungalows built over a rumbling fault, concerns the precariousness of relationships grounded on mutual misunderstandings and unfulfilled expectations. The locale is symbolic; in this world that is "one big hospital," not only is the house in danger of collapsing but everyone is subject to "nervous tremors" of fear, loneliness, loss of self-esteem, and a sense of diminishment. On a deeper level, the play exposes the way in which sex and gender stereotypes, perpetuated by the myths of advertising and popular culture, control and distort human behavior. Two early middle-aged couples—one in the midst of separation, the other newly married, and both undergoing periods of adjustment—come together on Christmas Eve. The newlyweds' problem is sex: the student nurse Isabel finds George too sexually forthcoming for her inhibited nature; they reach a happy accommodation, however, after their host, Ralph, counsels him that sex should not be "an offensive weapon," that love making must not be "rape," and that he should try a little tenderness.

The older couple's problem has more to do with negotiating power, with maintaining one's self-image and independence as two attempt to become one so that they can trade single beds marked "His" and "Hers" for a double decorated with "Ours." Now that Ralph has entered those "conformist" middle years when "a spooky shadow" of mortality has materialized, he feels he sacrificed his youth to marry the psychologically frigid Dorothy. The too magnanimous Dotty takes pride in Ralph's breaking free of dependency by quitting his demeaning job. Unfortunately, Williams, apparently without being satiric though maybe as a necessary sop to Broadway audiences of the late Eisenhower years, offers a seriously retrograde resolution. Without any war to fight as a proving ground, and with space colonization still in the future, the two men set out to recapture the "agrarian, pastoral existence" of the frontier by buying a ranch where they can raise herds of cattle for television westerns. Potentially divisive sex roles are firmly upheld. As Ralph, supposedly the most sympathetic and "deeply" caring of the foursome, says, "we got a *man's* world coming up, man! Technical! Terrific! And it's gotta be *fearless!*" They will be a part of it, while "the little woman," as in the TV commercial that opens the play, does the wash with a "miracle . . . cleanser" that leaves her rested enough "at sundown to light up the house with the sunshine of her smile." To his credit, Williams came to consider *Period of Adjustment* "unambitious" and "not important."

Williams wrote two other plays during the 1960s and one in the 1970s that might be designated "comedies" of a sort. *Kingdom of Earth*

(The Seven Descents of Myrtle) (1968), which the playwright termed a "funny melodrama," in many ways reworks the body/soul tension explored in *Summer and Smoke*. What was a conflict between two opposite characters in that play here becomes a triangle, with newlywed Myrtle Ravenstock forced to choose between her dying husband, Lot, an effeminate aesthete, and his animalistic half-brother, Chicken. More than anything else, though, these characters are parodic, even camp, versions of earlier ones; Chicken, for instance, seems to be Stanley Kowalski taken to extremes. Myrtle, fearful of losing her life in the encroaching flood waters, has little trouble deserting the transvestite Lot—who inhabits his mother's parlor and dresses in her clothes in an attempt "to create a little elegance in a corner of the earth we lived in that wasn't favorable to it"— for life with Chicken. It takes, in fact, only four rather than seven descents down the stairs before Myrtle, a former burlesque entertainer and Queen for a Day, succumbs to Chicken's demands that she fellate him, which, in a virtual mockery of Williams's notion of physical sexuality as transcendence, results in her feeling "saved" and looking "as if she had undergone an experience of exceptional nature and magnitude." To compensate for his marginalized position as both illegitimate and of mixed races, Chicken must exact vengeance by attaining sexual dominance, ensuring that he will father a child by a white woman and inherit the Mississippi land.

Much gentler and neither earthy nor campy in tone is the decidedly minor *A Lovely Sunday for Creve Coeur* (1979), a bittersweet comedy of misapprehensions and miscommunication. Dorothea, a high school civics teacher in St. Louis in the late 1930s consigned to a lower-middle-class urban existence, relinquishes her "romantic illusions" about the principal who has taken advantage of her when she, like Laura in *Glass Menagerie*, discovers he is engaged to someone else. Now she must settle for a life of picnic outings at Creve Coeur with her roommate Bodey, who is inordinately attached to her own twin brother, Buddy. Fearful of losing either him or Dorothea, or perhaps attempting to possess Buddy through Dorothea, Bodey will continue trying to arrange a marriage between them. Dorothea realizes that heartbreak can, indeed, be endurable, as she expresses in a line that encapsulates Williams's attitude: "we must pull ourselves together and go on. Go on, we must just go on, that's all that life seems to offer—and demand."

In *Slapstick Tragedy* (1966), which Williams called a "black" or "grotesque" comedy, the pain is physical as well as emotional and psychological. "The Gnadiges Fraulein," the second of the two one-acts that make up this double bill, in its techniques if not its vision constitutes Williams's closest approach to the theater of the absurd: a narcissistic actor plays the blond "erotic fantasy" Injun Joe, the Dark Angel of Death reportedly carries off at least one of the transients every night, and huge attacking birds swoosh overhead. Played out on the southernmost coastline of "these Disunited Mistakes" on a nonrealistic set that resembles a design by Picasso, "Gnadiges Fraulein" features a former B-girl who once performed before the crowned heads of Europe as part of a seal act and now competes with the giant cocalooney birds to catch raw fish. So tenacious is she in sallying forth on her quest that the local gossip columnist will "pay tribute to her fighting spirit."

Death, in the person of Jack in Black, hovers as well over "The Mutilated," the gentle fantasy curtainraiser of *Slapstick Tragedy*. Here, Trinket Dugan's mutilation from breast cancer, which has embittered her and kept her loveless, symbolizes the physical, emotional, or spiritual mutilations from which everyone suffers. When Trinket forgives Celeste, who has humiliated her publicly, Celeste smells roses and "receive[s] the invisible presence of Our Lady in [the] room," and the pain in Trinket's breast miraculously disappears. The Christmas Carollers, whose hymn punctuates the action, sing of all "the strange, the crazed, the queer," "the wounded and the fugitive, the solitary," "the wayward and deformed . . . the lonely and misfit" for whom "the dark," perhaps even death, will be "held back a little while" through some "miracle" like Trinket's forgiveness. Such temporarily salvific acts of grace figure prominently throughout Williams's works, as they do in his one indisputably major play from the post–1960 period, *The Night of the Iguana*.

"Acts of Grace"

Night of the Iguana opened on 28 December 1961, starring Margaret Leighton and Bette Davis, and achieved a run of 316 performances, making it the dramatist's last Broadway success. As both a summation of the themes he expressed in his string of important works during the 1940s and 1950s, as well as a harbinger of new concerns about the artist's need for tenacity and endurance that he would explore in a series of more personal plays to come, it is a watershed in the playwright's career. A more tranquil and reflective work than most of his earlier ones, *Night of the Iguana* seems appropriately wise and profound. Though still depending heavily on symbolism for its meaning—Williams describes it as "more of a dramatic poem than a play [and so] bound to rest on metaphorical ways of expression" (*Where I Live*, 146)—it remains the most realistically conceived among the dramatist's major plays. Set in 1940 on the verandah of the Costa Verde Hotel perched high above the Mexican coast (Williams had stayed in a similar hotel late that summer, complete with Nazi tourists celebrating the firebombing of London), the design features "a line of small cubicle bedrooms" across the back well; visually, they concretize the universal human condition of locked doors and walls of incommunication, whereas "broken gates" between people constitute what we "know of God." Arriving at the hotel is the Reverend T. Lawrence Shannon, a defrocked Episcopalian priest serving as tour guide to a group of Baptist women who are particularly irate because of his physical intimacies with the teenage Charlotte.

Like the iguana caught and tied to the verandah for much of the play, Shannon feels at the end of his rope, depressed and daydreaming of achieving peace and "painless atonement" with a bottle in a hammock or, if that fails, through a long suicidal swim to China. Undergoing a dark night of the soul, he yearns not for any mystical union but simply for human communion. Williams believed that in Shannon he "was drawing a male equivalent almost of a Blanche DuBois" (*Conversations, Williams*, 80), who sought a similar surcease from isolation. Shannon's problem has always been an obsession with darkness and evil, an excess of guilt, and an inability to forgive himself or see himself as redeemed. Being human means to be flawed, but not so flawed as to despair, which may be the worst evil of all. His life, beginning when his mother caught him masturbating and promised God would exact punishment for his finding pleasure, has been a recurring cycle of sin, guilt, and prayer to a "senile delinquent" and "angry, petulant" God of vengeance who reveals himself in thunder and lightning, rather than to a God of calm who leads through "still waters." As preacher and later tour guide, Shannon has attempted to imbue others with his obsessive vision: "I've always allowed the ones that were willing to see, to *see!*—the underworlds of all places, and if they had hearts to be touched, feelings to feel with, I gave them a priceless chance to feel and be touched." Shannon's words sound akin to Williams's own artistic credo, where nothing that is human remains off limits, although there have always been critics such as Signi Falk who find his candor and lack of restraint excessive.

Among the other temporary guests is Hannah Jelkes, a wandering middle-aged spinster portraiturist with an "androgynous-looking" quality and something of the "ethereal . . . medieval saint" about her. She, too, has undergone a dark night (whether it involved coming to terms with her sexual aloneness or her awareness of limited artistic talent Williams leaves ambiguous), but she successfully beat back the "blue devil." Much like Maggie in *Cat on a Hot Tin Roof,* Hannah acts as a catalyst, helping Shannon to see something in himself worthy of being saved. Yet precisely because he realizes that there can never be any physical, in the sense of sexual, meeting between them, Shannon remains suspicious of her ability to help. At a crucial point, he inquires of Hannah whether she ever had a "love experience," and she wistfully recounts the time when she accommodated the desires of an underwear fetishist for a piece of her apparel; in response to Shannon's naming this a "sad, dirty little episode," Hannah insists on the loving nature of the act, for she was responding compassionately and nonjudgmentally, and at great expense to her normally fastidious nature, to a "degree or . . . depth of [loneliness]" she had never before encountered. And then she utters Williams's most explicit statement of his own moral code: "Nothing human disgusts me unless it's unkind, violent." Williams intended Hannah, he says, "almost as a definition of what I think is most spiritually beautiful in a person and still believable" (*Conversations, Williams,* 83).

Traveling in Hannah's care is her 97-year-old grandfather, Nathaniel Coffin, the oldest practicing poet in America (and a loving homage to Williams's own maternal grandfather), who struggles to complete one last work before he dies. In the defrocked minister's sympathy for her grandfather, whom she calls Nonno, Hannah recognizes the seeds of Shannon's renewed sense of worth. She urges him to build on that by releasing the trapped iguana, also "one of God's creatures." Only when he does so, after first tearing off the gold cross that had become a kind of albatross ever since he lost sight of God's forgiveness, can Nonno complete his poem. Hannah helps Shannon, who in turn frees the iguana—and the result is art. At one point in its composition Williams had titled the play *Two Acts of Grace.* The names of the three characters underscore the dramatist's point about human altruism and interconnectedness, for "Shannon" contains all the letters needed to spell the other two. If, as Williams once remarked, "Hell is the self," then only by reaching out to the "other" can God be found.

The work that Nonno completes before he dies relates closely in theme to Williams's play. A poem about the necessity of living after the fall without succumbing to despair, it draws upon the image of the ripe orange that plummets down to mix with the earth in "An intercourse not well designed / For beings of a golden kind." The artist beseeches the "courage" of the heart to live positively, despite knowledge of flawed, imperfect humanity and eventual mortality. This perpetual coexistence of the golden and the decayed, of the sublime and the animal-like, is evident as well in the German tank manufacturer and his family who wander in and out of the play; lighted so that they look all "pink and gold like baroque cupids," they sing their Nazi marching song, fiends from hell with the voices of angels as they cheer the news that London is burning.

An acceptance of frail humanity, as embodied in Hannah's un-selfish response to the desperately lonely man, puts into perspective the relationship that Shannon enters into at play's end with Maxine Faulk, the proprietress of the Costa Verde. Maxine, a gutsy recent widow with a zest for life, might at first seem all body to Hannah's all spirit. Williams is not, however, setting up a Manichean duality but rather insisting once again on the need for accepting "the *unlighted* side" of human nature; not everyone can reach and exist on the spiritualized plan of a Hannah. Maxine, albeit on the level of physical sexuality, will be able to sustain Shannon in a relationship that enables him to reaffirm life; she will get him "back up the hill," something he cannot do alone. The physical, so long as it is not predatory, is never denigrated in Williams. Yet if Shannon is able to rest in the bed of Maxine, Hannah's fate proves more Beckettian. Despite her prayer to the contrary, she can only "go on" alone, enduring until the end. But then "en avant" became Williams's own cry from the heart in his later years as both man and artist.

Portraits of the Artist

The early 1970s, like the early 1960s, began on an upbeat note for Williams professionally, with a promising production off-Broadway. As in *Night of the Iguana*, a caught animal dominates the visual stage symbolism of *Small Craft Warnings* (1972). Suspended above the bar in Monk's Place hangs a "sailfish, hooked and shellacked and strung up like a flag" as a challenge to "much lesser . . . creatures that never, ever sailed an inch in their lives." For the "vulnerable human vessels" who seek some safe mooring, Monk's saloon, like those other barrooms in American dramas by William Saroyan and Eugene O'Neill, provides a temporary "place of refuge." Monk, who suffers from heart trouble, treats with "affection" the customers who form a surrogate family, making him feel "not alone" and fortifying him in his desire to meet death unawares, in his sleep. At play's end, Monk will accede to Violet's "supplication" and invite her upstairs to share his bed, finding, in Doc's words, the "solace of companionship." Doc—whom Williams portrayed in his acting debut in hopes of extending the play's run—will not be so lucky. An abortionist with a suspended license, he must hit the road, laughing darkly in "ultimate recognition of human absurdity and . . . self-loathing" after allowing a woman to hemorrhage to death rather than risk calling for an ambulance. If birth and death are "holy miracles," they remain "*dark mysteries*" to Doc. Doc thought the bright star over the trailer court signaled that he was "going to deliver a new Messiah," but the baby was stillborn. In a world where, at best, God has "no light on his face" and "moves in the dark," these transient souls must find ways to create their own divinity. Violet, for instance, can discover her answer only in physical sexuality; hands-under-the-table groping at men becomes an almost trancelike religious experience, "worshipping her idea of God Almighty in her personal church."

Williams expanded *Small Craft Warnings* from his one-act play, "Confessional." In keeping with that title, Williams structures his work through a series of 10 extended monologues; if the cell-like cubicles in *Night of the Iguana*'s stage setting symbolized the walls between individuals, here the long soliloquies indicate aloneness. Increasingly during the second half of his career Williams turned to using monologues, oftentimes recited in an area of light that simulates the cinematic close-up; however, he came to regard *Small Craft Warnings*, which he hoped would announce a major revival of himself as playwright, as "not a major work. It's badly constructed, with one monologue after another" (Spoto, 301). What made it endearing for audiences was Williams's "compassion" for his characters, though even that was not unalloyed because of the absolute honesty in their presentation.

In Quentin, the second-rate screenwriter, Williams draws the first openly gay character in his dramas, but the portrait emerges tinged with cynicism and disapprobation; although now finally uncloseted in Williams's work, the spiritually desiccated, aging homosexual Quentin is presented so "negatively" and stereotypically in the eyes of at least one critic that he judges *Small Craft Warnings* "a virulently heterosexist play" (Clum 1992, 164). Furthermore, by that time, as Bigsby points out, "The power which [Williams] had once been able to draw on from the public expression of sexuality was now lost to him as its open and joyous expression undermined its subversive power" (Bigsby 1992). Perhaps because Williams sensed that his own promiscuous behavior over many years threatened to deaden his sensibilities, he has Quentin claim that "hard," "brutal," "coarse" homosexual experiences without a lasting commitment have so impacted other areas of his existence that he has lost "the capacity for being surprised" and no longer feels "lightning-struck with astonishment" over being alive. If the shackled fish were freed and seen swimming in his bedroom, all Quentin could say would be "just 'Oh, well' " rather than " 'My God!' "

In contrast, the young Bobby, whom Quentin tries to pick up, has—like the persona of Keats's "On First Looking into Chapman's Homer"—maintained the innocent awe to see "with wild surmise"; everything is still "in 'caps' " for him. He is, in short, the perfect audience for the creations of both God and humankind, that is, of the artist. Morally untainted by the prejudices of society, Bobby returns Quentin's touch because it seems the natural thing to do; and he refuses to demean what was a purely human response by taking money from Quentin. Bobby reminds Leona of her brother, the anniversary of whose death-day she is marking. A violinist who was "too beautiful to live," his music had provided Leona with the "one beautiful thing" essential "to save [her] heart from . . . CORRUPTION!" If, in *Night of the Iguana*, the artist's vocation consists in transcending humankind's fallen nature and making it bearable and not mired in despair, in *Small Craft Warnings* that vocation appears less unflinchingly and more sentimentally: the artist's function is defined only by analogy, as Leona speaks about training her brother as a beautician "to lay his hands on the heads of the homely and lonely and bring some beauty out in them."

The decade between *Night of the Iguana*, William's last commercial success, and *Small Craft Warnings*, which seemed an augury of renewed hope for William's resurgence as a major dramatist, might be called his dark night of the soul, emotionally, psychologically, and creatively. He himself referred to the period as his "stoned age," a long agony of drink and drugs and depression that only deepened with the death from cancer in 1963 of Frank Merlo, his companion and lover for more than 14 years. In "Too Personal," a brief essay intended as "a preopening piece" before *Small Craft Warnings*, Williams worried over whether "the materials of [his] life" had become too much "the materials of [his] work." He justified any similarity on the basis that creative works can be only "synthetic" unless they "express those things most involved in [the writer's] experience." At the same time, it remains "the frightening responsibility of an artist" to universalize the purely personal, a process that remains in question, especially when linked with stylistic experimentation. As he comments in the *Memoirs*, "my stoned age had partial remissions, mostly coincident with theater productions in the sixties, all of them disastrous—due to my inability to cope with the preparations for them and with a turn, in my work, toward a new style and a new creative world with which the reviewers and the audiences found it very hard to empathize so abruptly" (707).

The Milk Train Doesn't Stop Here Anymore received two Broadway productions, neither of them successful, the first starring Hermione Baddeley in 1963, the second Tallulah Bankhead in 1964; Spoto considers it Williams's "attempt . . . to come to terms with his relationship to Merlo, to articulate in death what was unspoken in life" (260). Like the medieval coming-of-death plays, *Milk Train*, which might be termed "an allegory" or "a sophisticated fairy tale," departs strikingly from realistic conventions in the two "stage assistants that function in a way that's between the Kabuki Theatre of Japan and the chorus of Greek theater." The setting on Italy's Divina Costiera assures that the archetypal sea, source of both life and death, will be visually and aurally present. The villa's proprietress, Flora "Sissy" Goforth, an enormously wealthy former Follies girl widowed either four or six times, has become "a legend" and is now dictating her memoirs.

The Angel of Death arrives in the person of a "battered" yet "undefeated" poet and sculptor schooled in Hinduism, Christopher Flanders, who discovered his true vocation when he helped a dying old man to drown. Flora, who insists she will "go forth" to death, to "nothing" and oblivion (Williams, too, could never bring himself to believe in an afterlife), only when "she's ready," at first thinks that a physical relationship with Chris will restore her youth and vitality. Chris, however, teaches her two things: that "you need somebody or something to mean God to you, even if it's a cow on the streets of Bombay, or carved rock on the Easter Islands"; and that death should be accepted with dignity rather than defiance. The Angel of Death thus becomes the Artist of Death, counseling the dying to "go gentle." Finally admitting that she "can't make it alone," Mrs. Goforth beseeches Chris's presence until it is all over. Harmonic music seemingly issuing from Chris's fatalistically named mobile, "The Earth Is a Wheel in a Great Big Gambling Casino," suggests calm resignation. Studded with bits and pieces of pseudo-philosophizing, *Milk Train* finally proves less memorable than Albee's much briefer "Sandbox," which encompasses similar effects less didactically and more poignantly.

Williams's final play of the 1960s, *In the Bar of a Tokyo Hotel* (1968), a work full of fractured lines of dialogue in which characters complete one another's sentences and of almost Pinteresque ambiguities and gnomic utterances, centers on the death of the artist himself. In *Sweet Bird of Youth* a decade before, Williams had combined into one character the actress fearful of aging and the artist facing rejection. Here, that character is, in a sense, split into two in a middle-aged wife and husband, Miriam and Mark; Miriam even speculates at one point: "Are we two people, Mark, or are we . . . Two sides of! . . . One!" Miriam, who considers as enemies all "calendars, clocks, watches" that chart time's passing, has become a sensualist, attempting to seduce the Oriental barman as a denial of the inevitability of lost youth. Rejecting Mark's dependence on her, Miriam claims to need "a little time of space between [them]"; this ultimately fatal apartness finds visual confirmation in the circular areas of light in which Williams's separate characters are often caught on stage.

The "ravaged" and tormented Mark is the artist in extremis. Among his many phobias, some shared by Williams himself, are fear of confinement, of symbolic castration, of confronting the empty canvas, of madness. Mark, for whom venturing into a "new style" means entering "jungle country"—reminiscent of *Dragon Country*, the collective title of the volume of shorter plays in which *Bar of a Tokyo Hotel* appears—is totally self-absorbed by his art. Potentially, the artist achieves a godlike creation; Mark intones "In the beginning" and speaks of discovering "the imperishable things . . . color and light." As for Vee Talbot in *Battle of Angels* and *Orpheus Descending*, art for Mark should be akin to mystical vision: "I've understood the *intimacy* that should, that has to exist between the, the—painter and the—I! It! . . . The oneness, the!" Yet the Jackson Pollack–like spray-painted canvases on which Mark crawls around naked look like "circus-colored mudpies." Ironically, Mark, who fears confinement, is so completely turned in upon himself as artist that his art imprisons rather than renews. As Williams remarks, this artist "hasn't the comfort of feeling with any conviction that any of his work has had any essential value" (Spoto, 278).

Three ambitious plays from the last half-dozen years of Williams's life—he died in 1983 from choking on a pill bottle cap—which Ruby Cohn deems "major" works that "probe the cost of creating,"[1] round off his theatrical career by bringing him full circle, in a sense, back to his first success, *The Glass Menagerie*. As a memory play, *Vieux Carré*, which opened and closed abruptly in the spring of 1977, shares structural and stylistic similarities with *Glass Menagerie* in its use of a narrator/central character as well as music and nonrealistic lighting to achieve the effect of subjectivity and interiority. By the time of its composition,

however, Williams had published his *Memoirs* (1976), and so the homosexuality that he suppressed—except for vague hints in *Glass Menagerie*—could now be dramatized openly. Set in a cheap boarding house
in the "bohemian" section of New Orleans, *Vieux Carré*, essentially a
series of vignettes, treats three of the dramatist's recurrent concerns: the
universal human malady of aloneness ("God's phone's disconnected"); the
end of existence in the nothingness of death (the "oblivion" of "another
dimension"); and the nature of the artist and his social function.

The Writer, whom Williams explicitly identifies as "myself those
many years ago," that is, in the late 1930s, is affected by the loneliness
resulting from his unrealized sexual needs as well as by the death of
his grandmother (Williams based *Vieux Carré* partly on his short story
"Grand," written in homage to his maternal Grandmother Dakin). The
dying homosexual painter, Nightingale, urges the Writer to find the
strength to accept and survive and to move beyond loss. He initiates the
Writer into his first sustained homosexual relationship; he even points to
the Writer's cataract (an affliction Williams also suffered from) as symbolic of the heart becoming cold and calcified, a fatal illness for an
artist. The Writer is finally able to reciprocate Nightingale's attentions;
afterward, he experiences an apparition of his Grandmother in the form
of a comforting and forgiving Angel. Through his Writer character,
Williams emphasizes the artist's responsibility to be a truth-bringer,
avoiding "cowardly!—evasion." Furthermore, the Writer underscores the
close link between William's own life and his creativity, calling "writers
. . . shameless spies" who use, and ideally transmute, the events and
people around them in their art. The boardinghouse that had seemed
like a "madhouse" or "psycho ward" has actually been an education and
preparation for the Writer, a "waiting station into the world." When he
leaves with the jazz clarinetist Sky to travel out West, as Williams himself
did, he ventures into the unknown; "this house is empty now" as the
ghosts of the past begin to fade from memory. The Writer must go out
and go on, but for someone whose art builds so closely on his life as to
be virtually coterminus with it, that going forth is tinged with a fear that
someday the house of memory/imagination will be depleted. Should that
happen, it will mark the end of art.

Williams's *Out Cry*, perhaps because it is so intensely "personal,"
even private, a work—his "own human outcry"—was always thought by
the playwright to be more successful than it has proven; Williams termed
it "my best play since *Streetcar Named Desire*" (*Conversations, Williams,*
255). Yet the text, in its various versions over several years, as *The Two-*

Character Play in London in 1967 and then under its new title in Chicago in 1971 and New York in 1973, always eluded a production that would confirm the dramatist's own judgment. *Out Cry* announces its lineage back to *Glass Menagerie*, first in its production note that "Images . . . [having] a subjective quality . . . may be projected on the stage backdrop," but mostly in its brother/sister dyad, which, like that of Tom and Laura in *Glass Menagerie*, provides an alter ego for Tennessee and his sister, Rose. Locked in a theater that is possibly an asylum, a probably "insane" brother and sister team, Felice and Clare, enact "The Two-Character Play," an incomplete play-within-the-play that tells of their shamed lives in a southern town after their father killed their mother and then himself, which leaves them afraid to venture forth. Since the play they perform is unfinished and lacks closure, the metatheatrical *Out Cry* simulates, in the manner of Pirandello, an aura of the improvisatory. Felice and Clare will become completely "lost" in it at the point where a loaded revolver becomes a major stage property; now "the end will simply happen." Just as the house imprisoned and the theater imprisons, so the plot becomes a kind of prison, inevitably working itself out. Role and reality, art and life become one. Not only as characters but as actor and actress, Felice and Clare have no choice but the theater/asylum/art in which to play out and end their lives.

What makes *Out Cry*, in Williams's own words, perhaps "too personal" and "too special" for most audiences may be the confession it contains of the brother and sister's relationship. As Williams writes in his *Memoirs*, "Some perceptive critic of the theater made the observation that the true theme of my work is 'incest.' My sister and I had a close relationship, quite unsullied by any carnal knowledge . . . And yet our love was, and is, the deepest in our lives" (119–20). In his "Author's Notes," apparently written around 1970 but never published with the play text, Williams reveals, "There may be no apparent sexuality in *The Two-Character Play*, and yet it is actually the *Liebestod* of the two characters from whom the title derives," rendering the play itself "as vulnerable as Clare and Felice, and as deviant."[2] Despite the author's disavowal of any "apparent sexuality," *Out Cry* both verbally and visually treats more openly than any of his other long plays the incest theme. At one point, Felice and Clare "rush into . . . a compulsive embrace—like two lovers meeting after a long separation," after which the brother utters a line from the *Song of Solomon* that serves also as the play's epigraph: "A garden enclosed is my sister." And dominating the stage set are two images: "a huge, dark statue" suggesting "things anguished and perverse

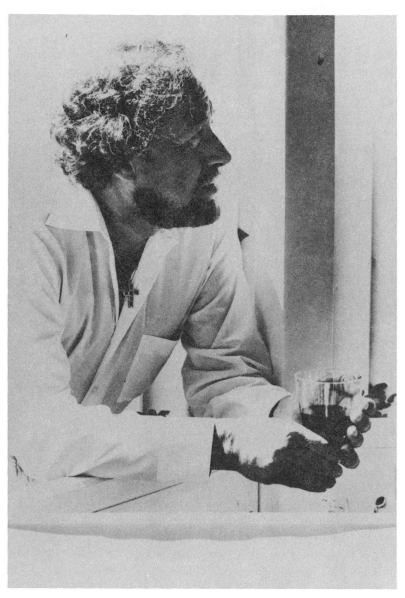

Tennessee Williams in the early 1970s. *Photographer unknown. Given to the author by Mr. Williams.*

(in [Felice's] own nature?)" that Clare will later refer to as "unnatural," "obscene," and a "monstrous aberration"; and a projection of a phallic "two-headed sunflower taller than a two-story house [that] seems to be shouting sensational things about us." Like the play, it is "the poem of two and dark as—Our blood? Yes, why don't you say it? Abnormality!"

The central characters of *Clothes for a Summer Hotel* (1980), Williams's last new play to be produced on Broadway during his lifetime, are nominally not a brother and sister but F. Scott Fitzgerald and his wife, Zelda. Yet Williams continues to examine here the symbiotic union between himself and his sister, this time acknowledging and exploring incestuous desire, however repressed, not from a physical or psychological perspective but as it is fulfilled through sublimation in art, making it even more "A Ghost Play" (which is its subtitle) than *Vieux Carré* or *Glass Menagerie*. "Words," as Zelda claims, "are the love acts of writers"; writing and the sex act are bound up together. Yet if, as Williams comments through his alter ego in *Vieux Carré*, "writers are shameless spies," then they prey upon and use the "other" as source and inspiration for their art. Along with this motif of betrayal, *Clothes for a Summer Hotel* reiterates many of the motifs central to Williams's later plays: fear of confinement; the connection between madness and art; the trauma of sexual difference for the artist; and the artist's despair over the waning of creative power with the passage of time.

Scott, a ghost of his legendary younger self, comes to visit Zelda in the Asheville Asylum, where she is confined and will burn to death in 1947, from that other place of make-believe, Hollywood, "a sort of madhouse, too." Androgynous in appearance, Scott seems uneasy about his masculinity and sensitive to the possibility of suppressed homosexuality, though as Hemingway assures him, "duality of gender can serve some writers well" in the creation of character. A romantic artist, he feels "robbed of youth." Life, in a bow to absurdity that Williams makes frequently in his late plays, can be nothing but endurance from the "wail" of birth to the "gasp" of death, only "an arranged pattern of—submission to what's been prescribed for us unless we escape into madness or into acts of creation." As an artist, however, Scott becomes jealous of Zelda and so needs to restrict her creativity. The role Scott would like to impose on her as southern wife and mother "pinches," and so Zelda rebels against her "shadow of an existence as Mrs.—Eminent Author." Since "Work" is that "loveliest of all four letter words," she demands freedom to pursue her own career. Furthermore, she feels preyed upon and devoured by Scott, who has used her as the model for his heroines, appropriating her life for his art.

Herein Fitzgerald and Williams most converge, for what the novelist did to Zelda the playwright has done to Rose. The play becomes, in fact, an apologia, an admission of "betrayal" as at the very core of creative endeavor when art draws upon the life of another, as Williams's did incessantly on his sister's. When the asylum burns, the place of illusions is reduced to ash; the homonymic pun on the word "clothes" in the title might even suggest the closing down of the house of the imagination, an apocalyptic moment for the artist, just as the loss of Rose would have been for Williams as writer. Apocalyptic fire constitutes an important image throughout Williams's theatrical canon, beginning with his early play *Battle of Angels*, in which the orchard associated with illusion is blowtorched to the ground.

A Political Turn

Apocalyptic imagery also holds a central position in *The Red Devil Battery Sign* (1977), which closed in Boston before ever reaching New York in a production starring Claire Bloom and Anthony Quinn, though it later opened in London. Williams here presents not just the destruction of art or illusion, as in *Battle of Angels/Orpheus Descending* or *Clothes for a Summer Hotel*, but of Western culture and civilization itself, making *Red Devil* its author's most political drama since *Orpheus Descending* and *Sweet Bird of Youth* 20 years earlier, both of which condemned racial bigotry and demagoguery. Williams regards *Red Devil* as a more "conventional" work than his other post–*Night of the Iguana* efforts and thus a return stylistically to the more theatrically successful plays of the 1940s and 1950s, though it still strains against the bounds of realism, especially in expressionistic sound and images. *Red Devil* dramatizes two relationships, a central one between King del Rey and The Woman Downtown and a quite subsidiary but simultaneous one between King's daughter, Nina, and McCabe, in both of which physical sexuality is humanizing, life restoring, and regenerative, in short, an "act of God."

The Woman Downtown's entire life has been a succession of confinements, most recently at the Paradise Meadows Nursing Home, where before escaping to the Yellow Rose Hotel she was subjected to electric shock treatments because of her familiarity with decoded documents belonging to the Red Devil Battery group, whose henchmen have invaded all walks of life, including the entertainment business. The secret organization is a military-industrial complex involved in the handing over of Asian democracies "to rule by power conspiracies" out to protect their "huge, secret investments"; their dedication to "genocide for profits undeclared" will lead to ever greater American involvement in an ever widening war. Williams recounts in his *Memoirs* his personal opposition to the "atrocity" of Vietnam; in 1971 he actually spoke at an antiwar rally in New York's Cathedral of St. John the Divine, which would later award him its first Arts Medal.

King del Rey and Woman Downtown's relationship plays out against a nightmarish background of urban unrest and chaos, with ominous wasteland sounds of wolf calls, warning trumpets, and quadraphonically distorted music, and with explosions and flares and draft resisters blowing up police squad cars. Above the city (downtown Dallas, where President John F. Kennedy was assassinated in 1963) is the neon Red Devil Battery sign that "pulses like blood." In a fantastic ending after King's death, "the play stylistically makes its final break with realism" as "the wild young denizens of the Hollow," led by Wolf, embrace the Woman Downtown as "Mother of all." Uttering the "awesome . . . defiant outcry of the she-wolf," she joins the rebels who advance to the front of the stage and, in a Brechtian moment of both castigation and challenge, confront the audience "who have failed or betrayed them." Williams implies that civilization has become so corrupted by the drive for power and money that it can be restored only by beginning a painful evolution up from savagery, with a matriarchy overthrowing and replacing the values of the patriarchy, an idea with seeds as far back as Blanche's warning to Stella about civilization's demise in *Streetcar Named Desire*.

Audiences and critics never questioned the validity of Williams's insistence on the role of art as a civilizing agent or the need for the human heart to respond with compassion to the outcry of the other, and yet the majority of the plays after the very early 1960s failed to hold them enraptured in the theater, as his previous masterworks had. If Williams won admiration for enduring as an artist, for the grace he showed in continuing to write under the pressure of near-continual rejection by critics and audiences during the last 20 years of his life, his hope for a late play that would be, like Nonno's deathbed poem in *Night of the Iguana*, his "most beautiful," eluded him. While recognizing the evident deficiencies of many of the later works, Walter Kerr could still justly claim in the late 1970s that "Tennessee Williams's voice is the most distinctively poetic, the most idiosyncratically moving, and at the same time the most firmly dramatic to have come the American theater's way—ever. No point in calling the man our best living playwright. He is our best playwright, and let qualifications go hang. In fact, he has already given us such a substantial body of successful work that there is really no need to continue demanding that he live up to himself, that he produce more, more, more, and all masterpieces" (quoted in Spoto, 326). Williams, however, suffered from the flaw—or is it the supreme virtue?—endemic to the most serious of American writers: demanding from himself a continued and sustained level of artistry. As he writes near the end of his *Memoirs*, "the passion to create . . . is all that we know of God" (242).

9

Lorraine Hansberry: Exploring Dreams, Explosive Drama

Shortly before A *Raisin in the Sun* opened on Broadway in March 1959 and catapulted Lorraine Hansberry, its 29-year-old author, to instant fame, she attempted to define the wellsprings of her art by reference to the social dislocations, sometimes nearly apocalyptic, through which she had lived since her birth on 19 May 1930 on Chicago's racially segregated southside: "I was born in a depression after one world war, and came into my adolescence during another. While I was still in my teens the first atom bombs were dropped at Nagasaki and Hiroshima, and by the time I was twenty-three years old my government and that of the Soviet Union had entered into the worst conflict of nerves in human history—the Cold War. I have lost friends and relatives through cancer, lynching and war. I have been personally the victim of physical attack which was the offspring of racial and political hysteria."[1] Her contemporaries in the theater experienced most of these individual and national traumas, though Hansberry's plays often reflect them more explicitly. What distinguishes Hansberry, however, is the conjunction of two other facts to which she accorded priority: "I was born black and a female."

An outsider by both race and gender, and so doubly erased in a predominantly white male theatrical world, Hansberry, because of her privileged social class and education, experienced still further exclusion from vast numbers of her own race, which some critics would take as reason for questioning the depth of her social commitment. Hansberry's father, Carl, was a U.S. deputy marshall who lost a bid for Congress, while her mother, Nannie, was a Republican ward committeewoman who gave her little daughter a white fur coat for her fifth Christmas, provoking taunts from her classmates. In the late 1930s, the family bought a home in a white neighborhood, which incited open hostility and resulted in a brick being flung through a window and barely missing Lorraine. Although the state courts ordered their eviction, Carl successfully appealed the decision to the U.S. Supreme Court, which struck down restrictive covenants based on race.

The Political Basis of Art

During Lorraine's high school years, the Hansberry home welcomed such luminaries in the black movement as W. E. B. Du Bois, the sociologist and author of the classic *Souls of Black Folk* (1903), under whom Lorraine would study African history; Paul Robeson, the prominent Shakespearean actor and activist with whom she would work on the journal *Freedom* in the early 1950s; Langston Hughes, the leading poet and playwright of the Harlem Renaissance and author of the poem, "A Dream Deferred," a line from which would provide the title for *Raisin in the Sun*; and her uncle, William Leon Hansberry, an early professor of African studies who became Lorraine's mentor after her father's death. She always subscribed to the Pan-Africanist notion that the destinies of the African and African-American peoples are intertwined. Throughout her brief life she affirmed the responsibility of the writer to speak for those without public voice who share in one or another aspect of her "otherness"—biological, racial, sociocultural—and face oppression because of it.

"The Negro Writer and His Roots: Toward a New Romanticism," written in 1959, contains Lorraine Hansberry's aesthetic credo, outlining facets of her dramatic theory and analyzing the sources of her political radicalism. For her the writer's vocation is ordinarily inseparable from a political agenda. She asserts the duty of black authors to dispel a number of myths or "illusions rampant in contemporary American culture," chal-

"A JOYOUS LAUGHTER-FILLED EVENT!" — CBS-TV

LAST YEAR'S **LONGEST RUNNING OFF-B'WAY HIT!**

Lorraine Hansberry's

TO BE YOUNG, GIFTED & BLACK

Adapted by **ROBERT NEMIROFF**   Original Production Directed by **GENE FRANKEL**

"AN EXTRAORDINARY ACHIEVEMENT! It is a whirl of probing, celebrating, hoping, laughing, despairing and moving on...a thrust of spirit...so brilliantly and tenderly alive."
— Nat Hentoff, N.Y. TIMES

"MAGNIFICENTLY AMUSING" "SUPERB!"
— NEWARK NEWS   — Los Angeles TIMES

"A TRIUMPH!" "WONDERFULLY MOVING"
— N.Y. POST   — Clive Barnes, N.Y. TIMES

"MARVELOUS!" "BEAUTIFUL THEATER"
— James Baldwin in ESQUIRE   — WALL STREET JOURNAL

"SHE STANDS AS THE ULTIMATE BLACK WRITER FOR TODAY"
— Julius Lester, VILLAGE VOICE

"MIRACULOUS — one marvels at the range!"
— THE VILLAGE VOICE

"THE WORDS AND IMAGERY OF A BLACK O'CASEY"
— THE GUARDIAN

"A MILESTONE!"
— TIME MAGAZINE

"The Finest Stage Work in New York... YOU MUST SEE IT!"
— Emory Lewis, THE RECORD

Theatrical flyer for the off-Broadway adaptation of Lorraine Hansberry's *To Be Young, Gifted, and Black*. From the author's collection.

lenging first "the notion put forth that art is not, and *should* not and, when it is at its best, CANNOT possibly be 'social.' " Ibsen's well-made problem plays exemplify Hansberry's dictum, following Arthur Miller, "that there are *no* plays which are not social and no plays that do not have a thesis." She singles out three additional destructive illusions subverting the American mindset: that somehow people can "exist independent of the world around them"; that the homogeneity in American society allows "one huge sprawling middle class" to be regarded as universally representative of what is a pluralistic and diverse culture and world; and, finally, "that there exists an inexhaustible period of time" during which this "nation may leisurely resurrect the promise of our Constitution and begin to institute the equality of man" (3–6).

Hansberry professes a balanced perspective on the topic of race, rejecting destructive stereotypes on both sides. Blacks as well as whites can be slaves to "ridiculous money values," to a perverted notion of "acquisition for the sake of acquisition" that elevates materialism over the possession of self and personal freedom. Blacks as well as whites can romanticize "the black bourgeoisie" and "Negro urban life," idealizing as eccentric and attractive what is actually evil and diseased. Blacks as well as whites can be politically naive, turning over their cause to those ambitious for power. Finally, well-meaning blacks might try to deny their "slave past or . . . sharecropper and ghetto present [as] an affront to every Negro who wears a shirt and tie" rather than analyze their history of oppression as a step toward overcoming it. Hansberry's analysis reveals a society in need of radical transformation, one still deficient in guaranteeing voting rights to all its citizens, one without equal job opportunities, one where lynchings still occur (she mentions Emmett Till, kidnapped and murdered in 1955), and one committed to racial genocide, since "the social and economic havoc wreaked on the American Negro takes some ten to fifteen years off the life-expectancy of our people." For these reasons, "the Negro writer has a role to play in shaming, if you will, the conscience of the people and the present national government" (8–10).

Acts of Empowerment

When Hansberry's *Raisin in the Sun* opened in 1959, it established, if belatedly, a mature black authorial presence in the previously white commercial theater on Broadway. From that perspective, 1959 might have been as decisive for the diversifying of American drama as 1956—which saw the premiere of John Osborne's *Look Back in Anger*—had been in moving modern British theater from the drawing room to the kitchen and in establishing the rebel against conservative mores and traditions as the contemporary antihero. Given Hansberry's insistence that the black writer concern herself with issues of race, it might seem surprising to find critics of *Raisin in the Sun* questioning the strength of her commitment to the black movement. Yet the play's very embrace by New York reviewers (exclusively white) and wide acceptance by audiences (again, predominantly white) may have contributed to the suspicion, by inevitably raising the specter of compromises in characterization and message that Hansberry's play must have calculatedly made to, in Bigsby's terms, "accommodate itself to the orthodoxies of Broadway" (Bigsby 1992, 11).

Hansberry, however, insisted that *Raisin in the Sun* is "definitely a Negro play before it is anything else,"[2] as confirmed by two of her fellow African-American writers. Novelist and later playwright James Baldwin, remembering the play's pre-Broadway run in Philadelphia, claimed "I had never before in my life seen so many black people in the theater. And the reason was that never before, in the entire history of the American theater, had so much of the truth of black people's lives been seen on the stage."[3] The more militant poet and playwright LeRoi Jones/ Amiri Baraka confessed 25 years later that those "taken with Malcolm's coming, with the immanence of explosion . . . missed the essence of the work—that Hansberry had created a family on the cutting edge of the same class and ideological struggles as existed in the movement itself and among the people."[4]

The first work on the Broadway stage directed by an African-American—Lloyd Richards, who in the 1980s would direct the plays of August Wilson and Athol Fugard—*Raisin in the Sun* chalked up 530 performances during its initial run, starring Sidney Poitier, Claudia Mac-Neil, Ruby Dee, and Diana Sands; it won the New York Drama Critics' Circle Award, making Hansberry the first black, only the fifth woman, and the youngest playwright so honored. (The film version, for which Hansberry wrote the first draft of the screenplay, received the Cannes Film Festival Award in 1961.) The play was by no means, however, the only notable work about the black experience to be seen on the American stage in the two decades beginning in 1940. Early in the period, Paul Green collaborated with Richard Wright on the stage version of the latter's novel, *Native Son*, in 1941; Abram Hill adapted Philip Yordan's *Anna*

Lucasta for black, rather than the original Polish, characters in 1944; and among musicals *Cabin in the Sky* and *Carmen Jones*, a black version of Bizet's opera, were notably successful.

Probably the most significant such play, and of greatest interest in the context of *Raisin in the Sun*, is Louis Peterson's *Take a Giant Step* (1953). Ostracized by his ethnic buddies, whose girlfriends refuse to be seen with a black man, and suspended from school for smoking in the lavatory after being openly rebellious against a white history teacher who knew nothing of the role of African-American soldiers during the Civil War, Peterson's central character, Spencer Scott, feels himself "an outcast." Ordered by his parents, who have become submissive to the materialistic value system of the white majority, to demean himself and apologize (his mother says, "You're a little colored boy—that's what you are—and you have no business talking back to white women . . . try and remember your place"), Spence tells his nurse, Christine, who will initiate him sexually, "I hate being black. . . . I hate the hell out of it." Left even more alone after the death of his feisty and supportive grandmother, he is faced with the choice between truth to his racial identity or acceptance by the white community. In deciding to do "the right thing" and break from the gang, Peterson's protagonist provides a prescient glimpse into the failure of integration under the pressures of racism. Though not many critics would likely agree with Bigsby that *Take a Giant Step* "is more subtle and affecting than Lorraine Hansberry's much praised play" (380), Peterson's drama does present a powerful, and prophetic, early image of black separatism.

If Peterson's play explores what happens to a black family *after* they have integrated a white New England neighborhood, Hansberry's emotionally charged drama about securing one's dignity within a system that not only discriminates against but even enslaves its racial minorities focuses on a family in the process of deciding to move into a segregated neighborhood. Crowded into a Chicago tenement apartment, the Younger family (the widowed Lena, "Mama," and her adult children— a son, Walter Lee, husband of Ruth and father of Travis, and a daughter, Beneatha) await the arrival of a $10,000 insurance payment on Walter, Sr., in the expectation that dreams too long deferred might finally be realized. From one point of view, the surname "Younger" may be seen as ironic, for this family's slave and sharecropper ancestors probably antedated on these shores those of many of the ruling white majority; from another, it seems particularly apt, since the "younger" generation of this family exists on the verge of discovering an adult identity and coming into their moral maturity. As the two children lay claim to the money, Walter to buy into a liquor store and Beneatha to pay her medical school tuition, Mama responds instead to the disintegrating family's need for a modest place in the sun to nurture and hold them together, and so makes a down payment on a home in a previously all white neighborhood.

Hansberry links Lena Younger with her ancient lineage by likening her posture in carrying herself to "the noble bearing of the women of the Hereros of Southwest Africa"; maintaining her dignity against the servility that society attempts to enforce upon her is one of Lena's most endearing traits. She secures that dignity with her moral integrity, with her respect for the "loveableness" of all life, even—perhaps most especially—at its moments of greatest weakness, and with the sheer doggedness with which she endures adversity and pursues her commitment to bettering conditions for her family. The three stage symbols associated with Lena attest to that dignity. The hat she dons whenever she leaves the apartment to work as a housekeeper or to do business in the world, rather than merely a protective crutch needed to face the outside, might better be seen as an assertion of her own position as a human being. The plant, starved for sunlight yet clinging to life, as are her children, encapsulates Mama's primary role as caregiver and nurturer. The garden plot at the new house signifies, as for Willy in *Death of a Salesman*, a little part of the promised land that she can cultivate with her own hands, her piece of the dream to own and inhabit, unlike the land her ancestors slaved on.

Mama can be, however, a hard taskmaster. She demands that her children accept and embrace *her* system of religious values as their own; she proclaims restrictive notions about the kind of economic opportunities blacks should seize—dignified work, yes, but entrepreneurship may be overreaching; finally, she too tenaciously clings to her position of authority in the household after Walter, Sr.'s, death, reining in her adult children. Her preventing Walter Lee, Jr., from attaining his share of the dream by investing in a business she finds morally repugnant has prompted some commentators to regard Mama as an emasculator who tears down rather than builds up the man and his position within the family. The widespread notion of the black matriarch as hostile destroyer instead of supportive protector is a myth long persistent in fiction and film. It is a construct from the outside, that is, from the white male perspective—and not unlike that equally pernicious Victorian stereotype of "the Angel in the House"—through which to situate the blame for continued subservience, built on racist images of the black "mammy" who, as "economic mainstay of the family"[5] must put duty toward her employer before all else.

In this regard, Hansberry alludes to the character of Berenice Sadie Brown in Carson McCullers's prize-winning stage adaptation (1950) of her novel, *The Member of the Wedding.* Though applauding the poignancy of that "lovely," delicate coming-of-age play about the need to "belong to a 'we,' " Hansberry could nevertheless still see how Berenice Sadie Brown's characterization was skewed along predictable lines, since "the intimacy of knowledge which the Negro may culturally have of white America does not exist in the reverse."[6] So in McCullers's drama Berenice turns her protective attention first to her white charge and surrogate son, John Henry, and only secondarily to her rebellious foster brother, Honey Camden Brown, who says, "No more 'boy this—boy that'—no bowing, no scraping" and asserts his equality by pulling a razor on the bar owner who refuses to serve him.

Hansberry, however, portrays Lena Younger's nurturing and prodding in a positive light, for Mama motivates Walter to develop self-respect. To raise Walter up from an anguished defeatism, she will even entrust the insurance money to him, enthroning him as heir to his father and "head" of the family. As Hansberry herself so eloquently wrote of Mama: Lena "is the black matriarch incarnate, the bulwark of the Negro family since slavery, the embodiment of the Negro will to transcendence. It is she who in the mind of the black poet [Hughes's "Washerwoman"] scrubs the floors of the nation in order to create black diplomats and university professors. It is she, while seeming to cling to traditional restraints, who drives the young on into the fire hoses. And one day simply refuses to move to the back of the bus in Montgomery" (*Les Blancs,* 210). Hansberry's fictional Mama, like the historical Rosa Parks before her, embarks on an analogous revolutionary path by moving into the previously all-white neighborhood. Her refusal to allow the word "nigger" in her house and her insistence that no one is meant to be a servant indicate a nascent militancy that finds explicit expression in a clarifying scene with their neighbor Mrs. Johnson, cut from the original Broadway production but resurrected for its twenty-fifth anniversary.

Mrs. Johnson righteously brandishes a newspaper reporting " 'bout them colored people that was bombed out their place" and predicts a similar fate awaiting such a "proud-acting bunch of colored folks" as the Youngers. Her warning tells what had occurred at the end of Hansberry's original draft, recalling what had faced the playwright's own family when they integrated a previously white neighborhood, as well as making palpable the violence that the Youngers could well experience after the curtain falls. The ending of the play, therefore, is by no means as unambiguously comfortable, or comforting, as is sometimes supposed. Mrs. Johnson's visit gives Mama an opportunity to counter the ameliorative racial attitudes her neighbor picked up from Booker T. Washington, whom Mama proclaims a "fool" for espousing that the blacks be given industrial training in lieu of university "Education [that] has spoiled many a good plowhand." Lena Younger's denunciation of Washington's program echoes the criticism leveled at him by one of the dramatist's mentors, W. E. B. Du Bois. In *The Souls of Black Folk*, Du Bois criticizes Washington for advocating a policy of survival "through submission" that would validate "the alleged inferiority of the Negro races" by demanding that black people relinquish "political power, . . . insistence on civil rights, [and] higher education of Negro youth," all for economic advancement.[7]

An instructive counterpart to Lena Younger in her movement toward a revolutionary, activist ideology is the slave mother Rissa in *The Drinking Gourd* (1960), Hansberry's unproduced teleplay commissioned as the first offering in a series on the Civil War but then rejected as too inflammatory. Subtitled "The Peculiar Institution"—in reference to the slavocracy that Hansberry equates with the Holocaust for victimizing not just blacks but also the poor whites who support the system along color lines rather than side with their oppressed brothers along economic ones—the script dramatizes the blinding of Rissa's son, Hannibal, as punishment for having learned to read and write. When her master, Hiram (whom the script strongly intimates took Rissa as mistress and fathered Hannibal), comes to the cabin, she chides him for failing to be master over his viciously racist son, Everett, and refuses to aid him as he lies dying of a heart attack. Rissa then steals Hiram's gun, symbol of his empowerment, and gives it to the blind Hannibal, who will escape north to freedom, a migration that will mark the demise of slavery as an institution; ironically, other migrations by blacks to the North 80 and 100 years later will culminate in new economic enslavement in the urban ghettos.

Mama in *Raisin in the Sun* gives her son, Walter Lee, two weapons against his oppressed existence, the first granted only reluctantly, while the second proves even more potent than the gun that Rissa entrusts to Hannibal. The one that Walter Lee begs for, money, carries with it only despair; the less tangible one, moral courage, comes as an unasked-for blessing that regenerates and transforms. The nature of these gifts is signaled, but in reverse order, at the play's opening. The images that greet an audience attending the play are of physical awakenings that portend later ones at deeper levels: the sleeping form of Travis, Walter Lee's son; the sleepy form of Ruth, his wife, coming in to wake him for school; and then a pajama-clad Walter, woken up unwillingly for another day as chauffeur for a white business tycoon.

The first substantive discussions in the play concern money, not only the hefty insurance check but Travis's pressing need for the 50 cents his teacher expects each child to have that day. To deny Travis the money would make the father appear inadequate in the son's eyes. For Walter, as for Miller's Willy Loman, giving material things *to* the son establishes proof of the father's love. Baraka has described his justly famous *Dutchman* (1964) as a play about what it means to be a man in America; the same could apply to *Raisin in the Sun*, in which Walter equates having money with being a man. He buys unquestioningly into the value system of the white oppressor class, including his willingness to pay graft down in the state capitol to facilitate getting a liquor license. Because he believes, to Mama's horror, money is synonymous with life, he divides all of life "[b]etween the takers and the 'tooken' "; the smartest take the most, while the rest "get to looking 'round for the right and the wrong; and we worry about it and cry about it and stay up nights trying to figure out 'bout the wrong and the right."

After Mama relents and entrusts him with most of the insurance money, he exuberantly take Travis aside (in a second important scene omitted from the original Broadway production) and regales him with his dream of success: a fancy house, two cars, a black caretaker he can patronize and demean just as he always has been, and a wife of leisure he can display as proof of having made it in America. The racism and sexism of his plans seem endemic to those possessing economic power. With the money in hand, Walter thinks that wife and mother have now, for once, given his dream the chance to become a reality, allowed him his manhood, and opened up a future of possibility rather than nothingness.

After his putative partner, Willy, bilks him and Bobo of their money in the liquor license scam, Walter Lee becomes willing to do what he would not when he had money: grovel like an Uncle Tom and take money to *not* move into the white community. When Lena demands that if he disgrace himself it be in front of his son, Walter Lee realizes that the white dream of success is not the right way for his family, and that they will move "into our house because my father—my father—he earned it for us brick by brick." Some critics have objected to the sudden-ness of Walter's change, arguing, as Gerald Weales does, "that his conversion seems imposed from the outside" (232). Yet such apparently abrupt reversals constitute a deliberate tactic of Hansberry's dramaturgy.

On one level, she writes what might be termed existential dramas, in which the processes of the characters' creating themselves, of defining who and what they are by the moral choices they make, is laid bare. On another level, she wants to establish, in the manner of her most decisive literary forbear, the Irish dramatist Sean O'Casey—whose influential *Juno and the Paycock* she first saw while a student at the University of Wisconsin—that only when a dramatist sees "the human person in its totality" and "tell[s] the truth about people," which necessarily entails presenting sometimes terribly flawed human beings, will the "genuine heroism which must naturally emerge" be credible. And yet, if she treasured O'Casey for his compassionate humanity, ironic humor, and implied belief in human potentiality, despite the foibles and failures that infuse his ghetto melodramas about the powerlessness of oppressed Dubliners living in the midst of enormous political upheaval, her social prescription departs from his: whereas O'Casey felt that the type of political order mattered little if there was not first an essential change in humankind itself, Hansberry blames the system and believes that change must begin there. Thus, on still a third level, Walter's capacity for dramatic change reflects his creator's belief, again shared with Miller, in the compelling interest of, and potentially tragic choice facing, the common man: "I happen to believe that the most ordinary human being . . . has within him elements of profundity, of profound anguish. You don't have to go to the kings and queens of the earth . . . but every human being is in enormous conflict about something" (*Young, Gifted, and Black*, 151).

The first gift that Mama gives Walter Lee, the money, plunges him to the depths; her second gift of moral acuity and authority helps him, as Mama exultantly proclaims, "come into his manhood . . . like a rainbow after the rain." And yet, the economic condition of this family remains unchanged, as is visually indicated by the worn furniture that will be moved from the tenement to the new house. When Mama slams the door she goes out, just as Nora in Ibsen's *A Doll House* does after that most famous of door closings in all modern drama, into a threatening world. Her return a few moments later for the wilting plant indicates this family will require nurturing to survive what lays ahead. They remain mired in subservient jobs and are likely to face, as Hansberry's own family did, bricks through windows from their racist neighbors. So *Raisin in the Sun*, rather than naively supporting integration or allowing its audiences to applaud, and thus to escape, protest directed against themselves, is in reality more subversive. "The dream denied," as the last line of Hughes's poem reminds, might not "dry up like a raisin in the sun," but rather "*explode*"—as America itself would in the 1960s.

The family member perhaps destined for greatest suffering under the continued economic burden is Walter Lee's work-weary wife, Ruth. Her plight underscores that Hansberry intends the play to confront not just issues of race and gender but those of social class as well; it is primarily economic realities, for instance, that prompt Ruth to make a down payment on an illegal abortion. When it appears after Walter loses the money that they will not be able to move, Ruth vows: "I'll work twenty hours a day in all the kitchens of Chicago . . . I'll strap my baby on my back if I have to and scrub all the floors in America and wash all the sheets in America if I have to—but we got to MOVE!" bell hooks's analysis in *Feminist Theory: From Margin to Center* of the dynamic of sexual oppression and exploitation at work within the lower-class black family finds an almost textbook application in the Youngers. According to hooks, black women like Ruth are objects of oppression: first by black men like Walter Lee, who must counter their own racial victimization and the resultant sense of themselves "as powerless and ineffectual in relation to ruling male groups" by "exaggerated expressions of male chauvinism [that] perpetuate [a] sexist ideology"; second by middle- and upper-class white women, themselves victims of sexism, who are yet able to exploit their servants and maids. The "double outsiders," so to speak, are then the "poor and working class women," such as Ruth and Mama, who "know from experience that work [is] for the most part exploitative and dehumanizing."[8]

The member of the Younger family with the best chance of escaping this net of gender and class discrimination is the college-age daughter Beneatha, through whom Hansberry—who admits that Beneatha is partially a self-portrait at a younger age—expresses her feminist, what she would call "womanist," agenda. Hansberry, in fact, once wrote that Simone de Beauvoir's "*The Second Sex* may well be the most important work of this century,"[9] and her female protagonists, such as Beneatha in *Raisin in the Sun* and Iris in *The Sign in Sidney Brustein's Window*, find themselves caught in the bind, explicated by de Beauvoir, between being a "sovereign subject" and a subservient object: "Now what peculiarly signalizes the situation of woman is that she—a free and autonomous being like all human creatures—nevertheless finds herself living in a world where men compel her to assume the status of the Other. . . . The drama of woman lies in this conflict between the fundamental aspirations of every subject (ego)—who always regards the self as the essential—and the compulsions of a situation in which she is the inessential. How can independence be recovered in a state of dependency?"[10]

Beneatha "looks for [her] *identity!*" as an adult, as a woman, and as a black. To discover it requires a certain rebellious spirit, sometimes affectionately parodied by the more mature Hansberry through a tone of playful exaggeration, a shedding of old selves and a trying on of new, much as Beneatha "experiment[s] with different forms of expression" through her hobbies, horseback riding last year, guitar playing this. To assert herself as a mature adult, she rejects the orthodox Christianity of her mother in favor of a rational humanism: "I get tired of [God] getting credit for all the things the human race achieves through its own stubborn effort. There simply is no blasted God—there is only man and it is *he* who makes miracles!" Such is Hansberry's "private" religion as well; acknowledging humankind's understandable need to "revert back to mystical ideas" when "we simply are confronted with some things we don't yet understand," she still regards these abstractions, as will Edward Albee, as illusions needed to get through life until reason, which is what "exalt[s] man," takes over: "I rather admire this human quality to make our own crutches as long as we need them. The only thing I am saying is that once we can *walk*, you know—then drop them" (*Young, Gifted, and Black*, 195, 197).

To claim independence as a woman, Beneatha chooses to pursue a nontraditional vocation as a doctor and denounces the attempts of her Nigerian boyfriend, Joseph Asagai, to use her as a sex object, claiming she's "not interested in being someone's little episode in America" and even suggesting that she might not ever marry—one of the few intimations in Hansberry's published works of her own lesbianism. Asagai's protestations to the contrary, sexual "feeling" between a man and a woman is *not* enough just "because that's what it says in all the novels that men write." To embrace her black identity and African heritage, Beneatha rejects George Murchison, the monied assimiliationist boyfriend in the Ivy League clothes, lets her hair go natural in an Afro, and in a show of anticolonial solidarity dons the native robes that Asagai brings back from Nigeria to perform a dance to African folk music.

Through Beneatha's discussion with Asagai at the opening of act 3 about the question of human progress and perfectability, Hansberry introduces into her work the debate between the absurdist and humanist views of history. Plunged into despair over the loss of the money for her education, Beneatha believes that she has now "stopped caring" about "being God" to others by curing their suffering. Because of her personal dilemma and disillusionment, she becomes cynical about the human condition: "Don't you see there isn't any real progress, Asagai, there is only one large circle that we march in, around and around." To which Asagai, who will return to his homeland to help move his "black countrymen" out of colonialism, perhaps only to be martyred for his efforts, counters that history, rather than a circle, "is simply a long line—as in geometry, you know, one that reaches into infinity. And because we cannot see the end—we also cannot see how it changes." Hansberry is neither so simplistic nor so sentimental as to deny the bleakness of the contemporary condition that she sees around her; intellectually, Hansberry may find Asagai's reading of human history more compatible with her own than Beneatha's, and yet, as Helene Keyser asserts, Beneatha's view more nearly reflects the family's condition at the close of the play.[11] At the same time, though, Hansberry believes that "man might just do what the apes never will—*impose* the reason for life on life" and thus use his unique "power to transform the universe" (*Young, Gifted, and Black*, 40). Her commitment to the possibility to alter one's destiny resembles that of the other great social dramatist of the American theater during the 1950s, Arthur Miller.

It finds further expression in her unproduced teleplay, *What Use Are Flowers?* (1961), a dramatic fable with appropriately flattened out characters, about rebuilding civilization after a nuclear holocaust. The Hermit, an English teacher who had escaped from the world into the woods 20 years earlier in misanthropic disgust, returns to find the children, refugees from the destruction, reduced to living in a prelingual state of Hobbesian savagery. The Hermit must act as a re-Creator by giving them names, as well as a vengeful Yahweh by renouncing them when they backslide; he must teach them the utilitarian skills required for physical survival, along with the "nonpractical" arts and civilizing graces—things like Beethoven's "Ode to Joy"—and emotions such as love and grief, which they must experience in order to be truly human. The final image of their trying to reconstruct the wheel that had been destroyed out of rivalry and jealousy places them on what Asagai would call the line of progress toward infinity, though the Hermit dies unsure that the line will remain unbroken. Hansberry pens here not an antitechnology fable but a plea that life be informed by aesthetic pleasure as well as pragmatic creation; in fact, the dichotomy of beauty versus use thematically situates this playlet securely in the Chekhovian tradition.

This debate over the validity of an absurdist epistemology and aesthetic, together with a strong emphasis on the indispensability of caring emotions, receives further elaboration in *The Sign in Sidney Brustein's Window* (1964), the only other Hansberry drama produced on Broadway during her lifetime.

A Challenge to Liberalism

A play about the need for caring, *The Sign in Sidney Brustein's Window* was kept alive on Broadway, in the face of less than enthusiastic reviews, by the commitment of Hansberry's friends and colleagues in the theater, finally closing after 101 performances on the night she died from cancer at the age of 34, 12 January 1965. Not as immediately emotionally affecting as *Raisin in the Sun*, and set outside the black ghetto in an ethnically and racially mixed cross-section of the liberal intelligentsia in the bohemian world of Greenwich Village, where Hansberry lived for a period in the 1950s, *The Sign in Sidney Brustein's Window* has a fuller canvas of characters and motifs; generally, critics felt it too cluttered. As James Baldwin explains, "It is possible . . . that [the play] attempts to say too much; but it is also exceedingly probable that it makes so loud and uncomfortable a sound because of the surrounding silence; not many plays, presently, risk being accused of attempting to say too much!" (xiv). Some audience discomfort may have stemmed from the work's central emphasis: the temporary disengagement and moral lapses that even the most well-intentioned intellectuals and artists and social activists are prone to as they do battle with cynicism and despair.

As the play opens, Sidney returns to the apartment he shares with his "Greco-Gaelic-[American] Indian hillbilly" wife, Iris, carrying crates of glassware, the remnants of a failed restaurant venture. Tired of taking on projects, he determines to "Presume no commitment, disavow all engagement, mock all great expectations," and celebrate the "death of the exclamation point." Angst-ridden, he desires to retreat, banjo in hand, to the mountains of Appalachia, where Iris can let down her hair and dance, a misguided, because apolitical, kind of Thoreauvian withdrawal, as their black friend Alton perceives. (Indeed, in a moment of reverie at the beginning of act 2, "the IRIS-of-his-Mind" will fulfill his daydream, "As he plays [and] the lighting shifts magically, and nonrealistically, to create the mountain of his dreams." Such interludes that move beyond merely factual realism are characteristic of Hansberry's otherwise almost naturalistic art, occurring also in *Raisin in the Sun*, as Walter mounts the kitchen table for his primitive dance, and in *Les Blancs*, during the ritual appearances of the African warrior goddess.) Yet, before long, Sidney takes over a newspaper; and although he promises to steer clear of politics, soon he is supporting Wally O'Hara for local office, complete with a sign in the window and a campaign song at rallies. When Wally unexpectedly wins, Iris reveals that he is controlled by corrupt political bosses and local drug lords; Wally himself rationalizes that to accomplish civic good requires "power" and money, which throws Sidney into despair.

Whereas earlier Sidney had mocked the absurdist philosophical position embodied in the plays of David, his homosexual neighbor, he now falls into cynical derision. As the only writer/character in Hansberry's canon, David might be expected to function as an authorial spokesperson. But Hansberry subjects the ideology underlying his art to strong criticism. His faddish off-Broadway play, featuring two characters who inhabit a refrigerator and positing a nothingness now and in the hereafter, reads like a parody of the works of such playwrights as N. F. Simpson and Eugene Ionesco. Hansberry herself engaged in a deliberate parody of Samuel Beckett when she wrote the unpublished playlet "The Arrival of Mr. Todog," and Sidney advises David to look to the social drama of Ibsen and Shaw rather than to the absurdists for models. Since, according to Steven Carter, "Hansberry agreed with Beckett and the other absurdists that existence has no preordained meaning, that past certainties and basic assumptions had indeed been tested and found wanting, [and] that much or even most of life is uncertain" (142), she could well understand the appeal of absurdism for post–World War II intellectuals who endured the Holocaust and the bomb. Nevertheless, she ultimately considered this philosophical stance as little more than a defeatist posture. In an expressionistic segment late in *The Sign in Sidney Brustein's Window*, marked by "deathly blue . . . and sensual fuchsia light," discordant "jazz sounds," and language with an unnatural "inton[ation and] a heightened, fragmented delivery," Sidney and David, together with Iris's sister, Gloria, join in "[a]n absurdist orgy . . . created in front of us—a disintegration of reality to parallel the disintegration in Sidney's world," defiantly mouthing the clichés of a too-easy despair over the human condition.

If Hansberry calls into question the ideology underlying David's plays, she scrutinizes him on the level of personal morality as well. Sidney, though nonjudgmental about David's homosexual lifestyle, suggests that he may be too exhibitionistic and self-pitying, employing his art to sublimate his anxieties. When the insecure young man temporarily sharing David's apartment demands the presence of a female voyeur before he can make love, David searches out someone to fill his partner's need; but in asking Gloria to watch, he would willingly reduce her to an object and demean her in her own eyes.

David's ethical failure, his desire to satisfy his lover but with total disregard for Gloria, is matched by Alton's inability to accept Gloria's past and marry her. When he discovers that she was a highly paid call girl, a "commodity" bought and sold like his slave grandmother, he refuses to take as wife "a white man's leavings." If Sidney's and Iris's moral lapses prove less hurtful to others than David's and Alton's, they still reveal a willingness to sell out, comparable to Walter Lee's in *Raisin in the Sun*. Sidney's act of corruption comes in trying to redeem his deteriorating relationship with Iris by helping shore up an acting career he has consistly belittled: if David will write a part for her into his next play, Sidney will respond with a favorable review in his paper. Even Iris, who no longer wants to satisfy Sidney's delimiting illusion of her as a mountain girl and yet fears being rejected as an actress, falls prey to moral lapses. Desperate to establish her independence and self-sufficiency, she will make commercials rather than serious work, even agreeing to spout erroneous advertising claims on screen.

Sidney insists, nevertheless, that he has retained the capacity to care: "It takes too much energy *not* to care. Yesterday I counted twenty-six gray hairs in the top of my head—all from trying *not* to care." And that capacity to be accountable is tested and reaffirmed in a most unexpected way, as Sidney feels compelled to make his own existential choice. Gloria, whose father called her "a tramp" on his deathbed for selling herself to survive, a truth she risked telling Alton, refuses to degrade herself as David wishes. Knowing that she is "better than this," and hoping that her father will forgive her, she commits suicide. Her decision to die rather than suffer further indignity paradoxically teaches Sidney that he must not continue through life refusing to stand up against the Wallys of this world, and that he and Iris must work through sorrow to arrive at strength: "hurt is desperation and desperation is—energy and energy can *move* things."

The father of the three sisters, Iris, Gloria, and the feisty if bigoted Mavis—who is limited by her bourgeois values but has, as Sidney empha-sizes, displayed courage by choosing the peculiar loneliness of staying in a loveless marriage—had changed their last name to Parodus. Referring literally to the chorus in Greek tragedy, here the name calls to mind all those who would watch from the sidelines, distanced and uninvolved, refusing to become engaged. Hansberry insists through Gloria's impact on Sidney that "people wanna be better than they are," that humankind must not fear commitment because of the pain it almost surely will exact but must instead rebel against passivity and inaction. As Sidney says when rejecting David's doctrine of the impossibility of progress: "The 'why' of why we are here is an intrigue for adolescents; the 'how' is what must command the living. Which is why I have lately became an insurgent again." That decision to pursue a path of revolutionary activism links him backward with Walter Lee and Mama of *Raisin in the Sun* and with Rissa and Hannibal of *Drinking Gourd*, and forward with the hero of the major stageplay Hansberry left unfinished at the time of her death.

The Revolutionary Commitment

Although Hansberry began writing *Les Blancs* in 1960–61—its title, "The Whites," alludes to Jean Genet's 1959 play, *The Blacks*—it was produced posthumously, in 1970, employing a text edited by Robert Nemiroff, the playwright's exhusband (they had divorced in 1964, less than a year before her death) and literary executor. Based loosely on Jomo Kenyatta, the drama is Hansberry's most ambitious in the sweep of its ideas, a powerful study of the ways in which Christianity, colonialism, and capitalism have conspired to oppress, enslave, and deracinate native Africans. Big business has come in, gouged out the earth, and hauled off the treasure, keeping the natives from progressing industrially into the twentieth century. The imperialists, represented by Major Rice, now call Africa "OUR HOME," employing the racist myth of the sacredness of white life to justify their tyrannical rule. The church, represented by the Schweitzer-like Reverend Neilsen, temporizes in matters of human rights by imposing foreign rituals that erase the cultural heritage of the natives and by undergirding a Eurocentric mentality and immorality.

Tshembe Matoseh, the focal figure in *Les Blancs*, is another of Hansberry's existential heroes who makes a series of moral choices that redefine him as a human being. Like Sidney Brustein, he moves from disavowing engagement to embracing commitment. Though he has not turned his back on activism as an ideal, now that he is married with a child in England he claims it is "all over with [him] and history"; having journeyed back to his homeland, unaware that he would be attending his father's funeral, he dismisses the rebel uprisings as "not [his] affair," saying he is no longer responsible. Yet historical events and processes force him to alter that resolve. To perform the tribal rites as eldest son, he must change from European to native dress, reminiscent of Beneatha's symbolic change of clothing in *Raisin in the Sun*; and wearing that garb, he confronts his brother, the middle son, Abioseh, a Catholic seminarian. Tshembe's African robes and primitive chants clash with the clerical dress and cross of his brother, who sees the rebels as terrorists who must be put down. The other man of the cloth, the Reverend Neilsen, not only had rejected the natives' petition for independence but had ostracized Tshembe's mother when she gave birth to a third son, Eric, fathered by the representative of the Empire, Major Rice. Eric is now being used as a sexual toy by the otherwise sympathetic Dr. Willy DeKoven, prescient enough to realize that he perpetuates suffering by participating in its cause. Neilsen, though a Christian minister still the most unregenerately racist of all, desired the mother and her mixed-race son dead, since God, he claims, had ordained absolutely "the natural separation of the races."

Tshembe, unlike those characters in *Drinking Gourd* who fail to see the connection between the black slaves and the poor whites, expresses sympathy for the white underclass, whose socioeconomic lot is little better than that of the Africans under colonialism and capitalism. He understands, too, that whites need the hatred of blacks to assuage their guilt for having oppressed them. Finally, he sees that the man of peace is no longer being heard, that the days of nonviolence are over. Even the American journalist, Charlie Morris, whose country's plane carrying bombs flies overhead, becomes a catalyst in urging Tshembe to actively involve himself in his fellow countrymen's fight for independence. Caught up in the primitive ritual dance, surreally lit, of the African warrior goddess, Tshembe discovers his new vocation. As Madame Neilsen, who had sheltered the exiled mother and child against her husband's wishes and who will die in a raid on the mission that marks the beginning of the end of colonialism, remarks: "Africa needs warriors." Tshembe's first act as a rebel must be to kill his reactionary brother Abioseh. His "animal-like cry of grief" that concludes the play is the cry of the totally engaged.

Tshembe's revolutionary act in *Les Blancs* seems of a piece with Rissa's decision in *Drinking Gourd* to refuse aid to Hiram and to arm Hannibal; yet because it entails the primal killing of brother by brother, it is more shockingly dramatic. It also reveals that if Hansberry had ever entertained integration as an answer to racial strife, she realized, however reluctantly, that there could come a time when violence becomes a moral necessity. As she wrote in a letter in 1962: "What I am saying is that whether we like the word or not, the condition of our people dictates what can only be called revolutionary attitudes. It is no longer acceptable to allow racists to define Negro manhood—and it will have to come to pass that they can no longer define his weaponry. I think, then, that Negroes must concern themselves with every single means of struggle: legal, illegal, passive, active, violent, and non-violent. They must harass, debate, petition, give money to court struggles, sit-in, lie-down, strike, boycott, sing hymns, pray on steps—and shoot from their windows when the racists come cruising through their communities" (*Young, Gifted, and Black*, 221–22).

Statements such as these, and plays such as *Les Blancs*, should indicate that those readers and critics to whom Lorraine Hansberry has appeared more interested in gaining acceptance from the largely white literary establishment than in speaking out unabashedly for the oppressed black minority are mistaken. Even the ending of *Raisin in the Sun*, with its potential for violence directed against the Youngers, belies the falsity of that impression, for, as Hansberry would also say: "I think it's very simple that the whole idea of debating whether or not Negroes should defend themselves is an insult. If anybody comes and does ill in your home . . . obviously, you try your best to kill him" (*Young, Gifted, and Black*, 249). While dramatizing her African-American characters' choices for self-hood and integrity, telling them to take up arms if necessary, she not only adamantly refuses to soothe her largely white audience's guilt over their responsibility for past racial inequities but increasingly challenges them in three powerful plays to adopt, if need be, an openly revolutionary stance aimed at ending those injustices. White audiences already of a liberal persuasion must now become radicalized. Some critics, such as Genevieve Fabre, have faulted Hansberry for employing the existing structures of "drama traditionally written by whites [that] requires catharsis" and thus not embracing experimental forms to express her revolutionary ideology.[12] Hansberry, however, always retains a primary focus on the dynamics of character change under pressure and manages, within the social/family problem play, to explode many of her audience's ingrained preconceptions about race and gender and to challenge them to be uncomfortable within existing social structures. Not only did her plays bring black drama to maturity. They charted the direction that virtually all later black theater in America would follow.

10

From the Margins: Edward Albee and the Avant-Garde

A compelling case can be made that the birthsites of modern American drama during the 1915–16 season were one of the nation's earliest "regional" theaters and an off-Broadway playhouse, when short works by Susan Glaspell, such as the protofeminist play "Trifles," and by Eugene O'Neill, such as the sea plays like "Bound East for Cardiff," were first produced at the Wharf Theater on Cape Cod and later at the Provincetown on Macdougal Street in New York. An equally compelling argument can be made that the birthsites of contemporary American drama during the 1959–60 season were again off-Broadway and out in the regions, with premieres in New York but away from Times Square of the first theatrical works by Edward Albee, Jack Gelber, and Jack Richardson and of plays in Cambridge, Massachusetts, by Arthur Kopit. Both groups of artists, separated by nearly a half-century, wrote against the Broadway establishment of their times and for audiences desiring something more than commercial pap. As Stuart Little remarks at the beginning of his historical survey entitled *Off Broadway: The Prophetic Theater*, "Off-Broadway is a state of mind, a set of production conditions, a way of looking at theater at every point at odds with Broadway's patterns."[1]

Kopit, whose *Oh Dad, Poor Dad, Mama's Hung You in the Closet and I'm Feeling So Sad* (for marquees large enough to accommodate it, the subtitle is: "A Pseudoclassical Farce in the Bastard French Tradition") finally reached off-Broadway in 1962, explains that these dramatists were committed to reinvigorating an American theater so fallen into desuetude that it bore "little more than superficial resemblance to the society and culture surrounding it" and so, unlike theater in most European countries, "lacked necessity" and did not matter.[2] In cultural histories of France, 1959 stands out as something of an annus mirabilis, with three important New Wave directors, Jean-Luc Goddard, Alain Resnais, and Francois Truffaut, all making first films that radically altered the grammar and style of the cinematic medium, *Breathless, Hiroshima, Mon Amour,* and *The 400 Blows.* The 1959–60 theatrical season in America would be hardly less a breath of fresh air, definitively announcing the end of the postwar era with Albee's "The Zoo Story," Gelber's *The Connection,* and Richardson's *The Prodigal.*

Richardson, Gelber, and the Off-Broadway Movement

Richardson's play, which like Sartre's *The Flies* and Anouilh's modern-dress *Antigone* adapts Greek myth for contemporary audiences, proves the least technically innovative yet most avowedly political of the three. Richardson's adroit re-visioning of the tale of Agamemnon's murder and the revenge of Orestes, his son, is openly critical of patriarchal authority in all its manifestations, in the family, in the state, in the military, in the writing of history itself. The playwright conceives of Orestes as a hater of pretense, possessing a strong sense of irony and a mocking laughter. Somewhat like Shakespeare's Prince Hal, he exercises the option of youth for "useless frolics" over civic duty; seeing that his father traded love for honor, for a "world to create," Orestes would rather retreat from public life, marry a fisherman's daughter, and be happy with his children. Particularly galling to him is society's tendency to assess the worth of a venture by the number of lives lost to accomplish it. Through his protagonist, Richardson seems intent on challenging civilization to question whether it can move beyond military might and mission as the sole means of measuring its power and influence. Yet discovering some means other than war and manifest destiny to validate it becomes difficult because of history's tendency to mythicize heroic exploits.

So Orestes rebels against the way "history," through the myths and legends woven around public figures, distorts reality and thereby constricts humankind's future rather than liberates it. After his father's assassination, Orestes must decide whether to continue fleeing from responsibility, rationalizing that his power to effect any social change will at best be minimal anyway, or to assume the burden of "thundering deeds." A skeptical, cynical Orestes finally submits to a historical process and destiny he feels incapable of fighting; claiming he "was not great enough to create something better," he "will go back, murder, and say it's for a better world, for this must be said to prevent insanity." Burdened with past history, he seems destined to assume a defeatist, antiheroic posture: "The world demands that we inherit the pretensions of our fathers, that we go on killing in the name of ancient illusions about ourselves, that we assume the right to punish, order, and invent philosophies to make our worst moments seem inspired."

Gelber's *The Connection*, premiered by The Living Theatre performance group founded by Julian Beck and Judith Malina, is smaller in scope, but no less impressive an achievement. On one level, Gelber's work—which incorporates a half-hour of jazz in the style of Charlie Parker into each of its two acts—is a Pirandellian play within the-making-of-a-play within the-making-of-a-movie that raises questions about the intersection between art and life and the writer's control, or loss of control, when a drama moves from page to stage. Gelber announces his drama's radical difference from the standard naturalistic Broadway play of the 1950s about dope addiction by having one of his characters allude dismissively to the ending of Michael Gazzo's *A Hatful of Rain* (1955), where a pregnant wife tries to save her junkie war-veteran husband by calling the police to come for him. Gelber's Jaybird, the author, wants his play to create the aura or illusion of improvisation; the actors are supposedly addicts off the street working for a few hours for money for a fix, even ready to take handouts from the voyeuristic audience during intermission. The question of whether this is all "really real" becomes clouded when Leach takes an overdose (he recovers), and Jaybird realizes that his desire "to do something far out . . . to have a little shock value" in order to neutralize the horror has gotten away from him and he, try as he might to prevent it, has "lost . . . the end." One of the photographers, certain that the movie they are filming will be cinema verité, keeps proclaiming of the action, "That's the way it really is"; once an action is staged before an audience, however, the line between life and art inevitably becomes drawn.

The Connection is not without its specific sociopolitical commentary that "Everything that's illegal is illegal because it makes more money for more people that way"; nevertheless, it remains close in its texture to that other, if less gritty, play about the need for artificial stimulants, some "dope dream" to sustain life, O'Neill's *The Iceman Cometh*. The men in Gelber's play are "waiting" for Cowboy, their heroin supplier, to arrive on "a white horse": "The connection is coming. He is always coming." Yet one of the addicts intimates that their Godot differs little from that awaited by everyone in the audience: "And like the rest of us you are a little hungry for a little hope. So you wait and worry. A fix of hope. A fix to forget. A fix to remember, to be sad, to be happy, to be, to be." Even Gazzo had employed the image of waiting: "the age of the vacuum, everybody's waiting—and no one believes." And Albee will continue the examination of the illusions humankind depends on to face what is sometimes perceived as a void.

Albee and the Absurd

Like O'Neill a half-century earlier, Albee chose initially to write what he calls "the brief play," and, in fact, he was introduced to New York audiences at the very same theater, the Provincetown Playhouse in Greenwich Village, where O'Neill had been. Nor had there been any dearth of important one-act plays during the 50 intervening years by American writers as various as Clifford Odets (*Waiting for Lefty*), Thornton Wilder ("The Long Christmas Dinner," "Pullman Car Hiawatha," "The Happy Journey to Trenton and Camden"), Tennessee Williams ("27 Wagons Full of Cotton," "Portrait of a Madonna"), and William Inge ("To Bobolink, for Her Spirit," "The Boy in the Basement"). In his landmark study, *The Theatre of the Absurd* (1961), Martin Esslin was the first critic to suggest that Albee, on the basis of his earliest one-act plays, should be grouped together with Samuel Beckett, Eugene Ionesco, Jean Genet, and company. Albee, in fact, refers to Ionesco's writings in his frequently reprinted essay, "Which Theatre is the Absurd One?" (1962). Playing with possible senses of the word "absurd," the dramatist's own answer to the question posed by his title is "the commercial Broadway one," for "what could be more absurd than a theater" that measures aesthetic quality by the amount of money taken in at the box office; that relegates the playwright to a collaborative position; that worships imports from London next to idolatry; and that in some seasons sees "not a single performance of a play by Beckett, Brecht, Chekhov, Genet, Ibsen, O'Casey, Pirandello, Shaw, Strindberg—or Shakespeare?" Albee goes on to propose "that the supposed Realistic theater" that encompasses most of the works produced on Broadway "panders to the public need for self-congratulation and reassurance and presents a false picture of ourselves to ourselves," whereas "The Theatre of the Absurd, in the sense that it is truly the contemporary theater," forces audiences to "face up to the human condition as it really is."[3]

Albee dramatizes the same point in his slight little sketch, "Fam and Yam" (1960), which is "An Imaginary Interview" between The Famous American Playwright of the post–World War II generation, probably William Inge, and The Young American Playwright of the nascent off-Broadway movement, almost certainly Albee himself. The playlet might be seen as his clarion call for a new American theater as opposed to the ailing and sickly old, which was characterized by "greedy" theater owners, "opportunistic" producers, "slick" directors, "assembly-line" critics, "pin-headed" theater parties, and playwrights who themselves elevated financial over artistic success.

Along with excoriating most commercial Broadway theater in his essay, Albee offers his personal perspective on what constitutes absurdist drama: "As I get it, The Theatre of the Absurd is an absorption-in-art of certain existentialist and post-existentialist philosophical concepts having to do, in the main, with man's attempts to make sense for himself out of his senseless position in a world which makes no sense—which makes no sense because the moral, religious, political and social structures man has erected to 'illusion' himself have collapsed" (147). Albee's works do, indeed, consistently explore the illusions that humankind creates in every area of endeavor to cushion and help make bearable the reality of that existence. In doing so, he recurrently employs many of the theatrical techniques—incomplete exposition; breakdown of causal connections; ambiguous closure; language games—that have come to be associated with one or other of the major Continental absurdist playwrights.

Yet there remain serious questions as to whether Albee in his early short plays does in fact subscribe to the central ideological tenets of the absurd. Brian Way, for instance, has argued convincingly that Albee "retreat[s] from the full implications of the absurd [wherein] the arbitrary, the disconnected, the irrelevant, non-reason, are seen to be the main principle or non-principle of the universe," because he "still believes in the validity of reason—that things can be proved, or that events can be shown to have definite meanings."[4] While Albee might at times embrace absurdism in style, he generally does not (except in his metaphysical drawing-room play, *Tiny Alice* [1964]) adhere to or advance an uncompromisingly absurdist philosophy. Ideologically, he remains a traditional liberal humanist, assuming much the same philosophical stance and political agenda as Lillian Hellman, Arthur Miller, and Lorraine Hansberry before him, exalting the natural virtues of an enlightened commitment to ideals of conduct guided by reason; a criticism of moral failure within a framework of compassion; and an overriding sense of responsibility to the community of humankind.

This is not to deny, however, Albee's leadership among the theatrical avant-garde, which he describes as "free-swinging, bold, iconoclastic, and often wildly, wildly funny." He continues by promising audiences, "If you will approach it with childlike innocence—putting your standard responses aside, for they do not apply—if you will approach it on its own terms, I think you will be in for a liberating surprise" (*Which Theater?* 150). Albee's fullest statement of his aesthetic goals appears in the introduction to his most experimental drama, *Box and Quotations from Chairman Mao Tse-Tung* (1968), where he speaks about the dual obligation facing the serious dramatist: "first, to make some statement about the condition of 'man' . . . and, second, to make some statement about the nature of the art form with which he is working. In both instances he must attempt change." Refusing to placate or be satisfied with the status quo entails, in turn, a commitment on the part of the playwright to "try to alter his society [and] to alter the forms within which his precursors have had to work." Nor does he omit his spectators or readers from the equation, for "an audience has an obligation (to itself, to the art form in which it is participating, and even to the playwright) to be willing to experience a work on its own terms." If they are to fulfill his own dicta, Albee's one-act plays, then, will partake in a spirit of anarchy, challenging preconceived ideas, theatrical conventions, and audience expectations.

Albee's One-Act Plays

First premiered in 1959 in West Berlin, before its New York opening on a double bill with Beckett's "Krapp's Last Tape" in January 1960, Albee's

"The Zoo Story," despite its brevity, establishes itself as emblematic of the age that produced it. A parable of alienation and spiritual dislocation in the nuclear age of anxiety, it dramatizes "the way people exist," afraid of aloneness yet equally leery of making contact, "everyone separated by bars from everyone else." The bench on a Sunday afternoon in Central Park, the only object on a minimally dressed stage, becomes symbolic of the space, so close and yet so distant, that separates and imprisons individuals within their own shells; and the park/garden itself intimates a fallen world of discord rather than harmony. Contemporary urban society is filled with outcasts, the marginalized and the disenfranchised. As Jerry catalogues them, in his roominghouse alone there live, among others, "a colored queen" who frequently plucks "his eyebrows . . . with Buddhist concentration"; "a Puerto Rican family" of husband, wife, and uncounted children; a "person in the front room whom [he's] never seen"; and a "woman who cries deliberately behind her closed door."

In a pattern he will repeat over and again in his later works, Albee brings a character from the outside into the playing space to challenge someone already there. On the park bench reading sits Peter, a fortyish, Madison Avenue type textbook editor who lives on the Upper East Side with his nuclear family, consisting of a wife and two of everything else, daughters, cats, parakeets, TVs—but no sons. Ironically, the happily conformist and complacent Peter is perhaps the most unknowingly isolated of all. Fulfilling the image of the perfect organization man in the gray flannel suit, he is so predictable as to be a nonentity, and thus can be described only by what he is not: "neither fat nor gaunt, neither handsome or homely"; through Peter's characterization, Albee removes the veneer from the "peachy-keen" Eisenhower era, revealing the shallowness and disquietude lurking underneath. Most damning of all for someone in the world of books and education who should be a sophisticated reader, Peter seems baffled by the narrative text that the intruder Jerry creates for him.

Jerry, whose handsome good looks have been replaced by "a great weariness," possesses an awareness of loneliness and death-in-life that Peter lacks. Orphaned at a young age (his memory box contains two empty picture frames), he experienced a loving homosexual relationship for a week when he was 15; now, however, Jerry is a "permanent transient" who finds himself unable to have sex with the same person more than once. Forcing the reluctant Peter to be his audience, in one of the wonderful verbal arias for which Albee will become known, he narrates "THE STORY OF JERRY AND THE DOG!" Standing guard for his "ugly,

Title page of program for first American production of Edward Albee's "The Zoo Story." *Courtesy of Billy Rose Theatre Collection, The New York Public Library for the Performing Arts, Astor, Lenox, and Tilden Foundations.*

misanthropic" landlady is a dog who, unlike almost everyone else, displays not just indifference to Jerry but open hostility. Disliking such antipathy, Jerry vows to break through and make "contact"; he determines to "kill the dog with kindness, and if that doesn't work . . . just kill him," first by feeding him hamburgers and then, if necessary, by poisoning the meat. The dog survives, but they do reach "an understanding." Moreover, Jerry, having tried to break down the bars between self and other "in this humiliating excuse for a jail," has "learned that neither kindness nor cruelty by themselves, independent of each other, creates any effect beyond themselves; and . . . that the two combined, together, at the same time, are the teaching emotion. And what is gained is love." His epiphany that "we neither love nor hurt because we do not try to reach each other" espouses Albee's belief that the necessity to break out of the shell of self and effect communion with the other can justify hurting that other to bring him or her to awareness. To be creative, love sometimes must be corrosive.

Peter fails to see that Jerry, in narrating the story of himself and the dog, actually tells the drama of himself and Peter as it acts itself out on a Sunday afternoon in Central Park. When Jerry as fabulist proves ineffectual because of the recalcitrance and lack of perception of his listener, he must employ other, increasingly brutal tactics. In answer to Peter's protest "I DON'T UNDERSTAND! . . . I DON'T WANT TO HEAR ANY MORE," Jerry first tickles Peter; when that does not work, in a version of the child's game King of the Mountain, he pushes him off the bench; and when that still fails to create the desired effect, he ultimately forces Peter to pick up a knife and hold it while Jerry impales himself on it and dies. Now, at last, Peter may no longer be "a vegetable" but at least "an animal" whose conscious life will never be the same. Some critics have interpreted Jerry's death as either a suicide that he was unable to effect on his own or a disguised homosexual act, and validity may inhere in both readings. But it seems that Albee, as Rose Zimbardo proposes in her seminal essay,[5] intended viewers of his own "story of Jerry and Peter" to understand Jerry's death as a potentially salvific sacrifice meant to raise Peter from the illusion of well-being and complacency to greater knowledge of what it means to be fully human, a reading that finds support in the biblical pharaseology ("So be it"; "I came unto you") that Albee employs near the startling close of his play.

Commissioned to provide a short dramatic piece for Gian Carlo Menotti's 1959 Festival of the Two Worlds in Spoleto, Italy, Albee decided to take the characters from another brief play on which he was working and place them into a different situation. What resulted was "The Sandbox," a near perfect little gem of a play, only around 20 minutes in performance, that blends symbolism with surrealism, dedicated to the memory of his much beloved grandmother. The minimalist setting is "a bare stage" against the sea and the sky. Mommy and Daddy, with a Musician in tow who provides flute accompaniment on cue to set the mood, enter carrying Grandma "under her armpits" and rather unceremoniously plop her down in a "child's sandbox" where, somewhat like Winnie in Beckett's *Happy Days* (1962), she proceeds to bury herself. Mommy and Daddy, whom the stage directions denote as presenile and vacuous, are deliberately flat stereotypes: she "imposing" and dominating, he "whining" and submissive, tending to respond with "Whatever you say, Mommy." They sit and, as Mommy says, "We . . . wait." As a number of commentators have remarked, waiting has become, after Beckett's seminal play, one of the central images of post–World War II theater. And "Sandbox," as a deathwatch, is a play of waiting. Yet the platitudinous Mommy and Daddy cannot respond with any true feeling, mouthing instead only the ready-made inanities familiar from greeting cards. The ritual exists for them stripped of any meaning, except getting Grandma out of their lives and "fac[ing] the future" with the same lack of awareness with which they have gotten through the past.

Just as nothing "real" exists beneath the outer shell of Mommy and Daddy, so, too, is the "well-built" young actor, not yet given a name or identity by Hollywood, all surface and role. But dressed in a bathing suit and doing calisthenics so that his arms resemble the "fluttering of wings," he plays well and sensitively his role as the Angel of Death. "Sandbox" achieves its forcefulness and, finally, real poignancy, in the way that Grandma, who experiences "puzzlement" and "fear" and tangentially decries the lack of respect shown aged parents, breaks through the predictable to experience genuine emotion. What at first she thought simply a game or role, playing at dying, becomes the reality of death, come for her and waiting to be accepted. She grows in awareness, in recognition and resignation. Functioning partly as mocking chorus of her children's phony responses as well as partly stage manager who orchestrates her own end provides her with a measure of control and contributes to the dignity and tranquillity of her death. Grandma can finally "go gentle into that good night" at what is for Albee at this point in his career an uncharacteristically tender close to the play.

In his preface to "The American Dream" (1961), Albee writes explicitly about the intention behind his lengthy one-acter: "The play is an examination of the American Scene, an attack on the substitution of artificial for real values in our society, a condemnation of complacency, cruelty, emasculation and vacuity; it is a stand against the fiction that everything in this slipping land of ours is peachy keen." He comments further about his work's manner: "Is the play offensive? I certainly hope so; it was my intention to offend—as well as amuse and entertain." In its use of flat, cartoonlike characters, banal and repetitious dialogue, and outrageous non sequiturs (Mommy greets a visitor by asking "Won't you take off your dress?" to which Mrs. Barker replies "I don't mind if I do"), "American Dream" comes closest of all Albee's plays stylistically to the absurdist drama of someone like Eugene Ionesco in *Bald Soprano* (1948), in which no soprano, let alone a bald one, ever appears. As satiric social criticism, Albee's work dramatizes the devaluation of the family—in a pluralistic society traditionally the main source of moral values—brought about through an embrace of material culture, a diminution of affective response, and a restrictive definition of sex roles that diminishes and delimits the individual.

Albee indicates this progressive deterioration in values by contrasting three generations. The wizened yet still wise Grandma hails from feisty "Pioneer stock"; the boxes in which she has packed the things "one accumulates" forge her link with the past. Now treated like a dog and bundled up to await the van man who will cart her off to the nursing home, something she would never have done to her own mother, she predicts that because it lacks a "sense of dignity" modern "civilization's doomed." She terms the present time an "age of deformity." Her daughter and son-in-law, expanded portraits of the Mommy and Daddy from "Sandbox" who bear the same name, are like a parody of the Strindbergian couple.

Mommy, whose more realistically portrayed antecedents in the American theater of the 1950s include the man-hating Ann from Joseph Kramm's *The Shrike* (1953) and the domineering Eliza Gant from Ketti Frings's stage adaptation of *Look Homeward, Angel* (1956), is the archetypal emasculator; she orders Daddy to "Pay attention" and deems Mrs. Barker's husband "adorable" since he is confined to a wheelchair. Marriage was entered into strictly as a business proposition, money to live off of in exchange for sexual favors; Mommy, nevertheless, is more than content that Daddy "has tubes now, where he used to have tracts," though she insults him for being "indecisive" and turned to jelly. Mommy adopts as her motto in all things the great American advertising slogan, "Satisfaction guaranteed or your money back." Unable to have a child of their own, Mommy and Daddy—unlike George and Martha in Albee's later masterpiece, "Who's Afraid of Virginia Woolf?" [1962], who refuse to blame each other for their sterility—adopt their little "bumble of joy" for use in the war against one another from the Bye-Bye (read "Buy, Buy") Adoption Agency. Finding him not to their liking, they mutilate him.

Now years later, baby arrives resurrected, so to speak, in the form of his twin brother, a "clean-cut, midwest farm boy type, almost insultingly good-looking in a typically American way," whom Grandma immediately dubs "the American Dream." Another actor like the Young Man from "Sandbox," he is a beautiful hulk on the outside, but spiritually undernourished, without feelings or moral sense within. For when his twin brother, whom he describes as "the rest of [him]self," underwent mutilation, he, too, "suffered losses. . . . A fall from grace . . . a departure of innocence" so that, cold and emotionless, he has "not been able to love anyone." His fall from grace evidences the blighting of the American Eden. Admitting that he will "do almost anything for money," he will stay as substitute son, ready to serve as stud-boy to Mommy.

Grandma finally becomes not only both stage manager/manipulator and detached onstage audience to these proceedings but also a choral commentator, speaking a tongue-in-cheek epilogue that sends the audience home while "everybody's got what he thinks he wants. . . . I mean, for better or worse, this is a comedy, and I don't think we'd better go any further." Her valedictory to this eulogy for the American Dream gone mad relates directly back to Albee's intention to shock his audience into an awareness that, if taken further, what he actually outlines here is closer to "the American tragedy."

The central image of marginalization of the "other," of the silencing of difference in all of Albee's one-act plays comes in The Death of Bessie Smith (1960). The playwright's coup de theater is to have the great blues singer never appear or be heard; her absence becomes in itself a powerful symbolic statement of the invisibility of blacks in white society, except when they can be commodified through their music, as Bessie was, or through their menial service, as the hospital Orderly willingly is. In life, Bessie had been answerable to her white producers and promoters, who lived off her financially and for whom she had to "hustle"; in death— and this forms the background of Albee's play—her body, shattered in a car crash, was shunted off from a segregated white hospital to a black hospital in Clarksdale, Mississippi, in 1937. (In a New York revival late in the 1960s, Albee agreed to the addition of original recordings and photographic slides of Bessie, which he had at first rejected as too emotional a ploy; indeed, the text would seem to invite such multimedia or even cinematic treatment.) Both the racial bigotry of the South, however, and the battles between the sexes are subsumed here under a more general examination of power structures, sometimes achieved solely through language.

The Nurse dominates all the men with whom she comes in contact. She belittles her father, who seems to have schooled her in prejudice, as a "hanger-on" and a "flunky." Reduced to using a cane, he no longer even wields that powerfully, but instead raps it in "a helpless and pathetic flailing." She patronizes the black Orderly for his deferential behavior, calling him "boy" and "ass-licker," sending him to fetch cigarettes and accusing him of bleaching his skin. Like Clay in LeRoi Jones/Amiri Baraka's *Dutchman* (1964), he has become an Uncle Tom, trying to "advance" himself by telling whites what they "want to hear" and buying into their value system. The Nurse both desires and derides the good-looking blond Intern, teasing him yet putting him off, reminding him of his place socially and economically, and abusing him physically. When he refuses her orders not to go outside and treat Bessie, she threatens to ruin his career at the hospital.

Some hazy writing on Albee's part leaves slightly blurry whether or not the Nurse recognizes the aloneness likely to result from her attempt to dominate others and so suffers self-hatred because of it; she professes a distaste for existence ("I am sick of everything in this hot, stupid, fly-ridden world. . . . I am tired of my skin. . . . I WANT OUT!") and is somewhere between laughter and tears as she ineffectually mocks the Intern's humanity. The apocalyptic image of "the great sunset blaz[ing]" that concludes the play hints that the Intern's earlier description of sundown, "The west is burning . . . fire has enveloped fully half the continent," might be read symbolically as pronouncing the decline of the West, consumed by exploitation, subjugation, and victimization of weaker by stronger, minority by majority, outsider by insider. Albee's archetypal Jerry, for example, is as socially, and perhaps sexually, marginalized as Inge's characters, who could only be true to their identity and feelings—that is, their essential humanness—when hidden away in closets or in basements.

Undeniably, some recurrent patterns in Albee's short plays—a character's arriving onstage to challenge the "other" to overcome fear of the unknown and awake to a fuller humanity; power conflicts in gender relationships; criticism of middle-class stasis and moral complacency—look forward to later, more major works by the playwright, such as *Who's*

Afraid of Virginia Woolf? (1962), A *Delicate Balance* (1966), and *Seascape* (1975). At the same time, however, the early one-acts serve as a culmination or summing up of many of the central emphases of post–World War II American drama. With their intimations of absurdity they speak, as do the works of Eugene O'Neill, of alienation and dislocation, mourning the estrangement of modern humankind from any source of ultimate meaning. They castigate, as do the plays of Lillian Hellman, Arthur Miller, and Tennessee Williams, an ethos of commodification that reduces culture to money and power and enshrines the material over the immaterial. Albee regrets, as does Miller, the replacement of a once empowering dream of an Eden regained by an enslaving devotion to competition and success. He reveres, as does Williams, the transmutative possibilities of art, the imaginative creation of a narrative/text or role/ mask as a grace-filled moment that is potentially educative and salvific. And like Lorraine Hansberry, his art tries to subvert those social structures and benighted attitudes that inhibit human progress and potential.

What Robert Motherwell, the American abstract expressionist painter, wrote about modern abstract art in 1951 as a response to "a feeling of being ill at ease in the universe" over "the collapse of religion, of the old close-knit community and family" provides a fit summation of the thrust of modern American drama from 1940 to 1960 as perfected by Albee and such forbears as O'Neill and Williams: "It is a fundamentally romantic response to modern life—rebellious, individualistic, unconventional, sensitive, irritable."[6] And also, Motherwell might have added, at its best moments, glorious.

chronology

Date	Drama, Literature, Art	World and National Events
1940	Robert Sherwood's *There Shall Be No Night* and James Thurber and Elliott Nugent's *The Male Animal* performed. Disney Studios release *Fantasia*.	Germany invades much of Europe. Fall of France and Battle of Britain. United States begins peace-time draft. Franklin Delano Roosevelt elected to third term as President of the United States.
1941	Lillian Hellman's *Watch on the Rhine* and Paul Green and Richard Wright's *Native Son* performed. Orson Welles's *Citizen Kane* released. Edward Hopper's "Nighthawks" displayed.	Lend-Lease program to aid Britain begins. Japanese attack Pearl Harbor 7 December.
1942	Thornton Wilder's *The Skin of*	Battle of Midway. Allies invade

	Our Teeth produced. T. S. Eliot's *Four Quartets* and Albert Camus's *The Stranger* published. Aaron Copland's *Rodeo* performed.	North Africa. Enrico Fermi splits the atom.
1943	Betty Smith's *A Tree Grows in Brooklyn* published. Richard Rodgers and Oscar Hammerstein's *Oklahoma* premieres. *Casablanca* opens. Abstract painter Jackson Pollock has one-man show.	Allies invade Italy. Wage-price freeze in United States.
1944	Mary Chase's *Harvey*, Tennessee Williams's *The Glass Menagerie*, and Sartre's *No Exit* performed. Aaron Copland's *Appalachian Spring* premieres.	D-Day, 6 June. Allies invade the Continent. Roosevelt elected to fourth term.
1945	Benjamin Britten's opera *Peter Grimes* and Rodgers and Hammerstein's *Carousel* premiere.	Roosevelt dies 12 April. Harry Truman becomes president. Germany surrenders 7 May. United States drops atom bomb on Hiroshima 6 August. Japan surrenders 9 August.
1946	Robert Penn Warren's *All the King's Men* and John Hersey's *Hiroshima* published. Eugene O'Neill's *The Iceman Cometh* and Arthur Miller's *All My Sons* performed. William Wyler's *The Best Years of Our Lives* released.	United Nations holds first session. Juan Peron elected President of Argentina. Italy becomes a republic. Verdicts reached in Nuremberg trials. Atomic Energy Commission founded. Xerox process invented. Bikini swimsuits make their appearance.
1947	Albert Camus's *The Plague* and Anne Frank's *Diary* published. Tennessee Williams's *A Streetcar Named Desire* premieres. Sculptures by Henry Moore and Albert Giacometti exhibited. Blacklisting of Hollywood filmmakers begins. Great Books program introduced.	Peace treaties signed in Paris. India proclaims its independence. U.S. Secretary of State George Marshall conceives European Recovery Program. U.S. plane flies at supersonic speed. Henry Ford (born 1863) dies. The Dead Sea Scrolls discovered.

1948   T. S. Eliot wins Nobel Prize for Literature. Norman Mailer's *The Naked and the Dead* and James A. Michener's *Tales of the South Pacific* published. Laurence Olivier's *Hamlet* released. Cole Porter's *Kiss Me, Kate* premieres.

Harry S. Truman elected thirty-third President of the United States. Mahatma Gandhi (born 1869), Prime Minister of India, assassinated. Modern Jewish State (Israel) comes into existence, with David Ben-Gurion as Premier. Long-playing records invented. World Council of Churches organized. Alfred Kinsey releases report on male sexuality. Babe Ruth (born 1895) dies.

1949   William Faulkner wins Nobel Prize for literature. Arthur Miller's *Death of a Salesman* and T. S. Eliot's *The Cocktail Party* premiere. Rodgers and Hammerstein's *South Pacific* opens. George Orwell's *1984* and Simone de Beauvoir's *The Second Sex* published. Bertolt Brecht founds The Berliner Ensemble.

People's Republic of China proclaimed under Mao Tse-Tung. Pandit Nehru becomes Prime Minister of India. Program of apartheid established in South Africa. U.S.S.R. tests atomic bomb. Hungarian Cardinal Mindszenty sentenced to life imprisonment for "treason."

1950   G. Bernard Shaw (born 1852) dies. Ezra Pound's *Cantos* published. Frank Loesser and Abe Burrows's *Guys and Dolls* premieres.

Korean War begins. Chiang Kai-Shek resumes presidency of Nationalist China. Alger Hiss found guilty of perjury. National Council of Churches formed.

1951   J. D. Salinger's *The Catcher in the Rye*, James Jones's *From Here to Eternity*, William Styron's *Lie Down in Darkness*, and Rachel Carson's *The Sea around Us* published. Robert Frost's *Complete Poems* issued. John Huston's *The African Queen* released. Gian Carlo Menotti's TV opera, *Amahl and the Night Vistors*, shown. *I Love Lucy* begins long TV run.

Winston Churchill becomes British Prime Minister. Color television introduced.

1952   Ralph Ellison's *The Invisible*

General Dwight D. Eisenhower

Man and Ernest Hemingway's *The Old Man and the Sea* published. Samuel Beckett's *Waiting for Godot* and Agatha Christie's *The Mousetrap* premiere. *High Noon* released.

elected thirty-fourth President of the United States. King George VI of England dies. Dr. Albert Schweitzer wins Nobel Peace Prize. First U.S. hydrogen bomb exploded. Contraceptive pill produced.

1953   Eugene O'Neill (born 1888) dies. Arthur Miller's *The Crucible* and Robert Anderson's *Tea and Sympathy* premiere. Buckminister Fuller designs geodesic dome. José Quintero's production of *Summer and Smoke* (by Tennessee Williams) inaugurates off-Broadway movement.

Stalin (born 1879) dies. Nikita Khrushchev appointed First Secretary of Communist party. Korean War ends. Elizabeth II crowned Queen of British Commonwealth. Dag Hammarskjold elected Secretary-General of the United Nations. Julius and Ethel Rosenberg executed for espionage. Alfred Kinsey releases report on female sexual behavior.

1954   Ernest Hemingway wins Nobel Prize for literature. Kingsley Amis's *Lucky Jim*, William Golding's *Lord of the Flies*, and J. R. R. Tolkien's *The Lord of the Rings* published. Federico Fellini's *La Strada* and Elia Kazan's *On the Waterfront* released. Newport (Rhode Island) Jazz Festival founded.

U.S. Supreme Court rules against segregation in public schools. Senator Joseph McCarthy censured by Senate. Atomic physicist J. Robert Oppenheimer's security clearance withdrawn.

1955   Vladimir Nabokov's *Lolita* and Graham Greene's *The Quiet American* published. Arthur Miller's *View from the Bridge*, Tennessee Williams's *Cat on a Hot Tin Roof*, William Inge's *Bus Stop*, and Lawrence and Lee's *Inherit the Wind* receive first productions. *Marty* (with Ernest Borgnine) and *Richard III* (with Laurence Olivier) released.

Anthony Eden succeeds Winston Churchill as Prime Minister of Great Britain. Black boycott of city buses in Montgomery, Alabama. A.F.L. and C.I.O. merge under George Meany. Albert Einstein (born 1879) dies.

1956   John Osborne's *Look Back in*

Eisenhower reelected President of

Anger, Albert Goodrich and Frances Hackett's *The Diary of Anne Frank*, and Eugene O'Neill's *Long Day's Journey into Night* premiere. Dramatist Bertolt Brecht (born 1898) dies. John F. Kennedy's *Profiles in Courage* and W. H. Whyte's *The Organization Man* published. Lerner and Loewe's *My Fair Lady* opens. Ingmar Bergman's *The Seventh Seal* released.

the United States. Abdel Nasser elected President of Egypt and seizes Suez Canal. Martin Luther King emerges as civil rights leader. Albert Sabin develops oral polio vaccine. Italian liner *Andrea Doria* sinks off Nantucket Island, Massachusetts. Elvis Presley becomes rock-n-roll sensation.

1957 Albert Camus awarded Nobel Prize for literature. Jack Kerouac's *On the Road* and Bernard Malamud's *The Assistant* published. Samuel Beckett's *Endgame* and William Inge's *The Dark at the Top of the Stairs* first produced. Leonard Bernstein's *West Side Story* opens.

Harold Macmillan becomes Prime Minister of Great Britain. U.S.S.R. launches Sputnik I and II, first earth satellites. Israel withdraws from Sinai Peninsula and hands over Gaza Strip to United Nations.

1958 Boris Pasternak, author of *Dr. Zhivago*, wins Nobel Prize for literature. Harold Pinter's *The Birthday Party*, Archibald MacLeish's *J.B.*, and Eugene O'Neill's *A Touch of the Poet* first produced. Van Cliburn wins Moscow Tchaikovsky piano competition. Guggenheim Museum, designed by Frank Lloyd Wright, opens in New York City. African novelist Chinua Achebe's *Things Fall Apart* published.

European Common Market established. Egypt and Sudan join to form United Arab Republic with Nasser as president. Governor Orval Faubus of Arkansas defies court-ordered segregation of schools. Angelo Cardinal Roncalli elected Pope John XXIII. Alaska becomes forty-ninth state.

1959 Saul Bellow's *Henderson the Rain King* and Philip Roth's *Goodbye, Columbus* published. First performances of Eugene Ionesco's *The Rhinoceros*, Lillian

Fidel Castro becomes Premier of Cuba. General Charles de Gaulle becomes President of France. U.S.S.R. launches rocket with two monkeys into space. Pope

Hellman's *Toys in the Attic*, William Gibson's *The Miracle Worker*, Edward Albee's "The Zoo Story," and Lorraine Hansberry's *A Raisin in the Sun*. Alain Resnais's *Hiroshima, Mon Amour* and Federico Fellini's *La Dolce Vita* released. U.S. Postmaster bans D. H. Lawrence's *Lady Chatterley's Lover* as obscene.

John XXIII calls first Ecumenical Council since 1870. Hawaii becomes fiftieth state.

1960   John Updike's *Rabbit, Run* and Harper Lee's *To Kill a Mockingbird* published. Alfred Hitchcock's *Psycho* and Alain Resnais's *Last Year at Marienbad* released. First performances of Edward Albee's "The American Dream" and Robert Bolt's *A Man for All Seasons*.

A U.S. U-2 reconnaissance airplane is shot down over the U.S.S.R. John Fitzgerald Kennedy elected as thirty-fifth (and youngest) President of the United States. Thirteen contestants arrested for perjury over rigging of TV quiz shows.

notes and references

Because virtually all of the works discussed in this book are readily available in a number of different editions and collections, no page references are provided for quotations from the plays within the text. Publication information about specific editions can be found in the Selected Bibliography.

Chapter 1

1. Chester E. Eisinger, ed., *The 1940s: Profile of a Nation in Crisis* (Garden City, N.Y.: Doubleday Anchor, 1969), xiv–xviii.

2. John Updike, quoted in David Lehman, *Signs of the Times: Deconstruction and the Fall of Paul de Man* (New York: Poseidon Press, 1992), 186.

3. Paul Fussell, *Wartime: Understanding and Behavior in the Second World War* (New York: Oxford University Press, 1989), 268.

Chapter 2

1. Eugene O'Neill, "Strindberg and Our Theatre," *Provincetown Playbill*, no. 1, season 1923–24.

2. Travis Bogard, *Contour in Time: The Plays of Eugene O'Neill* (New York: Oxford University Press, 1972), 406; hereafter cited in text.

3. Louis Sheaffer, *O'Neill, Son and Artist* (Boston: Little, Brown, 1973), 513.

4. Michael Manheim, *Eugene O'Neill's New Language of Kinship* (New York: Syracuse University Press, 1982), 206.

5. C. W. E. Bigsby, *Modern American Drama, 1945–1990* (New York: Cambridge University Press, 1992), 20–21; hereafter cited in text.

6. C. W. E. Bigsby, *A Critical Introduction to American Drama, Volume 1: 1900–1940* (New York: Cambridge University Press, 1982), 88, 103.

Chapter 3

1. Lillian Hellman, *Conversations with Lillian Hellman*, ed. Jackson R. Bryer (Jackson: University Press of Mississippi, 1986) 186; hereafter cited in text as *Conversations, Hellman*.

2. Lillian Hellman, *Scoundrel Time* (Boston: Little Brown, 1976), 45; hereafter cited in text.

3. Kenneth Holditch, "Another Part of the Country: Lillian Hellman as Southern Playwright," *Southern Quarterly* 25, no. 3 (Spring 1987):17; hereafter cited in text.

4. Lillian Hellman, quoted in William Wright, *Lillian Hellman: The Image, the Woman* (New York: Simon and Schuster, 1986), 168; hereafter cited in text.

5. Bonnie Lyons, "Lillian Hellman: 'The First Jewish Nun on Prytania Street,' " in *From Hester Street to Hollywood: The Jewish-American Stage and Screen*, ed. Sarah Blacher Cohen (Bloomington: Indiana University Press, 1983), 111, 116, 121.

6. Lillian Hellman, *An Unfinished Woman: A Memoir* (Boston: Little, Brown, 1969), 36.

7. Lillian Hellman, Introduction, *Six Plays* (New York: Modern Library, 1960), viii–ix.

8. Robert Brustein, quoted in Peter Feibleman, *Lilly: Reminiscences of Lillian Hellman* (New York: Avon, 1988), 359; hereafter cited in text.

9. Gale Austin, *Feminist Theories for Dramatic Criticism* (Ann Arbor: University of Michigan Press, 1990), 53.

10. Lillian Hellman, *Pentimento: A Book of Portraits* (Boston: Little, Brown, 1973), 10; hereafter cited in text.

11. Lillian Hellman, ed., *The Letters of Anton Chekhov* (New York: Farrar, Straus, 1955), xxvii.

12. Carl Rollyson, *Lillian Hellman: Her Legend, Her Legacy* (New York: St. Martin's, 1988), 276; hereafter cited in text.

13. Lillian Hellman, *Maybe: A Story* (Boston: Little, Brown, 1980), 42.

14. Caroline Heilbrun, *Writing a Woman's Life* (New York: Ballantine, 1988), 121.

Chapter 4

1. Arthur Miller, *Timebends: A Life* (New York: Grove, 1987), 115; hereafter cited in text.

2. Arthur Miller, Introduction, *Collected Plays* (New York: Viking, 1957), 29; hereafter cited in text.

3. Arthur Miller, *The Theater Essays of Arthur Miller*, ed. Robert A. Martin (New York: Viking Penguin, 1978), 73, 75; hereafter cited in text as *Theater Essays*.

4. Thomas E. Porter, *Myth and Modern American Drama* (Detroit: Wayne State University Press, 1969), 128–31.

5. Arthur Miller, *Conversations with Arthur Miller*, ed. Matthew C. Roudané (Jackson: University Press of Mississippi, 1987), 370; hereafter cited as *Conversations, Miller*.

6. Neil Carson, *Arthur Miller* (New York: Grove Press, 1982), 147.

7. Gerald Weales, *American Drama Since World War II* (New York: Harcourt Brace, 1962), 6.

8. David Savran, *Cowboys, Communists, and Queers: The Politics of Masculinity in the Works of Arthur Miller and Tennessee Williams* (Minneapolis: University of Minnesota Press, 1992), 42.

Chapter 5

1. Jordan Miller, "William Inge: Last of the Realists?" *Kansas Quarterly* 2, no. 2 (Spring 1970): 20, 26.

2. Tennessee Williams, Introduction, *The Dark at the Top of the Stairs* (New York: Bantam, 1958), viii.

3. Georges Sarotte, *Like a Brother, Like a Lover: Male Homosexuality in the American Novel and Theater from Herman Melville to James Baldwin* (New York: Anchor Doubleday, 1978), 133.

4. Elia Kazan, *A Life* (New York: Knopf, 1988), 604–5.

5. Janet Juhnke, "Inge's Women: Robert Brustein and the Feminine Mystique," *Kansas Quarterly* 18, no. 4 (Fall 1986): 106; hereafter cited in text.

6. Robert Brustein, "The Men-Taming Women of William Inge," *Harper's*, November 1958, 56–57.

7. Ralph Voss, *A Life of William Inge: The Strains of Triumph* (Lawrence: University Press of Kansas, 1989), 184.

8. Betty Friedan, *The Feminine Mystique* (New York: Dell Laurel, 1985), 18, 43; hereafter cited in text.

9. William Inge, quoted in W. David Sievers, *Freud on Broadway: A History of Psychoanalysis and the American Drama* (New York: Hermitage House, 1955), 354.

10. R. Baird Shuman, *William Inge, Revised Edition* (Boston: Twayne, 1989), 58.

11. William Inge, Foreword, *Four Plays* (New York: Grove, 1979), vi.

12. William Inge, quoted in Lewis Chandler, "An End to This Desperate Struggle, William Inge's Previously Unpublished Play 'The Love Death,' " *Studies in American Drama, 1945–Present* 5 (1990): 9.

13. C. W. E. Bigsby, *A Critical Introduction to Twentieth-Century American Drama, Volume 3: Beyond Broadway* (New York: Cambridge University Press, 1985), 16.

Chapter 6

1. Robert Brustein, *Seasons of Discontent: Dramatic Opinions, 1959–1965* (New York: Simon and Schuster, 1965), 284.

2. William Gibson, *The Seesaw Log with the Text of "Two for the Seesaw"* (New York: Knopf, 1959), 13.

3. Paddy Chayefsky, *Television Plays* (New York: Simon and Schuster, 1955), 132.

4. John Clum, *Paddy Chayefsky* (Boston: Twayne, 1976), 87.

Chapter 7

1. Tennessee Williams, *Conversations with Tennessee Williams*, ed. Albert J. Devlin (Jackson: University Press of Mississippi, 1986), 10; hereafter cited in text as *Conversations, Williams*.

2. Tennessee Williams, *Where I Live: Selected Essays*, ed. Christine R. Day and Bob Woods (New York: New Directions, 1978), 60; hereafter cited in text as *Where I Live*.

3. Tennessee Williams, *Memoirs* (Garden City, New York: Doubleday, 1975), 99; hereafter cited in text.

4. Tennessee Williams, "Poem for Paul," August 1941, unpublished; housed in the manuscript collection at Columbia University Library.

5. Jo Mielziner, *Designing for the Theater: A Memoir and a Portfolio* (New York: Bramhall House, 1965), 124.

6. Howard Barnes, quoted in Donald Spoto, *The Kindness of Strangers: The Life of Tennessee Williams* (Boston: Little, Brown, 1985), 138; hereafter cited in text.

7. Harold Clurman, *The Divine Pastime: Theatre Essays* (New York: Macmillan, 1974), 12.

8. C. W. E. Bigsby, *A Critical Introduction to Twentieth-Century American Drama, Volume 2: Tennessee Williams, Arthur Miller, Edward Albee* (New York: Cambridge University Press, 1984), 74; hereafter cited in text.

9. David Savran, *Cowboys, Communists, and Queers: The Politics of Masculinity in the Works of Arthur Miller and Tennessee Williams* (Minneapolis: University of Minnesota Press, 1992), 109; hereafter cited in text.

10. John Clum, *Acting Gay: Male Homosexuality in Modern Drama* (New York: Columbia University Press, 1992), 157, 161; hereafter cited in text.

11. Brenda Murphy, *Tennessee Williams and Elia Kazan: A Collaboration in the Theater* (New York: Cambridge University Press, 1992), 109.

Chapter 8

1. Ruby Cohn, "Late Tennessee Williams," *Modern Drama* 27, no. 3 (September 1984): 343.

2. Tennessee Williams, " 'Author's Notes' for *The Two-Character Play*," *Tennessee Williams Review* 3 (Spring/Fall 1982): 3–5.

Chapter 9

1. Lorraine Hansberry, "The Negro Writer and His Roots: Toward a New Romanticism," 1959, first published in *Black Scholar*, March–April 1981, 11; hereafter cited in text as "Negro Writer."

2. Lorraine Hansberry, *To Be Young, Gifted, and Black* (New York: New American Library, 1969), 128; hereafter cited in text as *Young, Gifted, and Black*.

3. James Baldwin, "Sweet Lorraine," in *To Be Young, Gifted, and Black* (New York: New American Library, 1969), xii; hereafter cited in text.

4. Amiri Baraka, quoted in Steven R. Carter, *Hansberry's Drama: Commitment and Complexity* (Urbana: University of Illinois Press, 1991), 25; hereafter cited in text.

5. Aishah Rahman, "To Be Black, Female, and a Playwright," *Freedomways (Lorraine Hansberry: Art of Thunder, Vision of Light)* 19, no. 4 (fourth quarter 1979): 258.

6. Lorraine Hansberry, *Les Blancs: The Collected Last Plays*, ed. Robert Nemiroff (New York: Vintage, 1972), 208–9; hereafter cited in text as *Les Blancs*.

7. W. E. B. DuBois, *The Souls of Black Folk* (New York: Bantam, 1989), 36–37.

8. bell hooks, *Feminist Theory: From Margin to Center* (Boston: South End Press, 1984), 15, 18, 97.

9. Lorraine Hansberry, quoted in Adrienne Rich, "The Problem with Lorraine Hansberry," *Freedomways (Lorraine Hansberry: Art of Thunder, Vision of Light)* 19, no. 4 (fourth quarter 1979): 250.

10. Simone de Beauvoir, *The Second Sex* (New York: Vintage, 1989), xli.

11. Helene Keysser, "Rites and Responsibilities: The Drama of Black American Women," in *The New Women Playwrights*, ed. Enoch Brater (New York: University Press, 1989), 231.

12. Genevieve Fabre, *Drumbeats, Masks, and Metaphor: Contemporary Afro-American Theatre*, trans. Melvin Dixon (Cambridge, Mass.: Harvard University Press, 1983), 241.

Chapter 10

1. Stuart Little, *Off-Broadway: The Prophetic Theater* (New York: Coward, McCann and Geoghegan, 1972), 13–14.

2. Arthur Kopit, "The Vital Matter of Environment," *Theatre Arts*, 45.4 (April 1961): 13.

3. Edward Albee, "Which Theater Is the Absurd One?" in *American Playwrights on Drama*, ed. Horst Frenz (New York: Hill and Wang, 1965), 169–70; hereafter cited in text as "Which Theater?"

4. Brian Way, "Albee and the Absurd: *The American Dream* and *The Zoo Story*," *American Theatre (Stratford-upon-Avon Studies 10)*, ed. John Russell Brown and Bernard Harris (London: Edward Arnold, 1967), 189, 191.

5. Rose Zimbardo, "Symbolism and Naturalism in Edward Albee's 'The Zoo Story,' " *Twentieth Century Literature* 8, no. 1 (April 1962): 10–17.

6. Robert Motherwell, quoted in Hilton Kramer, review of *The Collected Writings of Robert Motherwell*, *New York Times Book Review*, 28 February 1993, 24.

selected bibliography

Primary Works

Anthologies

Atkinson, Brooks, ed. *New Voices in the American Theatre*. New York: Modern Library, 1955.

Barnes, Clive, and John Gassner, eds. *50 Best Plays of the American Theatre*. 4 vols. New York: Crown, 1969.

Gassner, John, ed. *Best American Plays: Third Series, 1945–1951*. New York: Crown, 1953.

——, ed. *Best American Plays: Fourth Series, 1951–1957*. New York: Crown, 1958.

——, ed. *Best American Plays: Fifth Series, 1957–1963*. New York: Crown, 1963.

———, ed. *Best American Plays: Supplementary Volume, 1918–1958.* New York: Crown, 1961.

———, ed. *Best Plays of the Modern American Theatre: Second Series.* New York: Crown, 1947.

Halline, Allan, ed. *Six Modern American Plays.* New York: Modern Library, 1951.

Hewes, Henry, ed. *Famous American Plays of the 1940s.* New York: Dell Laurel, 1967.

Jacobus, Lee A., ed. *The Longman Anthology of American Drama.* New York: Longman, 1982.

Strasberg, Lee, ed. *Famous American Plays of the 1950s.* New York: Dell Laurel, 1967.

Works by Individual Playwrights

The bibliographies below generally restrict themselves to plays first produced between 1940 and 1960, except in instances where plays outside that time frame have been discussed at length in the text, in which case they are included here, or in instances when the author does not appear in the bibliographies to other volumes in this series. These primary bibliographies include as well collections of essays, letters, interviews, and memoirs—though not works of fiction or poetry written by these authors. The editions listed are the standard collected editions or else ones most readily available to readers in libraries or to students in paperback.

Edward Albee (1928–)

Plays

"The American Dream" and "The Zoo Story": Two Plays. New York: Signet, 1963.

"The Sandbox," "The Death of Bessie Smith" (with "Fam and Yam"). New York: Signet, 1963.

Interviews

Conversations with Edward Albee. Edited by Philip C. Kolin. Jackson: University Press of Mississippi, 1988.

Robert Anderson (1917–)

All Summer Long. New York: Samuel French, 1955.

The Days Between. New York: Samuel French, 1969.

I Never Sang for My Father. New York: Random House, 1968.

Silent Night, Lonely Night. New York: Random House, 1960.

Solitaire/Double Solitaire. New York: Random House, 1972.

Tea and Sympathy. New York: Random House, 1953.

You Know I Can't Hear You When the Water's Running. New York: Random House, 1967.

Paddy Chayefsky (1923–1981)

Gideon. New York: Random House, 1962.

The Latent Heterosexual. New York: Random House, 1967.

Middle of the Night. New York: Random House, 1957.

The Passion of Josef D. New York: Random House, 1964.

The Tenth Man. New York: Random House, 1960.

Jack Gelber (1932–)

The Apple. New York: Grove, 1961.

The Connection. New York: Grove, 1960.

The Cuban Thing. New York: Grove, 1969.

Sleep. New York: Hill and Wang, 1972.

William Gibson (1914–)

A Cry of Players. New York: Atheneum, 1968.

The Miracle Worker. New York: Bantam, 1964.

"The Miracle Worker" and "Monday after the Miracle". Garden City, New York: Doubleday, 1983.

Notes on How to Turn a Phoenix into Ashes: The Story of the Stage Production, with the Text, of "Golda." New York: Atheneum, 1978.

The Seesaw Log with the Text of "Two for the Seesaw." New York: Knopf, 1959.

Lorraine Hansberry (1930–1965)

Plays

Les Blancs: The Collected Last Plays of Lorraine Hansberry, ed. Robert Nemiroff. New York: Vintage, 1973. (Contains *Les Blancs, The Drinking Gourd,* and *What Use Are Flowers?*)

A Raisin in the Sun (complete version). New York: Signet, 1988.

A Raisin in the Sun/The Sign in Sidney Brustein's Window. New York: Signet, 1966.

Autobiography

To Be Young, Gifted, and Black: Lorraine Hansberry in Her Own Words. New York: Signet, 1969.

Lillian Hellman (1905–1984)

Plays

The Collected Plays. Boston: Little, Brown, 1972. (Contains *The Children's Hour, Days to Come, The Little Foxes, Watch on the Rhine, The Searching Wind, Another Part of the Forest, Montserrat, The Autumn Garden, The Lark, Candide, Toys in the Attic,* and *My Mother, My Father, and Me.*)

Memoirs

Maybe: A Story. Boston: Little, Brown, 1980.

Pentimento: A Book of Portraits. Boston: Little, Brown, 1973.

Scoundrel Time. Boston: Little, Brown, 1976.

An Unfinished Woman. Boston: Little, Brown, 1969.

Interviews

Conversations with Lillian Hellman. Edited by Jackson R. Bryer. Jackson: University Press of Mississippi, 1986.

William Inge (1913–1973)

Four Plays. New York: Grove, 1979. (Contains *Come Back, Little Sheba, Picnic, Bus Stop,* and *The Dark at the Top of the Stairs.*)

A Loss of Roses. New York: Bantam, 1963.

Natural Affection. New York: Random House, 1963.

Summer Brave and Eleven Short Plays. New York: Random House, 1962. (Includes "To Bobolink, for Her Spirit," "The Boy in the Basement," and "The Tiny Closet.")

Where's Daddy? New York: Dramatist's Play Service, 1966.

Arthur Laurents (1918–)

The Bird Cage. New York: Dramatists Play Service, 1950.

A Clearing in the Woods. New York: Random House, 1957.

Home of the Brave. New York: Random House, 1946.

Invitation to a March. New York: Random House, 1961.

The Time of the Cuckoo. New York: Random House, 1953.

Jerome Lawrence (1915–) and Robert E. Lee (1918–1985)

Auntie Mame. New York: Vanguard Press, 1957.

First Monday in October. New York: Samuel French, 1960.

The Gang's All Here. Cleveland: World Publishing, 1960.

Inherit the Wind. New York: Bantam, 1960.

The Night Thoreau Spent in Jail. New York: Bantam, 1972.

Archibald MacLeish (1892–1985)

The Fall of the City: A Verse Play for Radio. New York: Farrar and Rinehart, 1937.

Herakles: A Play in Verse. Boston: Houghton Mifflin, 1962.

J. B.: A Play in Verse. Boston: Houghton Mifflin, 1958.

Scratch. Boston: Houghton Mifflin, 1971.

This Music Crept by Me upon the Waters. Cambridge, Mass.: Harvard University Press, 1953.

The Trojan Horse. Boston: Houghton Mifflin, 1962.

Arthur Miller (1915–)

Plays

Collected Plays. New York: Viking, 1957. (Contains *All My Sons, Death of a Salesman, The Crucible, A Memory of Two Mondays,* and *A View from the Bridge.*)

The Man Who Had All the Luck, in *Cross-Section 1944.* Edited by Edwin Seaver. New York: Fischer, 1944.

Autobiography

Timebends: A Life. New York: Grove, 1987.

Essays

The Theater Essays of Arthur Miller. Edited by Robert A. Martin. New York: Viking Penguin, 1978.

Interviews

Conversations with Arthur Miller. Edited by Matthew C. Roudané. Jackson: University Press of Mississippi, 1987.

Eugene O'Neill (1888–1953)

Plays

Complete Plays, 1932–1943. New York: Library of America, 1988. (Contains *Ah, Wilderness!, Days without End, A Touch of the Poet, More Stately Mansions, The Iceman Cometh, Long Day's Journey into Night,* "Hughie," and *A Moon for the Misbegotten.*)

Letters

"As Ever, Gene": The Letters of Eugene O'Neill to George Jean Nathan. Edited by Nancy L. and Arthur W. Roberts. Rutherford, N.J.: Fairleigh Dickinson University Press, 1987.

Selected Letters of Eugene O'Neill. Edited by Travis Bogard and Jackson R. Bryer. New Haven, Conn.: Yale University Press, 1988.

"The Theatre We Worked For": The Letters of Eugene O'Neill to Kenneth Macgowan. Edited by Jackson Bryer and Travis Bogard. New Haven, Conn.: Yale University Press, 1982.

Notebooks

Eugene O'Neill at Work: Newly Released Ideas for Plays. Edited by Virginia Floyd. New York: Ungar, 1981.

Eugene O'Neill's Work Diary, 1924–1943. Edited by Donald Gallup. New Haven, Conn.: Yale University Press, 1981.

Interviews

Conversations with Eugene O'Neill. Edited by Mark W. Estrin. Jackson: University Press of Mississippi, 1990.

Jack Richardson (1935–)

Gallows Humor. New York: Dutton, 1961.

The Prodigal. New York: Dutton, 1960.

Xmas in Las Vegas. New York: Dramatists Play Service, 1966.

Tennessee Williams (1911–1983)

Plays

Clothes for a Summer Hotel: A Ghost Play. New York: New Directions, 1983.

A Lovely Sunday for Creve Coeur. New York: New Directions, 1980.

The Red Devil Battery Sign. New York: New Directions, 1988.

The Theatre of Tennessee Williams. Vol. 1. New York: New Directions, 1971. (Contains *Battle of Angels, The Glass Menagerie,* and *A Streetcar Named Desire.*)

The Theatre of Tennessee Williams. Vol. 2. New York: New Directions, 1971. (Contains *The Eccentricities of a Nightingale, Summer and Smoke, The Rose Tattoo,* and *Camino Real.*)

The Theatre of Tennessee Williams. Vol 3. New York: New Directions, 1971. (Contains *Cat on a Hot Tin Roof, Orpheus Descending,* and *Suddenly Last Summer.*)

The Theatre of Tennessee Williams. Vol. 4. New York: New Directions, 1972. (Contains *Sweet Bird of Youth, Period of Adjustment,* and *The Night of the Iguana.*)

The Theatre of Tennessee Williams. Vol. 5. New York: New Directions, 1976. (Contains *The Milk Train Doesn't Stop Here Anymore, Kingdom of Earth [The Seven Descents of Myrtle], Small Craft Warnings,* and *The Two-Character Play.*)

The Theatre of Tennessee Williams. Vol. 6. New York: New Directions, 1981. (Contains *27 Wagons Full of Cotton and Other Short Plays.*)

The Theatre of Tennessee Williams. Vol. 7. New York: New Directions, 1981. (Contains *In the Bar of a Tokyo Hotel and Other Plays*—which includes *Slapstick Tragedy.*)

Vieux Carré. New York: New Directions, 1979.

Autobiography

Memoirs. New York: Doubleday, 1975.

Essays

Where I Live: Selected Essays. Edited by Christine R. Day and Bob Woods. New York: New Directions, 1978.

Letters

Five O'Clock Angel: Letters of Tennessee Williams to Maria St. Just, 1948–1982. New York: Knopf, 1990.

Tennessee Williams's Letters to Donald Windham, 1940–1945. Edited by Donald Windham. New York: Holt, Rinehart and Winston, 1977.

Interviews

Conversations with Tennessee Williams. Edited by Albert J. Devlin. Jackson: University Press of Mississippi, 1986.

Secondary Works

General Works

Abramson, Doris E. *Negro Playwrights in the American Theatre, 1925–1959.* New York: Columbia University Press, 1969.

Adler, Thomas P. *Mirror on the Stage: The Pulitzer Plays as an Approach to American Drama*. West Lafayette, Ind.: Purdue University Press, 1987.

Austin, Gayle. *Feminist Theories for Dramatic Criticism*. Ann Arbor: University of Michigan Press, 1990.

Bernstein, Samuel. *The Strands Entwined: A New Direction in American Drama*. Boston: Northeastern University Press, 1980.

Bentley, Eric. *The Dramatic Event: An American Chronicle*. New York: Horizon, 1954.

———. *In Search of Theatre*. New York: Knopf, 1953.

Bigsby, C. W. E. *Confrontation and Commitment: A Study of Contemporary American Drama, 1959–1966*. Columbia: University of Missouri Press, 1968.

———. *A Critical Introduction to Twentieth-Century American Drama*. 3 vols. Cambridge, England: Cambridge University Press, 1982–85.

———. *Modern American Drama, 1945–1990*. Cambridge, England: Cambridge University Press, 1992.

———, ed. *The Black American Writer, Volume II: Poetry and Drama*. Baltimore: Penguin, 1969.

Brown-Guillory, Elizabeth. *Their Place on the Stage: Black Women Playwrights in America*. New York: Greenwood, 1988.

Bogard, Travis, Richard Moody, and Walter J. Meserve. *The Revels History of Drama in English, Volume VIII: The American Drama*. London: Methuen, 1977.

Bok, Hedwig, and Albert Wertheim, eds. *Essays on Contemporary American Drama*. Munich: Max Hueber, 1981.

Bonin, Jane F. *Prize-Winning American Drama*. Metuchen, N.J.: Scarecrow, 1973.

Broussard, Louis. *American Drama: Contemporary Allegory from Eugene O'Neill to Tennessee Williams*. Norman: University of Oklahoma Press, 1962.

Brown, John Russell, and Bernard Harris, eds. *American Theatre* (Stratford-upon-Avon Studies 10). London: Edward Arnold, 1967.

Brustein, Robert. *Seasons of Discontent: Dramatic Opinions, 1959–1965*. New York: Simon and Schuster, 1965.

———. *The Theatre of Revolt*. Boston: Little, Brown, 1964.

Case, Sue-Ellen. *Feminism and Theatre*. New York: Methuen, 1985.

Cohen, Sarah Blacher, ed. *From Hester Street to Hollywood: The Jewish-American Stage and Screen*. Bloomington: Indiana University Press, 1983.

Cohn, Ruby. *Dialogue in American Drama*. Bloomington: Indiana University Press, 1975.

Clum, John M. *Acting Gay: Male Homosexuality in Modern Drama*. New York: Columbia University Press, 1992.

Clurman, Harold. *The Divine Pastime: Theater Essays*. New York: Macmillan, 1974.

———. *Lies Like Truth: Theatre Essays and Reviews*. New York: Macmillan, 1958.

Downer, Alan. *Fifty Years of American Drama, 1900–1950*. Chicago: Regency, 1951.

Dusenbury, Winifred L. *The Theme of Loneliness in Modern American Drama*. Gainesville: University of Florida Press, 1960.

Esslin, Martin. *The Theatre of the Absurd*. Garden City, N.Y.: Doubleday Anchor, 1961.

Freedman, Morris. *American Drama in Social Context*. Carbondale: Southern Illinois University Press, 1971.

French, Warren, ed. *The Forties: Fiction, Poetry, Drama*. Deland, Fla.: Everett/Edward, 1969.

Frenz, Horst, ed. *American Playwrights on Drama*. New York: Hill and Wang, 1965.

Gassner, John. *Theatre at the Crossroads: Plays and Playwrights of the Mid-Century American Stage*. New York: Holt, Rinehart and Winston, 1960.

Gottfried, Martin. *A Theatre Divided: The Postwar American Stage*. Boston: Little, Brown, 1967.

Gould, Jean. *Modern American Playwrights*. New York: Dodd, Mead, 1965.

Heilman, Robert B. *The Iceman, the Arsonist, and the Troubled Agent: Tragedy and Melodrama on the Modern Stage*. Seattle: University of Washington Press, 1973.

Herron, Ima Honaker. *The Small Town in American Drama*. Dallas: Southern Methodist University Press, 1969.

Hewitt, Barnard. *Theatre USA, 1668–1957*. New York: McGraw Hill, 1959.

Jones, Margo. *Theatre-in-the-Round*. New York: Rinehart, 1951.

Kazan, Elia. *A Life*. New York: Knopf, 1988.

Kerr, Walter. *God on the Gymnasium Floor and Other Theatrical Adventures*. New York, Delta, 1973.

———. *How Not to Write a Play*. New York: Simon and Schuster, 1955.

Kolin, Philip C., ed. *American Playwrights since 1945: A Guide to Scholarship, Criticism, and Performance.* New York: Greenwood, 1989.

Krutch, Joseph Wood. *The American Drama since 1918.* New York, 1957.

Lahr, John. *Up against the Fourth Wall: Essays on Modern Theater.* New York, Grove, 1970.

Lewis, Allan. *American Plays and Playwrights of the Contemporary Theatre.* New York: Crown, 1970.

Lewis, Emory. *Stages: The Fifty-Year Childhood of the American Theatre.* Englewood Cliffs, N.J.: Prentice-Hall, 1970.

Little, Stuart. *Off-Broadway: The Prophetic Theatre.* New York: Coward, McCann and Geoghegan, 1972.

McCarthy, Mary. *Theatre Chronicles, 1937–1962.* New York, Farrar, Straus, 1961.

Meserve, Walter J. *An Outline History of American Drama.* Totowa, N.J.: Littlefield, Adams, 1965.

————, ed. *Discussions of Modern American Drama.* Boston: Heath, 1965.

Mielziner, Jo. *Designing for the Theatre: A Memoir and a Portfolio.* New York: Bramhall House, 1965.

Miller, Jordan Y., and Winifred L. Frazer. *American Drama between the Wars: A Critical History.* Boston: Twayne, 1991.

Mitchell, Loftin. *Black Drama: The Story of the American Negro in the Theatre.* New York: Hawthorne Books, 1967.

Nannes, Caspar H. *Politics in the American Drama.* Washington, D.C.: Catholic University of America Press, 1960.

Nathan, George Jean. *The Theatre in the Fifties.* New York: Knopf, 1953.

Poggi, Jack. *Theater in America: The Impact of Economic Forces, 1870–1967.* Ithaca, N.Y.: Cornell University Press, 1968.

Porter, Thomas E. *Myth and Modern American Drama.* Detroit: Wayne State University Press, 1969.

Quintero, José. *If You Don't Dance They Beat You.* Boston: Little, Brown, 1974.

Rich, Frank, and Lisa Aronson. *The Theatre Art of Boris Aronson.* New York: Knopf, 1987.

Sanders, Leslie Catherine. *The Development of Black Theatre in America: From Shadows to Selves.* Baton Rouge: Louisiana State University Press, 1988.

Savran, David. *Cowboys, Communists, and Queers: The Politics of Masculinity in the Works of Arthur Miller and Tennessee Williams.* Minneapolis: University of Minnesota Press, 1992.

Scanlan, Tom. *Family, Drama, and American Dreams.* Westport, Conn.: Greenwood, 1978.

Schlueter, June. *Metafictional Characters in Modern Drama.* New York: Columbia University Press, 1979.

———, ed. *Modern American Drama: The Female Canon.* Rutherford, N.J.: Fairleigh Dickinson University Press, 1990.

Schneider, Alan. *Entrances: An American Director's Journey.* New York: Viking, 1986.

Sievers, W. David. *Freud on Broadway: A History of Psychoanalysis and the American Drama.* New York: Hermitage House, 1955.

Simard, Rodney. *Postmodern Drama: Contemporary Playwrights in America and Britain.* Lanham, Md.: University Press of America, 1984.

Tynan, Kenneth. *Curtains.* New York: Atheneum, 1961.

von Szeliski, John. *Tragedy and Fear: Why Modern Tragic Drama Fails.* Chapel Hill: University of North Carolina Press, 1971.

Weales, Gerald. *American Drama since World War II.* New York: Harcourt, Brace, 1962.

Wood, Audrey, with Max Wilk. *Represented by Audrey Wood.* Garden City, N.Y.: Doubleday, 1981.

Selected Books about Individual Dramatists

Edward Albee

Bigsby, C. W. E. *Albee.* Edinburgh, 1969.

———, ed. *Edward Albee: A Collection of Critical Essays.* Englewood Cliffs, N.J.: Prentice-Hall, 1975.

Bloom, Harold, ed. *Edward Albee: Modern Critical Views.* New Haven, Conn.: Chelsea House, 1987.

Cohn, Ruby. *Edward Albee.* Minneapolis: University of Minnesota Press, 1969.

Debusscher, Gilbert. *Edward Albee: Tradition and Renewal.* Brussels: American Studies Center, 1967.

de la Fuente, Patricia, ed. *Edward Albee: Planned Wilderness.* Edinburg, Tex.: Pan American University, 1981.

Hirsch, Foster. *Who's Afraid of Edward Albee?* Berkeley, Calif.: Creative Arts, 1978.

Paolucci, Anna. *From Tension to Tonic: The Plays of Edward Albee*. Carbondale: Southern Illinois University Press, 1972.

Roudané, Matthew C. *Understanding Edward Albee*. Columbia: University of South Carolina Press, 1987.

―――. *"Who's Afraid of Virginia Woolf?": Necessary Fictions, Terrifying Realities*. Boston: G. K. Hall, 1990.

Rutenberg, Michael E. *Edward Albee: Playwright in Protest*. New York: Avon, 1969.

Wasserman, Julian, ed. *Edward Albee: An Interview and Essays*. Syracuse, N.Y.: Syracuse University Press, 1983.

Robert Anderson

Adler, Thomas P. *Robert Anderson*. Boston: Twayne, 1978.

Paddy Chayefsky

Clum, John M. *Paddy Chayefsky*. Boston: Twayne, 1976.

Lorraine Hansberry

Carter, Steven R. *Hansberry's Drama: Commitment and Complexity*. Urbana: University of Illinois Press, 1991.

Cheney, Anne. *Lorraine Hansberry*. Boston: Twayne, 1984.

Lillian Hellman

Adler, Jacob H. *Lillian Hellman*. Austin: Steck-Vaughn, 1969.

Falk, Doris V. *Lillian Hellman*. New York: Ungar, 1978.

Lederer, Katherine. *Lillian Hellman*. Boston: Twayne, 1979.

Rollyson, Carl. *Lillian Hellman: Her Legend and Her Legacy*. New York: St. Martin's, 1988.

Wright, William. *Lillian Hellman: The Image, the Woman*. New York: Simon and Schuster, 1986.

William Inge

Shuman, R. Baird. *William Inge*. Rev. ed. Boston: Twayne, 1989.

Voss, Ralph. *A Life of William Inge: The Strains of Triumph*. Lawrence: University Press of Kansas, 1989.

Arthur Miller

Carson, Neil. *Arthur Miller*. New York: Grove, 1982.

Corrigan, Robert W., ed. *Arthur Miller: A Collection of Critical Essays*. Englewood Cliffs, N.J.: Prentice-Hall, 1969.

Ferres, John H., ed. *Twentieth-Century Interpretations of "The Crucible."* Englewood Cliffs, N.J.: Prentice-Hall, 1972.

Huftel, Sheila. *Arthur Miller: The Burning Glass.* New York: Citadel, 1965.

Koon, Helene Wickham, ed. *Twentieth-Century Interpretations of "Death of a Salesman."* Englewood Cliffs, N.J.: Prentice-Hall, 1983.

Martin, Robert A., ed. *Arthur Miller: New Perspectives.* Englewood Cliffs, N.J.: Prentice-Hall, 1982.

Martine, James J., ed. *Critical Essays on Arthur Miller.* Boston: G. K. Hall, 1979.

Murray, Leonard. *Arthur Miller: Dramatist.* New York: Ungar, 1967.

Nelson, Benjamin. *Arthur Miller: Portrait of a Playwright.* London: Peter Owen, 1970.

Schlueter, Jane, and James K. Flanagan. *Arthur Miller.* New York: Ungar, 1987.

Weales, Gerald, ed. *"The Crucible": Text and Criticism.* New York: Viking, 1971.

———, ed. *"Death of a Salesman": Text and Criticism.* New York: Viking, 1967.

Welland, Dennis. *Miller: A Study of His Plays.* London: Eyre Methuen, 1979.

Eugene O'Neill

Alexander, Doris. *The Tempering of Eugene O'Neill.* New York: Harcourt, Brace, 1962.

Barlow, Judith. *Final Acts: The Creation of Three Late O'Neill Plays.* Athens: University of Georgia Press, 1985.

Berlin, Normand. *Eugene O'Neill.* New York: Grove, 1982.

Bogard, Travis. *Contour in Time: The Plays of Eugene O'Neill.* New York: Oxford University Press, 1972.

Cargill, Oscar, N. Bryllion Fagan, and William J. Fisher, eds. *O'Neill and His Plays.* New York: Oxford University Press, 1961.

Carpenter, Frederic I. *Eugene O'Neill.* Boston: Twayne, 1964.

Chabrowe, Leonard. *Ritual and Pathos: The Theater of O'Neill.* Lewisburg, Pa.: Bucknell University Press, 1976.

Chothia, Jean. *Forging a Language: A Study of the Plays of Eugene O'Neill.* Cambridge, England: Cambridge University Press, 1979.

Engel, Edwin. *The Haunted Heroes of Eugene O'Neill.* Cambridge, Mass.: Harvard University Press, 1953.

Falk, Doris. *Eugene O'Neill and the Tragic Tension*. New Brunswick, N.J.: Rutgers University Press, 1958.

Floyd, Virginia. *The Plays of Eugene O'Neill: A New Assessment*. New York: Ungar, 1987.

Frazer, Winifred D. *Love as Death in "The Iceman Cometh."* Gainesville: University of Florida Press, 1967.

Frenz, Horst, and Susan Tuck, eds. *Eugene O'Neill's Critics: Voices from Abroad*. Carbondale: Southern Illinois University Press, 1987.

Gassner, John, ed. *Eugene O'Neill: A Collection of Critical Essays*. Englewood Cliffs, N.J.: Prentice-Hall, 1964.

Gelb, Barbara and Arthur. *Eugene O'Neill*. New York: Harper's, 1962.

Hinden, Michael. *"Long Day's Journey into Night": Native Eloquence*. Boston: G. K. Hall, 1990.

Manheim, Michael. *Eugene O'Neill's New Language of Kinship*. Syracuse, N.Y.: Syracuse University Press, 1982.

Martine, James J., ed. *Critical Essays on Eugene O'Neill*. Boston: G. K. Hall, 1985.

Maufort, Marc, ed. *Eugene O'Neill and the Emergence of American Drama*. Amsterdam: Rodopi, 1989.

Miller, Jordan Y., ed. *Eugene O'Neill and the American Critics*. Hamden, Conn.: Archon, 1962.

Porter, Laurin. *The Banished Prince: Time, Memory, and Ritual in the Late Plays of Eugene O'Neill*. Ann Arbor: UMI Research Press, 1988.

Raleigh, John Henry. *The Plays of Eugene O'Neill*. Carbondale: Southern Illinois University Press, 1965.

Robinson, James. *Eugene O'Neill and Oriental Thought: A Divided Vision*. Carbondale: Southern Illinois University Press, 1982.

Sheaffer, Louis. *O'Neill: Son and Artist*. Boston: Little, Brown, 1973.

———. *O'Neill: Son and Playwright*. Boston: Little, Brown, 1968.

Stroupe, John H., ed. *Critical Approaches to O'Neill*. New York: AMS Press, 1988.

Tiusanen, Timo. *O'Neill's Scenic Images*. Princeton, N.J.: Princeton University Press, 1968.

Tornqvist, Egil. *A Drama of Souls: O'Neill's Natural Supernaturalism*. New Haven, Conn.: Yale University Press, 1969.

Tennessee Williams

Adler, Thomas P. *"A Streetcar Named Desire": The Moth and the Lantern*. Boston: G. K. Hall, 1992.

Boxill, Roger. *Tennessee Williams.* New York: St. Martin's, 1987.

Donahue, Francis. *The Dramatic World of Tennessee Williams.* New York: Ungar, 1964.

Jackson, Esther Merle. *The Broken World of Tennessee Williams.* Madison: University of Wisconsin Press, 1965.

Kolin, Philip C., ed. *Confronting Tennessee Williams's "A Streetcar Named Desire": Essays in Cultural Pluralism.* Westport, Conn.: Greenwood, 1993.

Londre, Felicia Hardison. *Tennessee Williams.* New York: Ungar, 1964.

Miller, Jordan Y., ed. *Twentieth-Century Interpretations of "A Streetcar Named Desire."* Englewood Cliffs, N.J.: Prentice-Hall, 1971.

Murphy, Brenda. *Tennessee Williams and Elia Kazan: A Collaboration in the Theater.* Cambridge, England: Cambridge University Press, 1992.

Nelson, Benjamin. *Tennessee Williams: The Man and His Work.* New York: Obolensky, 1961.

Parker, R. B., ed. *Twentieth-Century Interpretations of "The Glass Menagerie."* Englewood Cliffs, N.J.: Prentice-Hall, 1983.

Spoto, Donald. *The Kindness of Strangers: The Life of Tennessee Williams.* Boston: Little, Brown, 1985.

Stanton, Stephen S., ed. *Tennessee Williams: A Collection of Critical Essays.* Englewood Cliffs, N.J.: Prentice-Hall, 1977.

Tharpe, Jack, ed. *Tennessee Williams: A Tribute.* Jackson: University of Mississippi Press, 1977.

Thompson, Judith J. *Tennessee Williams's Plays: Memory, Myth, and Symbol.* New York: Peter Lang, 1987.

Tischler, Nancy. *Tennessee Williams: Rebellious Puritan.* New York: Citadel, 1961.

Van Antwerp, Margaret A., and Sally Johns, eds. *Dictionary of Literary Biography: Documentary Series 4 (Tennessee Williams).* Detroit: Gale, 1984.

index

The Author

Thomas P. Adler holds bachelor's and master's degrees from Boston College and a Ph.D. from the University of Illinois at Urbana-Champaign. Since 1970, he has taught dramatic literature and film at Purdue University, where he is professor of English and associate dean of liberal arts. His numerous articles, book chapters, and reviews on modern and contemporary British and American drama have appeared in leading journals and collections of essays in the field. He is the author of three books on drama—*Robert Anderson* (1978), *Mirror on the Stage: The Pulitzer Plays as an Approach to American Drama* (1987), and *"A Streetcar Named Desire": The Moth and the Lantern* (1990)—and a rhetoric text, coauthored with Leonora Woodman, *The Writer's Choices* (1985, second edition 1987).